Environment and Children

To Heddwen, Aloma, Brynach, Dewi, Martha, Owain, Tâl, Lukasz, Martyna, Jenny, Anna-Tora, and to all children, everywhere. May your generation heal the world from the wounds our generation has inflicted.

Environment and Children

Passive Lessons from the Everyday Environment

Christopher Day

with

Anita Midbjer

AMSTERDAM · BOSTON · HEIDELBERG · LONDON
NEW YORK · OXFORD · PARIS · SAN DIEGO
SAN FRANCISCO · SINGAPORE · SYDNEY · TOKYO
Architectural Press is an imprint of Elsevier

Architectural Press is an imprint of Elsevier
Linacre House, Jordan Hill, Oxford OX2 8DP, UK
30 Corporate Drive, Suite 400, Burlington, MA 01803, USA

First edition 2007

Notice
No responsibility is assumed by the publisher or authors for any injury and/or damage to persons or property as a matter of products liability, negligence or otherwise, or from any use or operation of any methods, products, instructions or ideas contained in the material herein.

Disclaimer
This book draws on many sources. Some are facts, some hypotheses, some opinions. Most – including many of my own statements – are mixtures. Even 'facts' are unavoidably selective and can rarely be guaranteed. Despite careful checking, neither I nor my colleagues or publishers can accept responsibility for any errors, misinformation or unsuitable advice. This also applies to opinions – particularly on issues affecting health and safety. As any recommendations must balance complex, often opposing, factors, not everyone will reach the same conclusions. In this – as indeed in every issue this book touches on – every reader must make up her or his mind, for which they alone must be responsible.

I offer the best advice I am capable of, but every circumstance is different. Anyone who acts on this advice must make their own evaluation, and adapt it to their particular circumstances.

British Library Cataloguing in Publication Data
A catalogue record for this book is available from the British Library

Library of Congress Cataloging-in-Publication Data
A catalog record for this book is available from the Library of Congress

ISBN: 978-0-7506-8344-9

For information on all Architectural Press publications
visit our website at www.books.elsevier.com

Typeset by Charon Tec Ltd (A Macmillan Company), Chennai, India
www.charontec.com

Printed and bound in Great Britain

07 08 09 10 11   10 9 8 7 6 5 4 3 2 1

Contents

Preface

Passive Lessons: Shapers of the Future

Environment affects how we think, feel and behave. It shapes our habits, expectations of normality and values. Affecting us physically and psychologically, it can support and nourish physical, mental and social development. But unless we consciously dedicate design to this end, it's more likely to hinder or unbalance development; it can even damage bodily health. Its influence, being largely subliminal, is potent. Children have even less defences against this than adults. Small children have virtually none.

Ninety per cent of physical environment is built, man-made. How does this affect children: their health, behaviour, education and development? To support them in these matters, what do we need to consider? How should what we offer evolve with age and circumstance?

Today's children will have to face unprecedented environmental challenges. How can we prepare them for this? Inspire them to work for environmental betterment? How can their surroundings help them in this? Can their influence contribute to a sustainable future? In particular, what passive lessons does everyday environment teach – all the time? It teaches these through every sense, through unvoiced – often unconscious – thoughts, assumptions and values, through behaviour expectations as well as concrete example. What lessons *should* it teach? Can these foster environmental and social awareness and responsibility?

What does all this mean for design? For schools and homes; playgrounds, parks and gardens; for children's everyday surroundings? How should we adapt places already formed, buildings already built, rooms already shaped? How can we make these into fitting environments for children?

Acknowledgements

I am indebted to many people for advice and information. From designing schools, kindergartens and child-centres by consensus with teachers, I have learnt a lot from too many teachers, parents and administrators to name. Without their observations and wisdom, these schools would not have been worth being in, and I would have known nothing worth writing about. In particular, without inspiring advice from Elvira Rychlak, Karl Partridge, Helen Brown, Maria Castella, Nim de Bruyne, Aleksandra Kaczmarek, Sue Fenoughty and my colleague, Anita Midbjer, this book would not have been worth reading.

PART 1

Environment *for* children

Design by adults: experience by children

Environment and child development

Does environment affect child development? Does it influence what children learn, the values they acquire, and the path they will choose through adult life? Can childhood experiences inculcate environmental responsibility?

Everybody knows children need love. This affects *everything*. It's critical for healthy psychological, social and bodily development – even influencing brain and nerves.[1] In fact, without love, children develop brains up to 30 per cent smaller than those who grow up enveloped in it.[2] But this is *human*, social environment. What about *physical* environment? This also influences brain development. From environmental experiences, the brain learns how it 'needs' to develop.[3] What other developmental, educational and motivational influences do buildings and places have? Do they affect children's – and subsequently, adults' – health? Their physical, mental and moral development? Their social and environmental awareness?

If so, this places great responsibilities on everyone who designs, alters and administers places. It also raises questions. How should places for children be? Will adult design criteria produce appropriate environments for children? If sunbathing isn't healthy for babies, what else do we need to look at in different ways?

Places as exploratoria

Children and adults view the world differently.[4] Buildings are designed by adults. But many, perhaps most, are used by children. When adults design buildings, practicality, energy-conservation, aesthetics and economy have major shaping influences. These are undeniably important – but have nothing to do with children's experience.

Adult experience centres on how we *use* places; we know what they are *for*. For children, it's more about what places 'say', how they meet and *experience* them. To them, the world is still fresh – one big sensory exploratorium. Hence railings and walls aren't for excluding trespassers, but for rattling sticks or bouncing balls. Paula Lillard distinguishes these approaches: 'children use the environment to improve themselves; adults use themselves to improve the environment. Children work for the sake of process; adults work to achieve an end result'.[5] This means places – for adults – are for pre-defined purposes;

but to children, they offer opportunities for things to do. This is a critical distinction.

Adults live (mostly) in a world of material facts – 'known' and unchanging. For children, the 'real' world is often servant to an imaginary world. Even single rooms, gardens or behind-the-shed forgotten places can be whole palettes of mood, whole geographies of mountains and jungles, harbours and shops – places to live out fantasy through action.

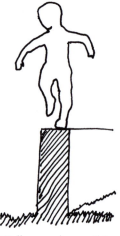

Experience and learning

How do children progress from a fantasy-shaped world to a fact-based one? How do they learn? Piaget considered that knowledge doesn't develop as a linear progression, but as a relationship-network, dynamically interweaving connected elements. Perception, action, interaction with others and

Walls are for walking along

reflection develop, modify and consolidate it.[6] *Abstract knowledge* doesn't last. Cerebral knowledge unsupported by experience is unsustainable. Much that children learn intellectually, they compartmentalize as nothing to do with life. Not surprisingly, everybody understands things more quickly, more deeply, more multifacetedly and more meaningfully by *experiencing* them. In fact, until children are six years old, they *only* learn through experience – by *doing* – never through commands.[7] They discover, understand and appreciate the world around them by active investigation.[8] This 'intuitive' learning is whole-body and multisensory.[9] As child psychologist Anita Olds observes, children 'live continuously in the here and now, feasting upon nuances of color, light, sound, odor, touch, texture, volume, movement, form and rhythm around them'.[10] (This persists into adolescence; how many teenagers do homework before the last minute?)

Innately compelled to learn about the world, children seek out concrete experiences. If these hold together – such as kitchens smelling, sounding, feeling and looking cosy – they can recognize *connections* and build a mental 'whole' from experiential 'parts'. Contradictory experiences – such as luxuriously soft, bouncy furniture in 'formal-behaviour-only' rooms, or 'leather' smelling of PVC, are confusing. Confusion reduces confidence. Educationally, as plastic things can *look* very different but feel identical to *touch*, they imply knowledge from different senses have no meaningful relationship. Fragmentary, non-related knowledge weakens interest, so is thought to contribute to low attention span.[11] In this age, plastic is barely avoidable. So, unfortunately is attention-deficiency. Sensory inconsistency is, of course, only one contributor amongst many probable causes.

Whereas adults already 'understand' things, children are still exploring the *relationships* between sensory messages. This makes them naturally creative. Sense-rich environments, by providing experience-experiments and imagination-opportunities of which we adults can't conceive, further creativity development.[12] In design, exuberant decoration can appeal to our sense of richness, but does it overburden children by excess? Does the decoration reinforce or confuse? Conversely, purely visual minimalism has a refined clarity and calm that can feed the soul. For adults, it can be an appealing aesthetic. But, if it doesn't feed the senses, can it nourish children? Sterile buildings are actively harmful. These say soul-state doesn't matter. They deserve no place near children.

Experience of place

Children and adults also *experience* places differently. Their mood-world is more differentiated than ours. We easily categorize rooms as single-mood places: living room, bedroom, kitchen, classroom, gymnasium … For children, one room can comprise five distinct places: four corners and a centre.

As lower eye-level shrinks spatial boundaries, children's space differs from that of adults. Smaller relative scale, reach and range make places (small, when revisited as an adult) feel huge. Their spatial consciousness is also different. Adults navigate within a Cartesian spatial grid. This organizes our spatial experience, and lets us think causally. Small children interact with space more through life-energy than prethought-out rational intention. In mid-childhood, their actions are mostly led by emotions. Only at the threshold of adulthood can they fully steer their life, and respond to space, through thinking.

View above table

View below table

Different thinking: different learning: different needs

Much conventional education focuses on intellectual development. But what about emotional development? Psychology often treats thought and feeling as opposites. Although, like Freud, Piaget separated their development, he recognized that whole understanding depends on a balance between emotional and intellectual comprehension.[13] Vygotskij observed that significance – hence *meaning* – is inseparable from feelings. He considered consciousness to be a dialogue of diverse mental forms, with feeling and thinking inextricably interlinked, but thought to be only a monologue to the world.[14]

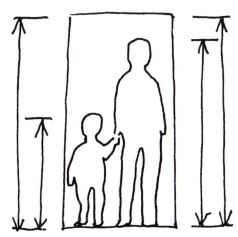

Proportional scales

Is there only one type of intelligence? Howard Gardner postulates seven: logical/mathematical, linguistic, musical, spatial, bodily/kinaesthetic, self-knowledge and social.[15] Different aspects of environment feed these different intelligences. Energy-conscious design, for instance, demonstrates causality. Spatial and kinaesthetic sensations are inseparable from experience of place. Architecture can both feed sense-of-self and help build society. Form- and space-language, harmony, melody, tempo and rhythm are its means.

These many intelligences raise questions about what it means to be human. Machines excel at logical intelligence. They'll soon be better at this than humans. (They're already better at remembering facts.) But unless balanced by uniquely *human* emotional, contextual and relationship-pattern thinking, this will bring a very one-sided – and meaningless – world.

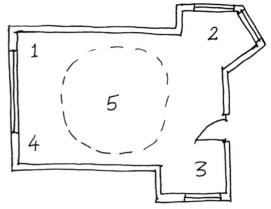

Child spaces in a room

Most of what children learn isn't taught, but 'found out' by exploratory play, both constructive and destructive. Smashing things, though fun, is quickly over. Creation, however, offers ever-increasing layers of experience – more fulfilling than destruction. Craftwork that links product directly to natural source brings an anchoring influence in a confusing world. The 'given' world – earth, water, growing plants – offer manifold creative opportunities[16] – from clay to dig, sieve, knead, form and fire, transforming mushy 'mud' into beautiful, waterproof and hard pottery; to willow to plant, coppice, cut, strip and weave into baskets. But, as some 80 per cent of Europeans are urban, our surroundings aren't normally mud and trees.[17] They're 90 per cent 'made' – mostly buildings. Can these also provide multiple layers of experience?

The built world is substantial, fixed. But it isn't *only* material. Into much of it is built artistic values. Anything artistic can't be wholly grasped with the intellect. Art isn't nature. Only humans can make or appreciate it. But, as Steiner pointed out, to do so, 'your soul must be attuned quite differently from your state of mind when you are concerned with earthly things … Art itself can be understood only if we realize that its task is to point the way beyond the purely earthly'.[18]

Innocently fresh, small children are naturally artistic. They don't, however, *consciously* evaluate aesthetics. They may say: 'Wow!' but never: 'This is a nice room'.[19] So do aesthetics matter for children? Or only for their parents? Early childhood experiences affect how they'll look at form, understand space and appreciate places as adults.[20] More importantly, environment influences children's emotional, social, intellectual and even physical development.[21]

Gender differences

Does gender affect environmental needs? Boys and girls are physically different. Having greater arm and shoulder strength, most boys can pull themselves up things by brute force. Girls often compensate with momentum, swinging up.[22] At rock-climbing, for instance, girls are usually better at sequences requiring grace – such as delicate-balance slabs; boys at moves demanding strength – such as overhangs. Activity equipment – not only climbing walls – therefore needs to provide for both.

Research finds other gender differences, but mostly smaller than differences between individuals. Which are due to testosterone and which to stereotyped expectations? Some are clear; most are disputed. Boys typically draw activity, movement; girls draw relationships, idealized characters and quieter situations.[23] In Baron-Cohen's view: 'The more a child produces, the less eye contact it makes after birth and the more it looks at inanimate objects'. From this develops a desire to systematize. Men, therefore, typically have greater interest in systems and the law-governed inanimate universe; women, the less-predictable sphere of social and emotional relationships[24] – a divergence visible even at four years of age.[25] Interested in systems of *things*, boys typically imagine saving someone from drowning with material aids: ladders, ropes and lifebuoys. Girls simply swim to the rescue.[26]

Boys and girls also relate to places differently – though it's not always clear why. Boys' alleged superior spatial abilities, for instance, are attributed to being allowed to roam more. Boys' games frequently develop over days, even weeks.[27] They often construct buildings (especially towers), usually unoccupied, whereas girls typically make 'rooms', then populate them.[28] This commonly develops into object- or place-focus. Girls have greater aesthetic interest in their surroundings, wanting beautiful colours and flowers.[29] Especially between the ages of 13 and 15 years, their place descriptions are more quality-rich than boys. In adulthood – at the extreme – this manifests in architecture as phallic tower-blocks or inhabitant-friendly interior design; in dentists' waiting-rooms, as car and home magazines.

Play preferences, however, are more often differentiated by adult expectations. Boys are usually more 'physical' so dominate playground central space, pushing girls to the periphery, where they develop 'perimeter' type games.[30] But is this preference or consequence?[31] Many people think the latter. In fact, *all* children need both places to construct things and to imagine worlds; both 'middle-of-the-room' and 'kick-about-field' sort of places for rambunctious play and 'low corner' and 'under-shrub' spaces for secretive conversations. Both places to use, adapt and build, and beautiful ones to *be* in.

Design for children

Development-wise, children are on a journey from energy-directed to thought-directed, but are never completely at either extreme. Paralleling this, their building needs evolve from form-mobility to structural-clarity. Light needs similarly progress with age. Babies can't handle much. Infants can feel insecurely exposed in bright light; but dreamy, enchanted, light encourages their imaginative fantasy. Teenagers need every aid to wakefulness and clear thinking. Likewise, colour-needs progress with age. Space-needs and social-supportive aspects of design are also age-related. A critical progression is that from *nurturing* to *inspiring* environments. Small children need protective support. Teenagers need motivation. The key motivating issue of our time is the challenge of sustainability. By the time today's children are adults, climate change will have made this central to every sphere of economic, social and technical life, and international relations.

What does this mean for design? How do built places meet children's needs? Most urban design assumes they'll just fit in. Most schools, most homes, are shaped foremost by practical concerns. Occasionally some 'childification' is superficially added. But although Mark Dudek, researching school architecture, concludes that 'aesthetic quality is fundamental in establishing an appreciation of their environment and raising self esteem',[32] concern for what children actually *need* is lamentably rare. How can the buildings and places we make or modify serve their deeper needs?

Children's aesthetic needs differ from those of adults. They're often given bright colours, 'kid's art', teddy-bear wallpaper, or fairyland 'film sets'. But bright colours are stimulating, unsubtle and oversubstantial; not magical. Magic is suggestion-rich; coming from 'another world', it's elusive, ungraspable. Disneyland-type film sets, however popular with children, do nothing for their imagination or intuitive sense of truth. Indeed by making the *un*true stimulating and appealing, they undermine their natural sense of reverent wonder – an important foundation for environmental responsibility in later life.

Although *people* are more important for children, it is *places* that they tend to remember better.[33] They intimately know every inch of their play territory: how every bit feels in different weathers. The experience of growing up in a predictable environment filled with 'character' creates personal identity, place identity and emotional security – all inextricably bound together.[34] Olds notes that 'such memories are indelible, as our own vivid images of childhood places substantiate'.[35]

The subliminal lessons children 'absorb' from values imprinted into buildings and places are almost irresistible. Infants also absorb the *quality* of their environment, and older children respond to how places *feel*.[36] Quality architecture is, therefore, at the heart of education for child development.[37] 'Quality architecture', however, means architecture for *children's* needs, not for adult criteria – an immense distinction.

But what *is* 'good' architecture? Opinions diverge widely. But appeal to architects, to style journals or even to most adults offers no guarantee of benefit to children. Nor do buildings whose main purpose is to make their architects' reputations. Whatever the adult accolades, unless their aesthetics nourish children they merely make places *less* like home, *less* something they can relate to. Consideration of children's needs may often require unconventional buildings. But their architecture should be design-reticent, child-development responsive. Children need buildings designed, not for magazines, but for children.

This means environment that both nourishes and inspires – in proportions according to age. Children need architecture not to *shape*, but to *serve* them; environment to strengthen and prepare them for the world we have unwittingly misshaped. This requires us to look with new eyes, with new understanding. This is an essential prerequisite if we are to design environments *for* children.

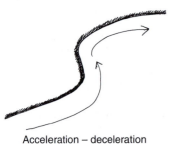

Acceleration – deceleration
dynamic asymmetry

Structure underlying fluid forms

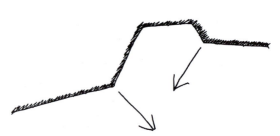

Mobility in harder forms

Notes

1 Olds, Anita Rui (2001) *Child Care Design Guide*. McGraw Hill.
2 Green, Jeff (2006) Sensing the world and ourselves. *New View*, Autumn.
3 Letter by 110 childhood professionals to the *Daily Telegraph*, 12 September 2006, and subsequent interviews on BBC Radio 4 *Today* Programme.
4 Already in the 1920s, Piaget recognized that children and adults think in different ways. Cited in Lundahl, Gunilla, ed. (1995) *Hus och Rum för Små Barn*. Arkus.
5 Lillard, Paula Polk (1972) *Montessori – a Modern Approach*. Schocken Books, quoted in Olds, Anita Rui (2001) *ibid.*
6 Ceppi, Guilio and Zini, Michele (1998) *Children, Spaces, Relations; Metaproject for an Environment for Young Children*. Reggio Children.
7 Skantze, Ann, Doctoral thesis, Stockholm University. Cited in Lundahl, Gunilla, ed. (1995) *ibid.* Also course booklet for Coordinators of Environmental Education Course, Alkmaar College of Education, The Netherlands, cited in Fenoughty, Susan (1997) *The Garden Classroom*. Churchill Fellowship report (unpublished).
8 Uijlings-Schuurmans, M. *Environmental Education in Primary Schools*.Alkmaar College of Education, The Netherlands, quoted in Fenoughty, Susan (1997) *ibid.*
9 Piaget's term quoted in Dudek, Mark (1996) *Kindergarten Architecture*. Spon.
10 Olds, Anita Rui (2001) *ibid.*
11 Green, Jeff (2006) *ibid.*
12 Lundahl, Gunilla, ed. (1995) *ibid.*
13 Piaget, Jean, cited in Lundahl, Gunilla, ed. (1995) *op. cit.*
14 Vygotskij, Lev Semënovic *Fantasi och kreativitet i barndom*. Daidalos (translated by Lindsten, Kajsa Öberg).
15 Gardner, Howard (1983) *Frames of Mind – The Theory of Multiple Intelligences*. Harper Collins. These also relate to Steiner's senses of language, thought/meaning, movement, health and individuality. Intelligence is no longer a simplistic concept. Other researchers have identified many 'intelligences', making this field a fluid and developing one.
16 Fenoughty, Susan (1997) *ibid.*, describing the exploration-rich environment at the Rudolf Steiner School, Norrköping, Sweden.
17 Szczepanski, Anders (director of Environmental and Outdoor Education at Linköping University) quoted in Fenoughty, Susan (1997) *op. cit.*
18 Steiner, Rudolf (1916) *The sense organs and aesthetic experience*. In Davy and Bittleston, eds, (1975) *The Golden Blade*. Rudolf Steiner Press.
19 There are, however, exceptions. As a Nant-y-Cwm teacher told me, one seven-year-old girl said of the kindergarten: 'I like this space'. If more places touched their hearts, would more children respond this way?
20 Research by Hjort, Bobo, cited in Lundahl, Gunilla, ed. (1995) *ibid.*
21 Lundahl, Gunilla, ed. (1995) *op. cit.*
22 Ministry of Education (1952) *Moving and Growing*. HMSO.
23 Aronsson, Karin (1981) *En spännande situation där någon är i fara och där någon kommmer till hjälp*. Lunds Konsthall (exhibition catalogue).
24 Professor Baron-Cohen quoted in Glaser, Karen (2003) *Written in the Womb*. Building Design, 23 May 2003.
25 MacDonald, Gaye (1996) University of California, Los Angeles, cited in Mark Dudek (1996) *ibid.*
26 Aronsson, Karin (1981) *ibid.*
27 Loni Miers from Viborg Seminariet, cited in Mark Dudek (1996) *ibid.*
28 Lundahl, Gunilla, ed. (1995) *ibid.*
29 Nordström, Maria (1990) *Barns boendeförställningar i ett utvecklinspsykologiskt perspektiv*. Doctoral thesis, Statens Institut för byggnadsforskning, Lund University, cited in Farnestam, Sandra (2001) *Arkitektur i skolan*. Unpublished dissertation, Umeå University.
30 Clarricoates, K. (1987) Child culture at school – a clash between gendered worlds. In Pollard, A., ed. (1987) *Children and their Primary Schools*. Falmer Press.

31 Sue Fenoughty, environmental education consultant.

32 Dudek, Mark (2000) *Architecture of Schools*. Architectural Press.

33 Olds, Anita Rui (2001) *ibid*.

34 Olds, Anita Rui (2001) *op. cit.*

35 Olds, Anita Rui (2001) *op. cit.*

36 Steiner, Rudolf (1996) *The Foundations of Human Experience*. (1919 lectures) Anthroposophic Press.

37 Nordtsröm, Maria (1990) *ibid*.

CHAPTER 2

Childhood: a journey

Childhood

What is childhood? What does it mean to be a child? We all know what these words mean. Or do we? Historically, culturally, philosophically, psychologically and educationally there is no simple unanimity. 'Childhood' itself is a relatively new, and Western, concept.[1]

In other times and places, children started work young. Many jobs – such as running errands or carrying drink to harvesters – were small, but made children proud to be useful, indeed indispensable. Many others, often lonely, burdensome and monotonous – such as guarding sheep or scaring birds – carried full adult responsibility for their family's survival. Others again – such as 'powder-monkeying' on warships, work down coal mines, in factories or up inside chimneys were harsh, dangerous and exhausting. This was a cruel way to grow up. It still happens. Despite widespread condemnation, many of the products we happily buy are made by Chinese children.

'Teenagehood' is even more recent, barely half a century old. Teenage rebelliousness is a particularly Western issue, linked to our culture of individualism, material progress and devaluation of the elderly. To young people, the new is inspiring – the future they'll grow towards. Old people represent not wisdom and oral tradition, but the old, irrelevant, restrictive and fuddy-duddy. This combines with peer-led escalating expectations of rights, but declining responsibilities. Even teenagers' new freedoms easily become decision-making burdens. Other cultures, where the wisdom of age is respected above new products and novel ideas, manifest none of this.

How fast should children grow up? Intellectual development is easy to accelerate, but emotional development doesn't keep up, leaving children with more to process emotionally than they're capable of.[2] Moreover, as Elke-Maria Riscke writes, 'civilization … upbringing and education, 'tear' … children out of their dreaming consciousness much too early and abruptly, pulling them into physicality and thus robbing them of the peace and strength which they need to build up their body in a healthy way as a physical basis for their soul spiritual development'.[3]

What are children ready for, when? What supports, inspires – or burdens, disenchants – them? What does this imply for their environment?

Children and environment: developing consciousness

Babies start life as part of their mother. Adults are independent beings, fully able to exercise *conscious choice*. But individuality doesn't come overnight; it takes a long journey. Even before birth, babies are aware of the spirit – goodness or disharmony, love or bitterness – around them. Growing into control of their bodies, children become increasingly 'earthly', until bodily consciousness predominates over spiritual. The next step is recognizing their separateness from everything and everyone around them – 'self'-consciousness. All this, however, is a slow process.

For very young children everything is a *oneness*. Unable to distinguish between themselves, how they're feeling and their surroundings, they say 'naughty table' when banging a head on one. As they accord emotional qualities to things and places, how toys *look* is less important than their 'animist' *being*. Things (for us, inanimate) are agents of soul and will. Hence 'Teddy feels sad' or 'The sun wants to shine'. In this way, they use their environment to understand themselves and their social relationships.[4]

As space consciousness (up, down, left and right) and time consciousness develop, so does '*I consciousness*': awareness of the self as separate and distinct from surroundings. One early manifestation is the concept 'mine'. On their journey to individuality, their own personal chair represents their 'own' space. Kindergarten teacher-trainer Margaret Meyerkort describes the stubbornness of the 'terrible two's' as 'simply a protective shield behind which hides a newly found sensitivity. The child is protecting the still tender plant of the Self ... The process of alienation from nature, from the surroundings, and from other creatures, starts on the level of the physical body with the attainment of verticality and then continues in the realm of the soul'.[5] Between three and five years old, children begin to distinguish *place* mood – and meaning – from their own mood. Between four and seven years of age, they become interested in how places can be *used*; they make 'places' with fabric, furniture and other things we adults assume had other functions.[6]

Cupboard or home?

They're not really little 'I's, however, until, around seven years, they're no longer bound to copy everything around them. Now feeling fully separate from their environment, imitation becomes eclipsed by a more aware recognition of authority. Their reactions and responses – and inspiration to learn things – begin to be led by how things make them *feel*.[7] They start to develop a vivid pictorial imagination. With their conscious emotional life waking up, they're drawn to dramatic stories where good confronts evil. They begin to distinguish right and wrong – albeit in black and white categories, hence cops and robbers games. While adults can view woodcutters as environmental despoilers and wolves as endangered species, young children's polarities are formed by archetype: Little Red Riding Hood's father is, therefore, the embodiment of good, the wolf of evil.

Around eight and nine years of age, their sense of *space* emerges. They can now model space and move around places in their thoughts.[8] Whereas younger children learn through their hands and bodies, children of this age now start to understand rules and principles. Rather than watch and copy, they're able to listen and allocate.[9] With increasing awareness of the 'individuality', they become conscious of belonging to social groups such as 'gang' or 'class'. Already concerned about 'fairness' – how others treat them – children begin to balance individual and group needs, particularly in team sports. By 11 years, no longer thinking things around them are the direct result of their existence, they can understand things through words, without needing bodily experience.[10]

The physical coordination of late childhood – manifest in avid tree climbing – disappears at puberty. With limbs growing too fast to control accurately, teenagers sprawl. Bodies growing rapidly to adulthood, but souls still on the journey of childhood, make hormonal changes and unfamiliar sexual feelings hard to deal with. No wonder mood swings are so common.

A developed sense of space lets older children imagine, design and make places.[11] Only between 13 and 15 years of age, however, do they give the aesthetics of their surroundings *conscious* values.[12] Whereas between seven and 11 years, they related to their environment through their senses, from 12 to 15 they're more reflective, judging it, others and themselves, with questions such as 'what do people think of me? Am I important?' Surroundings can make them feel positive – or negative – about themselves.[13]

Becoming aware of themselves as *individuals*, 'outsider'-thinking and painfully separate, teenagers want to understand the world. They no longer automatically believe what they're told, but must question and doubt everything. This critical outlook, and the desire to make their *own* unique mark, impel them to defy tradition, even rebel against everything – although peer group convention often makes rebellion conformist. So new is this individualized identity, that they sometimes have to fight to assert it. Though often painful, rejecting parental expectations, apparently stepping backwards, even losing the way, is an essential phase in growing-up. But it needn't take self-destructive, socially unacceptable or criminal forms. These stem in large part from feelings of betrayal: the world isn't true; it's not beautiful, not good – it offers no inspiring ideals to fight for, no *positive* way to make any contribution, only destructive or egotistical ways.

Teenagers develop abstract thinking.[14] This lets them construct idealistic utopias independent from anything they've ever experienced – visionary but often ungrounded.[15] Educationally, inspiration is an effective motivator; orders are usually counter productive. To deter teenagers from smoking, for instance, it's less effective to lecture them on adverse health effects (after all, at this age, they will live for ever) than to kindle outrage against cynically profiteering tobacco companies.

Inspiration by ideals is a hallmark of adolescence, but this can take many forms from environmental crusading to militant fundamentalism. Is it fed by hope? Or by despair? Do teenagers' surroundings speak of a world that deserves destroying? Or one they're inspired to improve? When inspiration is lost, thwarted, overwhelmed by hopelessness or sidelined by overpassive entertainment or drugs, this can turn into apathy or nihilism.

Inspiration is vital to see adolescents through this black-hole period – inspiring issues, inspiring people, inspiring places.

How much of today's crisis of adolescence is due to alienation, disenchantment? How much would be resolved, had children grown up in environments that valued them, and that they valued? Environments that matched developing needs as they grew?

The in-between world

Once children become aware of separateness from mother, they inhabit a world *between* self and environment, between fact and fantasy. Through imaginative fantasies, they organize thoughts and learn to manage feelings. Dolls, for instance, reflect and fulfil children's ever-changing emotional needs.[16] Their non-judgemental love forgives tempers, experimental haircuts and face illustration. Projecting their feelings onto such imagined 'friends', and treating them accordingly, helps children cope with life 'on their own'.[17] Fantasy is therefore full of symbolic meaning, and crucial to children's intellectual and emotional development.[18]

Combining experience and feelings, fantasy forms a bridge between the 'objective factual' outer-world and what is developing within the child. Vygotskij considered that, just as art and thought, aesthetics and rationality, belong together and balance life, so do fantasy and fact.[19] Through play, feeling, intellect and fantasy enrich each other.[20] Without fantasy, play isn't possible.

As dreams do, play situations can symbolize hard-to-face issues.[21] Like fairy-tales this helps children work through conflicts and problems of existence,[22] strengthening the emerging self.[23] By enabling children to 'handle' the unfamiliarities of the 'real world', this in-between phase sets the scene for all subsequent development. If they can't cope with a world made safe through imaginative fantasy, how will they manage the next stage: understanding the *essence* of things in a pre-rational, intuitive, way? To discriminate positive from negative, the forward-leading from reactive-denial, this is essential. Without this base, how can they – as teenagers – be inspired by the drama of good struggling against evil? What will motivate them to positive, deeply committed actions?

The outer – material, 'real' – world gains primacy over the inner – child-created, imagined – world only slowly, with much overlap. Older siblings may introduce disbelief in Santa Claus, but this only *fully* convinces when 'reality' is really more real than imagination. For many years, daydreams remain more engrossing than the factual world. Imagination, 'the golden gift of childhood' is an unsurpassed fertilizer of future creativity. Though natural to children and impossible to totally obliterate, we can all too easily unwittingly stultify it. Imagination-stimulating places are crucial to healthy development, but sterile buildings, play cubes and rectilinear rooms have had fantasy sucked out of them.

What about outdoors? Doesn't lots of space solve all problems? Small children's imaginative worlds, however, have an inward-looking scale. They need small subspaces, protectively gestured. Hence, shrub-edged woodland glades, having more 'rooms' than bare lawns, increase imaginative-play invitations, giving more 'room' for play. Moreover, places where you can't see everything at once *feel* significantly bigger. Although middle-school children need open, level space for social activity-based games, they also enjoy activities led by imagination, curiosity and inventiveness. These need identifiable 'places' – which are smaller.

Land where you can't see everything at once feels twice the size of open, level land

One space versus many 'rooms'

What about buildings and gardens? Although fixed, these form the stages on which fantasy dramas unfold. The more mood-evocative they are, the more starting points for fantasy dramas. Like theatre stages, adaptability – for instance, by fixing points for divisibility into subplaces or multiple lighting options – increases potential mood-range. Pre-made 'sets' deny children any creative input, so sap enthusiasm.[24] Also, the more fixed their

Imagination can make anything into anything

imagery, the narrower, so less engrossing, the story range. *Our* imagination, once concretized in film or toy, does nothing for *theirs*. Like colouring-in books and video fairy stories, places, play equipment and toys representing fixed things have already had the imagining done by somebody else. Moreover, a space rocket is *only* a space rocket, whereas a cardboard box can be boat, cauldron, house, car, shop, bed or TV; and tree-roots can be anything from dragon to moun-

Hard rectangular rooms softened by furniture

tain. With *things,* such as dressing-up clothes, utensils and sticks and blankets to build with, or sand and mud to mould, children build imagined worlds. But *places* are where these happen – or, lamentably often, can't.

Play: preparation for life

Play is no luxurious indulgence. To Winnicott, 'To play is to use imagination, the most important thing a person can do … Play is always an experience of creating, also of uniting time and space – so is fundamental to how we live'.[25] Play bonds outer experience to inner. Steiner considered it 'the work of childhood' – essential for children to experience their world with their whole being.[26] Imitation and imagination let children dramatize, learn to make sense of and manage their experiences – essential preparation for taking part in the grown-up world.[27]

From play, in all its forms, children gain a sense of achievement and self-security, develop cooperative abilities and outlook, and also respect both for themselves and others.[28] Its new opportunities and challenges teach children how to take control in unfamil-

Small children investigate everything

iar situations. Crucial to how we subsequently manage adult life, no wonder it takes great concentration. To Winnicott, anti-play, anti-creativity, 'everything must be justified as practical' attitudes reduce humans to the level of machines – producing the feeling that nothing matters and life isn't worth living.[29]

Play needs space – in cities, prohibitively expensive. Can virtual experiences replace outdoor play? These can be tailored for educational content and allow withdrawal into three-dimensional spaces players can control.[30] Unlike play, however, they weaken the distinction between outer, social, reality, and inner, imaginative, symbolic fantasy.[31] Also, after video games, it can take hours before basic orientation and coordination skills fully return.[32] Some things effortlessly learnt from real-life experiences can't even be accessed by electronic games: how can you experience virtual love, or virtual tree-climbing?[33] Moreover, unlike real-world society, you can just switch off computer games or e-chat whenever things aren't going right, so never *have to* learn to sort out problems. Socially, children playing together learn to intuit each other's needs. Playing video games, they don't.[34] Moreover, overstimulation and information-overload contribute to decreasing attention span generally,[35] and Attention Deficit Disorder specifically. These pressures – and others, such as educational competitiveness and advertising-led consumerism – stressfully reduce emotional digestion time. This is implicated in the rapid growth of childhood depression.[36] It's relevant to ask: who finances television? As this is mostly advertising, how can it *not* encourage consumerism? As it's expensive, how can it *not* be high-pressure, super-fast?

Physiologically, TV and video games retard the functioning of sensory neuron signals in the brain – probably irreversibly. The shortage of applicants capable of combining abstract thought with flexible imagination and instant decision-making, essential for aero-space work, is attributed to this.[37] Health-wise, television and computer games have produced an 'indoor generation' of children, with childhood obesity – threatening Type 2 diabetes and heart problems in middle age – already affecting one child in four.[38] Moreover, these entertainments often reduce children's sleep, resulting in a hormonal contribution to obesity.[39] Psychologically, kindergarten teacher-trainer, Margaret Meyerkort, warns that imagination pre-formed TV images and pre-planned video-game scenarios (albeit with multiple pathways) 'kill the creative forces in our children, induce lethargy in them, and bring about the conviction: I have a right to be entertained'.[40] Unbelievably, schools now have to teach children how to play. It doesn't help that a third of all children are too nervous of getting dirty to willingly do so.[41] Even more unbelievably, some children have no ability to imagine.[42]

Virtual play is so recent that the full physical, social, emotional, educational and ecological consequences in mature adults are yet to come. For healthy, whole-person, development, there's no substitute for outdoor social play – however expensive is space.

Environment and development

Children progress from *exploring* the world around them, to trying to *manipulate* it, physically, socially and emotionally. As materially conscious, cause–effect rationality increases, they start to *use* their environment: a resource, not a responsibility. By adulthood, conscious *understanding* has developed. Whether they now abuse, exploit or work symbiotically with nature, depends on attitude. Do they respect and treasure, and feel respected by, their environment? Or does it de-value them? Must they violently *demand* 'respect'?

For infants, the more magical their environment, the more fully can they live in their in-between world. The longer they do so, the better can they learn to manage the unfamiliar material world. The more secure they feel, the more confidently do they grow towards independence. Security progresses from parental (or similar trusted adult) proximity to having a secure physical base – trustworthy, durable and anchored. For small children, this implies heavyweight, solid buildings; and within them, private sanctuaries such as window-seats, hideaways, niches and platforms. Masonry and earthen buildings easily provide this solidity. Timber ones can compensate for lack of weight with the visual warmth of unpainted wood. Straw-bale buildings offer good environmental protection, but need to sound, feel – and be – as substantial as they look. Steel ones are strong, but look too lightweight to communicate this to the senses, only to the brain. They can suit teenagers, but never infants.

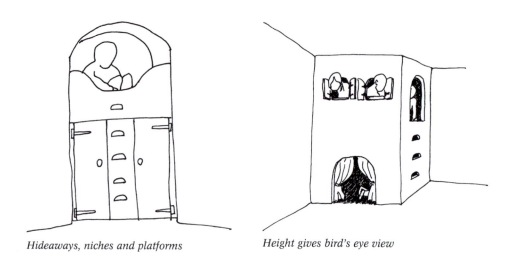

Hideaways, niches and platforms   *Height gives bird's eye view*

Though not always painless, play teaches children to overcome social problems. It encourages them to stretch themselves, sometimes subtly, sometimes adventurously, even dangerously. Surroundings rich in experiential possibilities encourage improvisation and resourcefulness. The more diverse their environment – especially outdoors – the greater the exploratory and creativity potential, and the wider the play- and social-scenario range.

For teenagers, this diversity need extends beyond school and home neighbourhood boundaries to the wider world within which these areas are enmeshed. They need more open buildings, flooded with light, outward looking and filled with a feeling of levity. This implies lighter-weight buildings. Between earth-bound, protective enclosure and upward-gestured bright openness, children's environmental needs evolve, paralleling their own developmental journey.

What environment best fulfils children's developmental needs? Design must tread a narrow path between nourishment and manipulation, between the reverent magical and the dramatically theatrical, fantastical; between the reassuringly secure and the creativity-stimulating challenging; between places that nurture and those that help them grow. Nourishment and challenge are opposites. These require a very delicate balance.

Development is what childhood is about. But for healthy development, undistorted by fears and worries, children need to feel valued and protected. They need both challenge and an ambience of security. The environment we offer children – at every stage – can be a support or hindrance they can carry far into life. With childhood itself under threat from the pressures of modern life,[43] this is too important just to leave to good intentions and good taste.

STATE   →   →   →   →

Trust	Wonder	Curiosity	Control	Determination to change the world

ENVIRONMENTAL QUALITY NEEDED

Integrity	Magic	Sensory exploration	Creative interventions	Inspiration

Evolving environmental needs

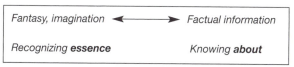

Fantasy, imagination ◄────────► Factual information

Recognizing **essence**   Knowing **about**

Evolving relationship to the world

Notes

1 *How* new is a matter of much argument. J.H.P. Plumb suggested it started at the end of the seventeenth century, with the design of clothes, games and books specifically for children. Cited in Dudek, Mark (1996) *Kindergarten Architecture*. Spon.

2 Lecture by child psychologist Amons, Christie (2005) at *The Integrity of the Child* conference. *Anthroposophy Worldwide*, No. 3.

3 Riscke, Elke-Maria (1985) Pedagogical aspects of kindergarten architecture. In Flinspach, Jürgen (1985) *Waldorfkindergärten Bauen*. Unpublished translation by Luborsky, Peter (1988).

4 Skantze, Ann, in Lundahl, Gunilla, ed. (1995) *Hus och Rum för Små Barn*. Arkus.

5 Meyerkort, Margaret *Kindergarten architecture and equipment*. Compiled by Elvira Rychlak. Unpublished.

6 Nordström, Maria (1990) Barns boendeförställningar i ett utvecklinspsykologiskt perspektiv. Doctoral thesis, Statens Institut för byggnadsförskning, Lund University. Cited in Farnestam, Sandra (2001) *Arkitektur i skolan*. Unpublished dissertation, Umeå University.

7 Steiner, Rudolf (1996) *The Foundations of Human Experience*. (1919 lectures) Anthroposophic Press.

8 Nordström, Maria. In Lundahl, Gunilla, ed. (1995) *ibid*.

9 Piaget, Jean, cited in Lundahl, Gunilla, ed. (1995) *op. cit.*

10 Piaget, Jean (1982) *Barnets själsliga utveckling*. Liber förlag (original 1964).

11 Nordström, Maria. In Lundahl, Gunilla, ed. (1995) *ibid*.

12 Nordström, Maria. In Lundahl, Gunilla, ed. (1995) *op. cit.*

13 Skantze, Ann (1989) *Vad betyder skolhuset? Skolans fysika miljø ur elevernas perspektiv studerad i relation till barns och ungdomars utvecklingsuppgifter*. Doctoral thesis,

Stockholm University. Cited in Farnestam, Sandra (2001) *ibid.*

14 Steiner, Rudolf (1996) *ibid.*

15 Piaget, Jean. Cited in Lundahl, Gunilla, ed. (1995) *ibid.*

16 Soft dolls with archetypically minimal facial expression can be imagined into whatever moods needed. Hard, full-featured ones are less versatile.

17 Winnicott, Donald Woods. Cited in Lundahl, Gunilla, ed. (1995) *ibid.*

18 Nordström, Maria. In Lundahl, Gunilla, ed. (1995) *op. cit.*

19 Vygotskij, Lev Semënovic () *Fantasi och kreativitet i barndom.* Translated by Lindsten, Kajsa Öberg. Daidalos.

20 Bettelheim, Bruno (1976) *The Uses of Enchantment.* Thames & Hudson.

21 Skantze, Ann. In Lundahl, Gunilla, ed. (1995) *ibid.*

22 Bettelheim, Bruno (1975) *ibid.*

23 Bergstrom, Matti. Quoted in Lundahl, Gunilla, ed. (1995) *ibid.*

24 A castle, improvised by children from scrap 'is worth a thousand perfectly detailed, exactly finished castles, made for them'. Alexander, Christopher et al (1977) *A Pattern Language.* Oxford University Press.

25 Winnicott, Donald Woods. Cited in Lundahl, Gunilla, ed. (1995) *ibid.* (Quotes translated from Swedish.)

26 Steiner, Rudolf, quoted by *Lifeways North America*, http://www.waldorfhomeschoolers.com/waldorfplay.htm.

27 Vygotskij, Lev Semënovic *ibid.*

28 Arq, Concepcion Laguna (1995) The children, the green area and the sense of community in Mexico City. *International Play Journal* 3, .

29 Winnicott, Donald Woods. Cited in Lundahl, Gunilla, ed. (1995) *ibid.* (Quotes translated from Swedish.)

30 Dudek, Mark (2000) *Architecture of Schools.* Architectural Press.

31 Jennings, Sue (1995) Playing for real. *International Play Journal* 3,

32 Green, Jeff (2006), Sensing the world and ourselves. In *New View*, Autumn.

33 Letter by 110 childhood professionals to the *Daily Telegraph,* 12 September (2006), and subsequent interviews on BBC Radio 4 *Today* Programme.

34 Source: Kaczmarek, Aleksandra, teacher.

35 Dudek, Mark (2000) *ibid.*

36 Letter by 110 childhood professionals to the *Daily Telegraph* (2006) *ibid.*

37 Scott, William B. (2002) *Aviation and Space Technology Journal,* 6 May 2002.

38 UK children are among the most unfit in Europe. Fenoughty, Sue, environmental education teacher consultant.

39 *Today* Programme, BBC Radio 4, 19 October 2006.

40 Meyerkort, Margaret, *ibid.*

41 Green, Jeff (2006) *ibid.*

42 Letter by 110 childhood professionals to the *Daily Telegraph* (2006) *ibid.*

43 See, for instance: Palmer, Sue (2006) *Toxic Childhood: How the Modern World is Damaging Our Children, And What We Can Do About It.* Orion.

CHAPTER 3

Developmental needs: challenge and certainty

Conflicting needs

'Contradiction' said Hegel 'is the root of all movement and liveliness'. This is especially true of children's developmental needs. No-one can develop without challenges to surmount. But children *also* need to feel safe. In various forms, these conflicting needs continue throughout life, but in childhood, the tension between the known and the unknown, between challenge, stimulation and reassuring constancy, is particularly acute.

Stimulation is essential to a healthy life. Without constant stimulus, our senses wither and life is boring. Unrelieved stimulation, however, is stressful. For a stress-free life, we don't need too much, and we need rests from it. For peaceful but invigorated balance, we need both sameness, predictability, and contrast, stimulus. Psychologists Fiske and Maddi call this 'difference within sameness'.[1] As background ambience, natural settings such as lapping wavelets, dancing leaf-shade patterns, gurgling streams or endlessly re-forming clouds combine, calming tempo, the security of a *reliably constant* world, with the life and delight of sensory stimulation.

Difference within sameness suggests buildings that are simultaneously unpretentious, quiet, and experientially, sensorially rich. This dynamic balance between stimulation and calm is reflected in children's conflicting needs for challenge, adventure, and reassurance, security; for the reliably unchanging and the chaos of creation. The optimum balance between these extremes progresses with age – babies principally need calm; teenagers, excitement – but both are always present. Stimulation and calm, risk and security are *external* factors; we need our environment to supply them. They involve, therefore, environmental design.

Reassurance by design

Confusing buildings make us feel at their Kafkaesque mercy. In easily interpreted ones, we know where we are, so feel more confident. For children, therefore, 'decipherable' architecture is crucial. Roofline, glazing, materials and façade gestures indicating rooms' uses, relationships and hierarchy help here.

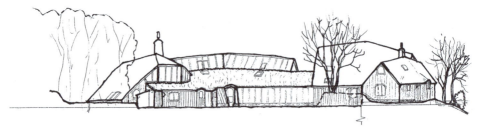

Building legibility: what rooms are for, their relationships and hierarchy

To feel safe, children need to know: 'How did I get in here? How can I get out? What is this space connected to?' Without visually obvious pathways from one place to another, their world can be confusing, even frightening.[2] Sensory connections – visual, acoustic or olfactory – between inter-related rooms allow them to know what's going on next door. Without these, they can feel alarmingly cut off.[3] In small clusters of rooms, it's reassuringly easy to know where we are, but what distinguishes one sealed box somewhere on a long corridor from another?

Anywhere confusing enough to need maps or signs seeds stress – even for adults. For children, it's much worse. Its lesson is that the world isn't reliable. Things aren't as they appear; they must be learnt and remembered. We can never be confident we're in the right place – perhaps *we*'ve done something *wrong*. This breeds guilt. To anthropologist Edward Hall: 'To be disorientated in space is to be psychotic'.[4] Such architecture actually hinders children's healthy development. In contrast, mood-individuality, meaningful unity and navigational clarity, by helping children know where they are, reassures them that life is safe.

Mood distinctions – such as cosy and warm or spacious and airy, hard and noisy or soft and quiet, light and open or dark and protected – give individuality to places. This helps us know where we are without needing to think. Turning ceilings down to walls or using beams as area-dividers enhances enclosure, distinguishing separate spaces. Lower-ceilinged alcoves make areas of special, quieter, mood – such as study-areas – feel more private. Such 'my house' effects make children feel territorially secure, so better able to concentrate.[5]

Perception psychologists know that we 'read' things of similar quality as inherently related.[6] Small children see the world as a wholeness of qualitatively related similarities. If it isn't, their world-view is undermined – confusing and unsafe. Difference-within-sameness has, therefore, implications for design. While distinctiveness is essential for identity, places without coherent unity lack harmony; their unstable relationships destabilize children's confidence. As traditional towns demonstrate, spatial unity doesn't depend on stylistic uniformity. It's more about compatible *form-generators*. Each palette of building materials or type of construction brings limitations that qualitatively unify forms, however diverse their shapes.

Metamorphosis works the same way. One *principle* manifests in different, but related, forms in different circumstances. In any metamorphic series we recognize different elements as belonging together: part of one 'individuality'. But the link, the principle, that unites them, isn't physically present; like a child's attention, it requires inner activity. Metamorphic variation both guarantees visual unity and expands the variety essential for navigation. As the variety is *meaningful,* not just stylistically indulgent, this strengthens both coherence and identity. These, in turn, support children's feelings of security.

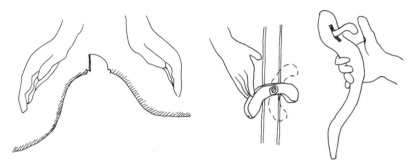

Metamorphosis: in different materials, circumstances

Metamorphosis of building form

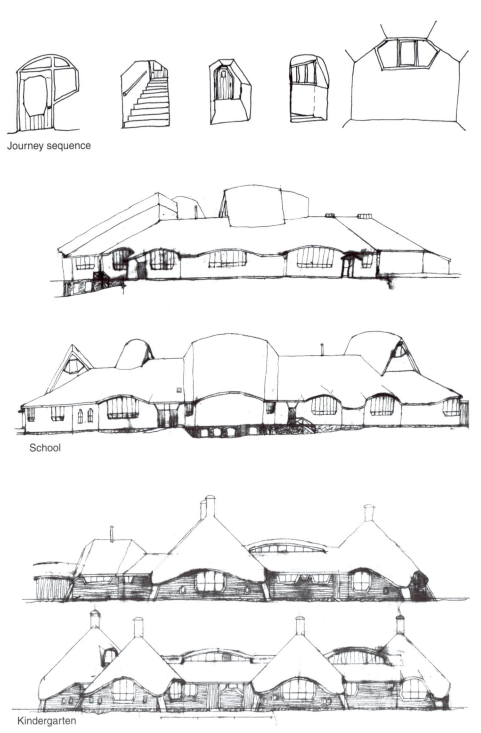

Journey sequence

School

Kindergarten

Metamorphosis in school design

Security to venture out from

Security is the prime need for babies and small children, but it's not long before the need to stretch – often frighten – oneself manifests. Toddlers peep at strangers from behind mother's skirt then hide again. Like chicks rushing back to mother hen, small children need a protective adult nearby. Consequently, in alcoves off kindergarten rooms, they feel secure, but if these become small *rooms*, they don't.[7]

Most people prefer seats where their back is to a wall. Unpredictable events behind us are stressful. Consequently, odd noises or doors opening behind children make them feel insecure. Even locked, never-used, doors feel unsafe to play in front of. Doubly insecure for infants because who knows what kind of monsters live behind them? This is the same if children can hear, but not see, what's about to happen nearby. Low or partially transparent boundaries keep them in visual 'touch', so they don't need to fear nasty surprises.[8] Windows connect room-world with outer-world and its happenings. (For attention focus, however, it's best if these don't view any activity.) Feeling in control of events frees children from worry, giving them the confidence to stretch themselves in play.

Semi-protected play

Very small children want parental (or similar) company to *feel* safe. Older ones don't. More independent and adventurous, they nonetheless still need adults within occasional view or earshot to *be* safe.

Children have *never* been completely safe, but there is a modern dimension. Until the 1950s, children playing on the street were surrounded by people who knew them – a constant multi-age community. This ensured a high level of casual supervision. But with modern traffic and without self-supervising street community, children can no longer run free.[9] Nowadays, we must specifically *design* places where they can play safely without over-restrictive control. Small children move fast. You can't chat to friends, read or comfort a child and assume other children will still be there. For relaxed adults and safe children, this means some sort of enclosure. But nobody likes restrictions. Semi-enclosures feel less confining. For safety, these depend on supervision, usually parental, but also sometimes just informally by neighbours. Domestic windows, open-fronted workshops or allotments surrounding courtyards, cul-de-sacs or park dead-ends ensure supervisory view. For greens encircled by private gardens, self-closing gates, latched above child reach, can keep children from wandering.

Even larger children need the security of a home to return to after their adventures. But whether or not buildings exude security depends, in part, on where they're placed. In the middle of open space, they feel exposed. Backed by trees or land-features, or tied into surroundings by hedges, walls or shrubbery, they feel as though they belong there, so are more durably rooted, reassuringly 'safer'.

Just as families picnic more by rocks than in mid-beach, few children play on feature-less flat lawns by tower blocks. Feeling safer near protective edges, they prefer playing

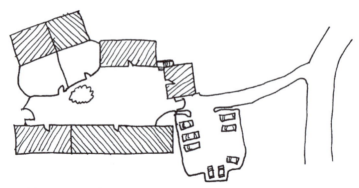

Informal supervision: courtyard

Play-space surrounded by gardens

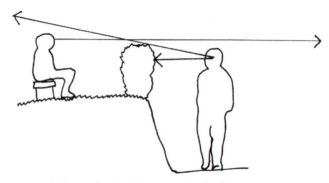

Elevating private ground about 3 feet (1 m) retains visual privacy

Neighbourhood green with good supervisory view from every kitchen window

near houses, trees or under porches.[10] Anchored to 'home', while allowing adventure-space, this edge-realm weaves between security and stimulation, the safe and the stretching. Such polarity interfaces also offer the richest and most varied activity opportunities. In nature, life is richest where elements meet; where field meets wood, land meets water; in human society, where culture interweaves with culture, activity with activity.

Just as animals beat well-trodden paths around their boundaries, children prefer enclosure *edges* for small-group social interaction.[11] In playgrounds, as kickabout and boisterous runabout activities tend to dominate centre spaces, edges better provide intimate, quieter spaces for fantasy play or privacy. 'Pleating' edges increases both 'nestle-places'

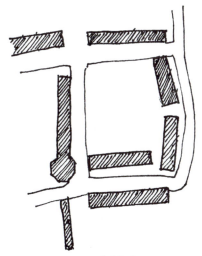

Play green surrounded by houses

and features to climb, command or hide behind. Just as lofts and elevated floor-levels give 'protected' views indoors, physically superior locations, such as balconies, terraces, uphill slopes, steps and sitting walls, give both better observation and psychological security.[12]

A few generations ago, most children lived near countryside, with almost limitless choice of safely wild places in which to play. Today, most live in cities, with countryside

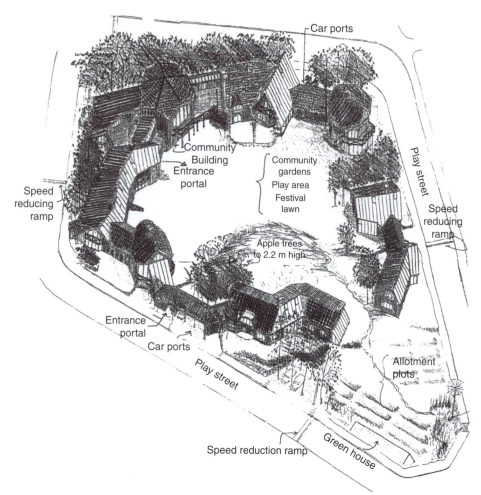

Car ports

Community
Building
Entrance
portal

Community
gardens
Play area
Festival
lawn

Play street

Speed
reducing
ramp

Speed
reducing
ramp

Apple trees
to 2.2 m high

Entrance
portal

Car ports

Allotment
plots

Play street

Speed reduction ramp

Green house

Eco-village: horseshoe of domestic windows with allotment activities closing open end

usually inaccessible – and sometimes toxic-sprayed. Many parks are unexciting and unappealing. Roadside playgrounds, though safety fenced, are neither stress-free nor healthy. Nowadays we have to *make* child-friendly places – traffic-safe, neighbourly, soft to eye and ear, climatically comfortable and sense-stimulating; they won't just happen.

Stretching boundaries

Growing up is about overcoming challenges. An early step to independence is making secret 'homes' – even if only blanket houses or chairs to hide behind.[13] These hidey-holes fulfil many functions: stage-sets for imagination-stories, 'sulk-bins' to withdraw into when upset,[14] and 'womb burrows' for security. (When something is too much to

Green cul-de-sac play-area in sun with long 'escape route' overlooked by neighbours' allotments, greenhouse, apartments for the elderly, gardens, roof-gardens and domestic windows

Vehicle accessible court, traffic calmed for play priority

In-between places to play in

Pleated edge

handle, children often hide; consequently, in house fires, firemen must, tragically, check cupboards and under beds.) Development-wise, hidey-holes provide a manageable 'microsphere', which prepares children for the complex 'social macrosphere' they'll soon encounter.[15]

Children feel impelled to test themselves in places increasingly distant from home, then to create their *own* 'homes' – dens.[16] Wendy-houses are for playing 'home', but a den is 'your own place in the world' – a concretization of your identity. Archetypally linked with nest-, home- and defence-making, dens are sacred, and therefore easily compromised by adult intrusion. This gives den-play an almost ritual quality. Although den-building rarely lasts beyond the age of 12 years, children missing out on this have a 'ritual gap'.[17] As Kong describes, '... the environmental experiences available for children, especially those in middle childhood when they encounter the world for themselves, away from grownups and parental control, are crucial in the development of sane, healthy adults'.[18]

Dens made *for* children, not *by* them, are neither challenging, created, nor secret – consequently, most are shunned. Kits of parts suggest – indeed *are* – someone else's design. Dens built of found materials are more 'your own'. Many found materials, however, such as nail-rich demolition planks, are dangerous. Straw bales, dead branches or live willow cuttings are safer. Bales, however, need to be provided – and, if light enough for children to lift, a building lesson would not go amiss.[19] Similarly, as children are forbidden to carry knives, willow cuttings – or secateurs – need to be provided. This, unfortunately, limits spontaneity.

Whereas dens – or buildings – of natural material return to earth gracefully, ones of industrial materials – such as polythene sheeting – just get so squalid nobody uses them. This is a lesson in living *with* nature. Grown materials lend themselves to gentler, more fluid, and *more imagination-demanding* forms. Tree houses demand even greater resourcefulness, imagination and freer thinking. Some schools even plant trees for this purpose.[20]

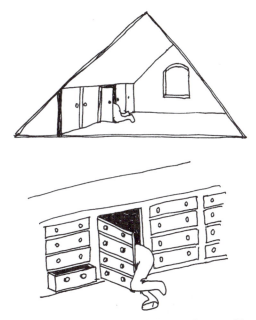

Some dens are real 'hidey-holes', undiscoverable to all except a select 'secret society'

But *where* can dens be built? As child-accessible 'wild' land contracts year by year, is den-making possible at school? At Björko Friskolan (Linköping, Sweden), the whole grounds – except the football field – are wooded for directed learning, spontaneous play *and* den-making.[21] Dens 'near' school may be acceptable, but dens *at* home are too tame. 'Far away' is more exiting. Urban waste ground, however, is often unsafe: syringes, toxic waste and rats, with reputations for mugging, dealing, bullying or teenage sex. The common adult view that 'cleaned-up is best' overcomes abandonment problems, but children also need 'wild' places: weeds, shrubs and unkempt trees – adventurous and apparently unsupervised. Will such places be safe from crime? This depends on many factors, including social and cultural ones. Defensible space measures, however, have significant effect. 'Portal' access makes places feel 'owned'. Buildings and activities visually commanding such 'gateways' make these feel policed. Such non-offensive defences depend on making intruders feel everyone knows they're there.

Whether in schools, on housing estates, parks or wasteland, there's a fine line between places that provide adventure, fun and den opportunities and forgotten, ownerless, 'no-places' that encourage vandalism, bullying and crime; between wild, unkempt places and derelict, squalid ones. Places that emanate messages of responsibility and value induce like attitudes and behaviour. Forgotten, uncared-for places do the reverse. This is about what places say.

Children's perspectives differ from adults'. A German friend, remembering his childhood in a bombed-out city, described it as wonderful, exciting and creativity-stimulating – unlike the bland playgrounds with activity pre-determining equipment where he now

A developer planned five houses on this 'wilderness' playground. The surrounding community suggested two – to complete the supervisory enclosure – and jointly buying the remainder (at three-plot value) to preserve it

teaches! Tidiness and order help adults cope. Children likewise need structure in their lives, but they *also need* the un-ordered – places where they're free to make *their own* adventures, create *their own* constructions and hidden places.

wild ←----→ care ←----→ neglect

Human imprint: nature-respectful or not?

There are other ways in which children territorially assert their independence. At home, they grow increasingly possessive of their bedrooms' privacy. Susan Isaacs' pioneering Malting House School reflected this by giving boarders their own individual bed-sitting rooms with lockable doors.[22] Nonetheless, there's no substitute for children making secret places themselves, for such places support their *development*.

Adventure

Children love adventure. It's about stretching, frightening yourself – an essential part of growing from dependent child to independent, self-directed adult. Overcoming fear is central to this. Balancing on walls, climbing trees, swinging high and cycling fast are overcoming-fear tests. So are babies' peek-a-boo and toddlers' hide-and-seek. These progress to real frights and real adventure.

Adventure may be essential to inner growth, but what about safety? This is a sensitive issue. Few parents want their children to play somewhere unsafe. Few children can resist the challenge of somewhere adventurous. Adventure can be dangerous. But life without challenge is development-stunting. The real issue, therefore, is how to maximize challenge, while minimizing injury risk. The more dangerous something *feels*, but safer it *actually* is, the better both for development and survival. This is known as 'safe danger'.[23]

Some things are easy, such as long swinging ropes over not-too-deep water or swings on slopes so you look a long way down – but wouldn't actually fall far. Slides built into hillsides increase opportunities for long runs with curves and varied slope (up to 40°). More exciting than freestanding slides, these are actually safer.[24] Also, they obviate the need for laddered platforms, off which children are easily pushed. Moreover, as more things can happen on hilltops,

Perceived risk: long view down but short fall

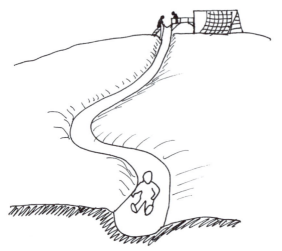

Slides built into hillsides for long runs

there's always something else to do, so fewer disputes and fewer feelings of defeat. Educationally, such slides look more at home in the landscape, so *enhance place* instead of imposing *purchased object*.

Scariness doesn't cause accidents. Things going wrong do. Children don't have the experience to anticipate these. Many safety aspects are solely about anticipatory planning; they have nothing to do with perceived danger. Swings, for instance, need twice their suspension-length clearance and, like cable-rides, carousels and all moving devices, are safer near playground edges, backed by fences.[25] Sharp corners – whether of play equipment, furniture or buildings – hurt more than 'softer' forms. What about ground surface? Safety matting can't reduce accidents. It's environmentally polluting, expensive and looks artificial – but does it minimize injury? Natural surfaces, such as grass and bark-mulch are equally effective – and also cheaper. Of all outdoor surfaces, wood chips are the safest to fall on.[26] They also smell good. (But, as they crumble with use, need occasional replacement.) Sand is widely used in Sweden, such a safety-conscious country that even tricycling toddlers wear crash-helmets. Though sand is dual-purpose – safety surface and play – sand-*pits* should never be under climbing trees. Apart from leaf contamination, falling onto children isn't considerate.

Water-play and tree-climbing are two things children love. But neither is safe. They're fun just *because* they're so important to their development. The 1952 Ministry of Education recognized this: 'In climbing a tree, a child becomes more versatile as he finds his way round an awkward angle, up a place where a long stretch is necessary, and along a branch where he must wriggle full-length. He begins to know

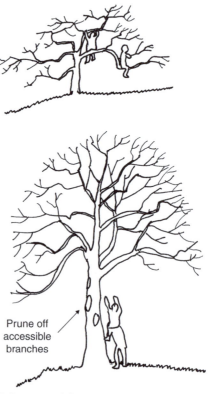

Prune off accessible branches

Safe trees and dangerous trees

Trawl-net draped across low spreading branches makes sociable tree-top 'nests' for minimal risk

more about trees and about himself, and he gains new realizations of height, width, depth, weight and resilience'.[27] Like kittens, however, children climb first and look down later, making tall trees dangerous. Lower, spreading ones (such as apple, pear and cherry) are as good to climb, but not so far to fall from. Five feet (1.5 m) up means nine feet (2.7 m) eye-level – for children, adventurously high. Nets and ropes allow children to make a wide range of constructions.[28] (As abrasion and ultraviolet deteriorate cordage, it needs regular inspection.[29]) Trawl-nets draped across low spreading branches make sociable tree-top 'nests' for hanging out and chatting. If these are hard to climb into, older children feel important, as only *they* can get in.

Water play isn't about risk; it's about water. Beguilingly inviting, its dangers are invisible. No wonder water-sprites look appealing but draw you to your doom! Nonetheless, few ducks drown. They're used to water. Likewise children have always lived by sea, rivers, lakes and ponds. Mostly safely. But anyone – from infant to alcoholic adult – unable to raise their faces, can drown in inches. Under five years of age, children's heads are so proportionally large that they float head down. Small children *always* need supervision. For them, water should never be more than 8 inches (200 mm) deep, and must not have unexpected depth changes.[30] Hard surfaces, especially concrete, grow slime underwater – invisibly dangerous. Bricks do too, but – like gravel – their joints let feet mechanically engage. Invisible risk makes places more dangerous than they look, they are turned into 'traps' – doubly hazardous. It's essential, therefore, that water *looks* more dangerous than it actually *is*. Large ponds or wide canals, with shallow gradients and without entangling weeds, achieve this. Small deep ponds should be fenced, filled with rocks, or covered with non-corroding mesh or decking. While it's a rare fence that is permanently childproof, brambles, roses, thorny shrubs and nettles deter climbing or burrowing. (Also the thorns are good for small birds, the nettles for butterflies.) Infants can't easily get into raised pools and streams, making these safer. But these look artificial, so teach nothing about water in topographical context.

Unfortunately, no tree, water or anything adventurous is *completely* safe. But what in life is? And what fun is life when neurotically overprotected? To Lady Allen, adventure playgrounds should include: 'Danger. This is what children want'.[31] She considered that *perceived danger* modifies behaviour, encouraging care and responsibility. Also it helps safety awareness become habitual for any situation.[32] As an element of danger means that they have to keep an eye on, and out for, each other, children develop social and spatial awareness. Developing this, 'cooperative adventure playgrounds' make adventurous activities impossible without cooperation.[33] Educationally, risk requires children to focus intently on task. As little else in life does to a comparable degree, experience of risk is important to cultivating attention.[34] Danger, therefore, has developmental, social and educational benefits. But Nietzsche's aphorism: 'what doesn't kill you makes you stronger' is perhaps *too* uncompromising. Danger, after all, is still dangerous. Should we accept previous generations' level of risk? Life is no longer 'cheap'. Should safety standards reflect this?

Although statistics show as many accidents in 'safe' as in 'dangerous' playgrounds,[35] litigation-conscious design increasingly closes sand-heaps (for hygiene), forbids tree climbing and limits 'high' equipment to five feet (1.5 m), making parks too 'safe' to be fun, so less played in.[36] Is less fun a reasonable price to pay for increased safety? Unfortunately, children denied opportunities for adventure seek them out – often in *really* dangerous places, such as railway tracks and building sites.[37] Consequently, the Royal Society for the Prevention of Accidents recommends playgrounds should *not* be safer than 'necessary'.[38] As over 700 children are killed by traffic each year in Britain, 'dangerous play' that keeps them off roads is, in fact, usually safer for them.[39] Also, danger-thrill deprivation leads teenagers to even greater risks – both driving and with narcotic experiments. But what is the 'right' level of danger? Any answer is sure to be wrong. Nobody can responsibly recommend real danger, but without perceived danger, risk is displaced and many times multiplied.

Perceived risk and the *stimulus* of new challenges are what children need. These are essential ingredients for developing self-reliance and self-esteem. It's the task of design to provide these whilst keeping *actual* risk – unfortunately never wholly avoidable – to acceptably low levels. Unfortunately, things can go wrong when, with only a few years life-experience, children try to stretch confining limits, try the unfamiliar. But never growing beyond the dependency of infanthood would be worse for everybody!

Creativity: known meeting unknown

Children are naturally creative. At the beginning of their life journey, they're searching for meaning – what they mean, the world means, life means. This brings openness to try everything. Unlike adult outlook, already shaped – hence blinkered – to use things 'properly', they enthusiastically do things wrongly. Still thinking flexibly, they quickly understand computers, video recorders, mobile phones and anti-child locks.

Vygotskij considered creativity – the entertaining of an unknown future – another form of consciousness; an aspect of truth, richer than conventional material-facts 'truth'.[40] In the brain, creativity is born where chaotic impulses from the brain-stem meet signals from the brain-surface that order the impressions from the outer world.[41] In life also, creativity flourishes where order and chaos interpenetrate, where inner drive meets outer stimulus – often in the form of obstruction.

Imagination – from within – and creativity – adapting that which is around – feed each other. Enchanted mood and sensory richness readily trigger imagination. Craftwork and art stimulate creativity. What facilities do these need? Some crafts can be done anywhere, but some need fully equipped workshops. Others are better outdoors, but roofed. Greenwood turning, for instance, needs outdoor air-humidity. Metalworking forges and ceramics kilns are fire risks, so safer in detached sheds. To encourage children to think with their hands, Reggio Emilia pre-schools have 'ateliers' off every classroom, with the 'real' tools even small children always want to use. (Though potentially dangerous, sharpness increases effectiveness – and, as this gives better control, some say is safer.) Art is possible anywhere. Steiner (junior) schools, feeling art should be inseparable from life, do it in classrooms. Reggio Emilia consider that studios increase the scope of what can be done. Mess-wise, it's certainly easier in studios. These need specific environmental conditions: plentiful north light, large walls for easy paper mounting, multiple overhead fixing points and ample sinks. Generous floor-space, high ceilings and calm colouring – white or pale greys – help counteract clutter and over-busyness.

But what *environments* stimulate more creativity than others? Rene Dubos observed how many creative people had grown up in New York's Lower East Side or on small family farms. Although widely contrasting environments, both situations provide a wide range of experiences, encourage resourcefulness and flexible imaginative thinking, and link consequences to actions.[42] Rich exploration opportunities foster creativity. For small children, this is *sensory* exploration. Consciously directed, intellectually understood exploration only comes with age. Artistic exploration encourages knowing things in multiple ways. Unlike hard rectangular forms and spaces, 'living' ones – especially ever-changing, soft-edged living nature – elude definition and increase imaginative opportunities. Box environments encourage box thinking. Living-formed surroundings require flexible, living, interpretation, stimulating living thinking.

Designing exploratory opportunities into children's surroundings, but

Soft space instead of hard space; ever-changing space instead of fixed

knowing how they should be explored, imposes the same limitations as 'educational' toys. Only *unknown* challenges stimulate creativity. Although essentially working beyond the limits of our knowledge, creativity depends upon intuitive direction: where the process will lead. This requires multiple ways of looking, of developing concepts. The childhood faculty that imagines into being whatever we *want* to be there, matures in adulthood into the ability to penetrate the essence of what *is* there but cannot be readily seen. This is all about *knowing* rather than knowing *about*.

Only through creativity can we ever make anything *new*. Remembered knowledge can only *reproduce*. To Steiner, past-based knowledge ('reproduction') needs to be balanced by future-based striving towards the unknown (creativity). In unfamiliar situations, reproduced knowledge is irrelevant. Without creativity we're victims to the winds of life.

The known and the unknown

Development depends on challenge. But children can't face this without disabling fear unless they feel secure. They need to be enfolded by a world they can rely on. To venture into the uncharted unknown, they need the reassurance of the known.

How much challenge, how much security do children need? The balance point is sensitive: too much known, too safe, and development is stultified by the easy but unchallenging. Too much unknown, and it's unbalanced by stress they're too young to handle. This balance point isn't static; it evolves with age.

Environment can provide both challenge and reassurance, adventure and safety. But, for small children, the greatest challenges and feelings of protectedness are *social*. Social stresses and security aren't random. They're significantly influenced by physical surroundings. These determine how children meet, the atmosphere in which they do so, and how easily they can do things together. Socially as well as physically, these establish relationships between known and unknown.

Childhood: a journey of evolving needs

Notes

1 Fiske and Maddi (1961) *Functions of Varied Experience*. Quoted in Olds, Anita Rui (2001) *Child Care Design Guide*. McGraw Hill.
2 Research by Prescott and Jones (1967) cited in Dudek, Mark (1996) *Kindergarten Architecture*. Spon.
3 Olds, Anita Rui (2001) *Child Care Design Guide*. McGraw Hill.
4 Hall, E. (1976) The anthropology of space. In Prohansky, Ittleson and Rivlin, eds, *Environmental Psychology: People and their Physical Settings*. Holt Rinehart and Winston, quoted in Dudek, Mark (2000) *Architecture of Schools*. Architectural Press.
5 Dudek, Mark (2000) *op. cit.*
6 Arnheim, Rudolf.
7 Riscke, Elke-Maria (1985) Pedagogical aspects of kindergarten architecture. In Flinspach, Jürgen (1985) *Waldorfkindergärten Bauen*. Unpublished translation by Luborsky, Peter (1988).
8 Olds, Anita Rui (2001) *ibid.*
9 In fact, child road-deaths have been declining for half a century. But the number of places in which children can play and the range over which they roam have shrunk many times faster.
10 Olds, Anita Rui, *ibid.*
11 Olds, Anita Rui, *op. cit.*
12 Olds, Anita Rui, *op. cit.*
13 Marcus, Claire Cooper (1995) *House as a Mirror of Self*. Conari Press.
14 Bayes, Kenneth (1967) *The Therapeutic Effect of Environment on Emotionally Disturbed and Mentally Subnormal Children*. The Gresham Press.
15 Hart, R. (1993) Summer in the city. *International Play Journal* 1, 3 September. Quoted in Dudek (2000) *ibid.*
16 Marcus, Claire Cooper (1995) *ibid.*
17 Marcus, Claire Cooper, *op. cit.*
18 Kong, L. (2000) Nature's dangers, nature's pleasures: urban children and the natural world. In Holloway, S. and Valentine, G., eds, *Children's Geographies: Playing, Living, Learning*. Routledge. Quoted in Enns, Cherie C. (2005) *Places for Children*. University College of the Fraser Valley.
19 Mini-bales are increasingly rare.
20 For instance Harte Skole, Kolding, Denmark, descried in Fenoughty, Susan (1997) *The Garden Classroom*. Unpublished Churchill Fellowship report.
21 Fenoughty, Susan (1997) *op. cit.*
22 This dated from 1924. Dudek, Mark (2000) *ibid.*
23 Kong, L. (2000) *ibid.*
24 Olds, Anita Rui (2001) *ibid.*

25 Olds, Anita Rui (2001) *op. cit.*
26 Pofesssor David Ball interviewed on *The Learning Curve*, BBC Radio 4, 25 June (2002).
27 Ministry of Education (1952) *Moving and Growing*. HMSO.
28 Sue Hutchinson of Loopy Soow, playleader.
29 Nylon rope lasts well, but polypropylene deteriorates rapidly in ultraviolet light, first becoming splintery, then weak.
30 Olds, Anita Rui (2001) *ibid.*
31 Lady Allen (the pioneer of adventure playgrounds in Britain from 1969): archive interview in *The Learning Curve*, BBC Radio 4, 25 June (2002).
32 Sue Hutchinson of Loopy Soow, playleader.
33 As, for instance, in a forest on Norrbyskär island, Umeå, Sweden.

34 Green, Jeff (2006), Sensing the world and ourselves. *New View*, Autumn.
35 Professor David Ball (2002) *ibid.*
36 Professor David Ball (2002) *op. cit.*
37 Professor David Ball (2002) *op. cit.*
38 *Today* Programme, BBC 4, 15 June (2006).
39 UK figures, 2006.
40 Vygotskij, Lev Semënovic *Fantasi och kreativitet i barndom*. Daidalos (translated by Lindsten, Kajsa Öberg).
41 According to brain surgeon Matti Bergström, as described in Lundahl, Gunilla, ed. (1995) *Hus och Rum för Små Barn*. Arkus.
42 Dubos, Rene (1973) *the Biological Basis of Urban Design*. Ekistics April 1973, quoted in Venolia, C. (1988) *Healing Environments*. Celestial Arts.

PART 11

Health: physical, developmental and social

CHAPTER 4

Social relationships and place

School society

Children's social horizons normally expand slowly. Until playgroup or kindergarten, most live in a home-based society – unchallenging and securely small. This makes the unfamiliar social exposure a *sudden* jolt. To some extent, however, mother's absence is moderated by the feeling of constant protection by adults close nearby. But while kindergartens enfold, schools open up. Children are more 'on their own'. They now have to learn *social* responsibilities.

Schools are insular societies, often walled-in, with their own un-homelike conventions and rules. Architect Hans Scharoun described them as hierarchical urban microcosms: homes (classrooms) opening off streets (communal spaces); community neighbourhoods (classroom groups with associated rooms); and town-hall (assembly hall).[1] Outdoors, a common hierarchy is that from 'urban' to 'natural': from building-surrounded tarmac to playing-fields. Sometimes this spans from courtyard, through amphitheatre and garden to wood. Character distinctions between hierarchical layers can be emphasized by thresholds. Indoors, fire-doors, passage-constrictions and darker or light-flooded places can provide these. Outdoors: tree-arches, ground-surface changes and bridges.[2] Most intergroup social life, however, occurs in the *public* spaces between buildings or rooms. Unfortunately, not all of this is good.

Bullying

Children's social life isn't automatically harmonious. Shyness, possessive ownership, dog-in-the-mangerism aren't uncommon. Nor is bullying.[3] Whether verbal or physical, this can scar for life. Though partly age-related, and worst around 12 to 13 years of age,[4] it particularly occurs when children are crowded, bored and out of adult view.[5] Such environmental factors are avoidable.

Most bullying takes place at or near school – usually in public spaces, such as toilets, cloakrooms, corridors, playgrounds and their hidden edges. But bullying isn't just opportunistic. It has multiple roots. These include animal behaviour[6] (hens in confined spaces 'hen-peck' the weakest to death), competitive dominance,[7] violence at home[8] and compensation for insecurity: animal, social, cultural and individual-spirit levels.

Although primarily societal, social-scale, friction, role-models and insecurity have architectural implications. This raises the question: do schools unwittingly *teach* bullying?

In schools, competitiveness, domination and aggressive shouting are all magnified by scale. Scale itself is an issue. Groups larger than 20 dominate and frighten small children.[9] Primary school society isn't cohesive if too big: at 30 children, social bonds are intimate and strong. At 100, everyone still knows everyone else; but not at 300. Larger children need larger society, but alienation grows with increasing numbers. By 1000 children, it's strong – a recipe for bullying. Contrast this with village schools. Parents meet there; social, political and cultural events take place there. All ages use playgrounds and sports fields out of hours. All this keeps the village shop going, reinforcing social cohesiveness. Such small schools have limited facilities, but give children the breadth of multi-age play, events and social groups. As they feel supported by a known community, vandalism, violence and theft are normally uncommon.

Cramped space and perceived scale – both building and social – are architectural issues. But how much space do children need? Before gardenless apartments made it impossible, parents used to tell bickering children to 'go play outside!' When they do, disputes usually evaporate. With teenagers, space to keep away from trouble reduces it. In school, more space means fewer conflicts.[10] In childcare centres, less than 30 square feet (3 m²) of primary space per child increases aggression (but over 50 square feet (5 m²) reduces social integration). Reggio Emilia preschools therefore specify 42–45 square feet (115–125 (10.5–11.5 m²) including adult and service space).[11] Primary-school children are less active in class, so only need 40 square feet (4 m²) each (20 (1.9 m²) is minimum).[12] Adolescents take up more space with their sprawling bodies; they need 30 to 50 square feet (3–5 m²) each.[13] Such figures aren't cast-iron. Cultural expectations and behaviour, racial body-size, climate, educational policy and room design affect whether children need more or less space.

Another architectural issue is unsupervised out-of-sight spaces. The design principles for 'defensible-space' crime reduction and bullying are identical: territoriality, natural surveillance, access control and opportunity reduction.[14] Feeling that parts of public spaces are 'their own' strengthens year-groups' social identity and reduces perceived scale, revers-

ing alienation. Unless *all* groups have adequately defined gathering places, however, this can cause conflict.[15] Blind spots and inactive edges often have a reputation as places for smoking and drugs. Pupils recognize this with comments such as 'dead-end-dangerous'

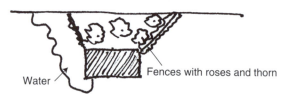

Water

Fences with roses and thorn

Sealing off hidden space

and 'stay away, only drug dealers and smokers allowed here'.[16] Supervisory site-lines are, therefore, essential. Likewise, adding life to an area improves both safety and quality of play.[17] Well-defined routes and areas of activity clarify who does what, where, but congestion points, such as narrow alleys, often generate friction and provide opportunities for intimidation.[18]

But how can we identify problem spots? Walking around shows up many. (The more people involved, the broader the viewpoint.) How can activity be brought to dead places? Light and mood-levity to gloomy bits? Attractiveness to the unloved?

Additionally, where – and when – do fights and bullying occur? Are there common features, such as colliding-into-each-other spaces or out-of-sight back-lands? It's important, however, that improvements aren't just localized to problem areas, or undesirable activities are merely displaced. But what about new designs, with no *actual* places to observe? Here, imagining walking round, and being in *every* part, shows up potential problems.

Does dominating, aggressive architecture subliminally encourage bullying? Many schools were built when forceful architecture was in fashion. Their architects proudly called them *brutal*ist. These manifest an *attitude* to design; an attitude easily absorbed by children. Change the architectural aims from *powerful impact*, style-assertive, to child-*friendly*, harmonious and reticent, and dominance and aggression disappear. But what about schools already built? Though some have induced so much vandalism that they've been demolished, it is too expensive to demolish many. Fortunately, *softening* buildings – even 'brutal' ones – isn't prohibitively costly. Building-on elements to humanize façade scale, vegetation-

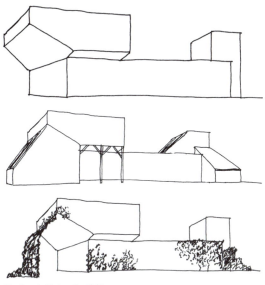

De-brutalizing buildings

cloaking or tree-screening can achieve this. Although shrubs and trees can obstruct sight-lines, greenery has a more than compensating de-aggressivizing influence. Pruning for supervisory view is, however, a wise additional precaution.

Can places that obviously *value* children mitigate any anger children bring with them? Those that *don't*, certainly magnify it. Unfortunately, many schools, as environmental education consultant Sue Fenoughty describes, 'are becoming "fortresses", surrounded by prison-like fencing, locked entrances and security cameras; inside this "compound" children are herded onto tarmac squares'. Is it surprising that anti-social behaviour is a growing problem?[19] Just as overtly vandal-proof design attracts vandalism, treating children as ruffians encourages rough behaviour. In schools that look like prisons, with everything sterilized to deter vandalism, criminal damage flourishes.[20]

On a limited patch of tarmac, 1000 children milling, running and playfighting make disputes, baiting and bullying almost inevitable. Contrast this with Fenoughty's description of a landscaped playground: 'Although it was halfway through break time when we arrived, there were no children careering round the playground and no signs of adult intervention. Instead, there were groups of self-motivated children engaged in a variety of ad hoc activities, made possible by the design of the grounds'.[21] As 85 per cent of schools that have improved their grounds found this reduced bullying, it's well worth the relatively small expense.[22]

Young and old

Children are drawn to children of like age. Mono-age groups guarantee the same developmental stage – good for play and virtually essential for education. But, just as for adults, diversity is socially healthy. Multi-age groups bring valuable social integration challenges. Moreover, instead of just competing, everyone has something *different* to give. Different experience, attitudes and values foster multiple strengths. Children learn best from children, but increasing use of child-care centres and after-school clubs mean they're at home less. This reduces sibling interaction, increasing the importance of informal multi-age meetings.

What age-ranges are compatible? Can infants mix with teenagers? As small children automatically look up to them, teenagers don't *need* to force their domination to be 'boss'. The young ones, inspired by: 'this is how I will be one day', admire the older; teenagers, enjoying this admiration, feel 'important' and responsible. This tends to temper even tearaways' behaviour, allowing them to show a gentle side of themselves that they're normally too vulnerable to admit to. On this basis, the Green School in Austin, Texas, found looking after small children brought the best out of 'problem' (namely criminally inclined) teenagers. Steiner (Waldorf) schools often locate high schools near kindergartens. Alternatively, 14- to 15-year-olds (class 8) each individually 'sponsor' six- to seven-year-olds joining the school, greeting them on arrival each morning, and accompanying them at festivals.

What about shared playgrounds? Infant–teenager proximity sometimes works, but there can be problems. Some age-group needs contrast sharply: children over 10 years need open space for gathering, also for rambunctious play. Small ones need smaller places, of more comprehensible scale, with protected bays. Both groups need more 'private' protected spaces to withdraw to: the older for 'adult' conversations, the younger for fantasy-play realms. Small children are easily pushed over, and small equipment broken. Twelve-year-olds can run 100 feet looking backwards; woe betide anyone small in the way. Fences can protect fragile infants from robust older children, whilst allowing both groups to watch and be watched by each other.[23] And all can share *informal* meeting places, such as paths to school. This is about crossing paths, *facilitating* not *ordering* contact.

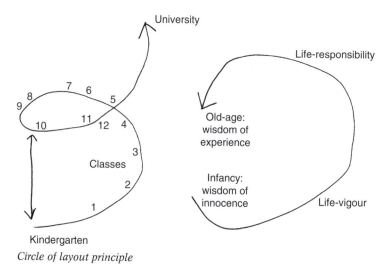

Circle of layout principle

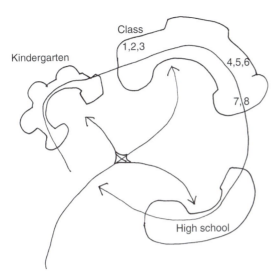

Kindergarten

Class 1,2,3

4,5,6

7,8

High school

Shared drop-off point

How about very young and very old? Are they compatible? Skateboarding teenagers endanger the frail elderly. (Fortunately, gravel or bark-chip paths deter skateboards.) Not all old people like having children around; they're noisy, rude and interfere with 'respectable' pastimes earned by a lifetime's work. Minimum age 'Retirement Villages' appeal to this outlook. Similarly, children can have wilder fun when adults are excluded. If this is what both groups want, what's wrong with age-segregation? Aren't some old people sour, some children brats? Actually, *all* are, but only some of the time. Young children, however, give old people energy; the elderly give the young peace – and unstinted time and attention. Enthusiasm and experience, energy and wisdom, compliment each other – closing the cycle of life.

Small children intuitively connect with older people. Whereas parents know *about* things and are busy with *doing*, grandparents emanate wisdom, knowing, being. Until relatively recently, parents were at work all day so most children were brought up by grandparents. They grew up in a reassuringly unhurried atmosphere. Grandmother's fireside stories, full of calm wisdom, were the heart-centre of home.[24] But three-generation families are rare today. Some Steiner kindergartens, therefore, arrange to have an older person to just sit and spin – a quiet presence to anchor the constantly swirling child energy.

What about outside school? Siting old peoples' homes beside schools maximizes noise nuisance and (over-rated) fear of perverts. In convivial public spaces, however, children learn how to meet grown-ups and widely varied adult conversations provide a model to emulate.[25] Wind-sheltered benches comfortable for the elderly (some higher,

more upright and with armrests, to ease getting up) near places where small children play – both intended, such as sandpits, and 'found', such as low-walls for balancing on – create meeting *opportunities* within parental view. Locating some in sun, some in shade, extends the season of use. Arranging *proximity* of children and elderly – not *forcing* them on one another – and providing environments that encourage conviviality are urban design issues, too

Infancy – old-age

often neglected. The issue is never one of age-compatibility, but of identifying proximity circumstances that bring out the best of both.

Learning sociability

Childhood society isn't just about fun. Inadequate socialization retards social development, increasing susceptibility to psychiatric illness in later life.[26] Modern life is increasingly private, individually separate. The many layers that formerly built community hardly exist today. Many people don't know their neighbours. Families – especially those living high above the ground – easily become insulated in their private homes. Though many children make friends quickly, some are shy, even withdrawn. Sociability isn't automatic. Children have to *learn* to meet.

Doing things together breaks much ice. Focusing more on task, which is cooperative, than on our personal defences, we suddenly realize we're at ease – no longer struggling to find something to say. *Activity*, whether work or play, is social – especially activities such as playing ball, impossible on one's own.[27] Equipment that needs at least two, such as water cascades with a pump to work and water-flow obstructions to arrange, *demands* cooperation.

Water-cascade and pump

Whereas swings may need queueing or fighting to get on, ropes are more fun with a crowd of arms and legs

Do seats guarantee conversation? In hospital waiting corridors: no. Design and location are significant. Positioned to observe things *going on*, you can just watch without *obligation* to talk. This makes conversation easier. Seats at an angle to each other are more sociable. They're more inviting if sunny or shady, as required. But seats are formal – not for the shy. Logs, sections of tree-trunk, low walls and fence-rails, even steps to sit on, are more casual. (For safety, side branches or flat undersides prevent rolling. Also logs must be too heavy for children to lift, then drop on toes[28].)

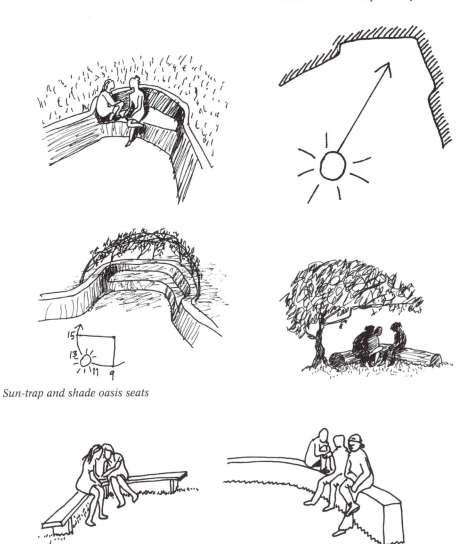

Sun-trap and shade oasis seats

Informal seats for sociability

Scale affects the ability to relax, and hence sociability. In big spaces, children easily feel lost, too exposed. In small spaces, proximity – hence meeting – is unavoidable. As adults, there are particular places we pause to talk in. We 'cross paths' with people on paths and stairs, in passages and doorways, greeting and often stopping to talk to them. Doorways both constrict and require us to pause; for children, they're anchoring reference points.[29] Threshold and transition spaces help children adjust mood and behaviour from loud to quiet, public to private, sociable to individually concentrating, outdoors to indoors. Sometimes children can't feel at ease without such public–private transition places.[30] Entries, garden gates and stair landings are intermediate zones between the security of house interior, private territory or upper step and the freedom of being outside, on the way somewhere. Here, it's 'safe' to be socially open, especially if one person is just about to go – hence traveller's goodbye syndrome: nothing to say on the platform, but plenty once one of you has boarded the train. Children do exactly the same.

To Aldo van Eyck: 'To go in or out, to enter, leave or stay away, are painful alternatives ... It is human to tarry. Architecture should take more account of this'.[31] Lobbies by doorways induce lingering and discussion. Is it coincidence that notice-boards usually end up here? Overhanging roofs near entrances make good chatting points and pushchair parks make for chat-inducing activity. When parents chat, children meet. When children chat, parents meet. Benefits for all.

Doorways make chatting-points

Overhanging roof for pushchair park

Linking places

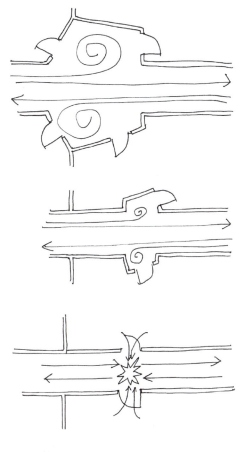

Adults often think in nouns: so 'circulation spaces' are just links between rooms. But children live in verbs and adverbs, so they experience school corridors as places where they're briefly free, but (inexplicably) forbidden to run. Different spatial arrangements affect *how* they interact socially. Do they more easily meet or collide? Pause and linger or push past, keep moving?

As children 'bump into' each other in 'circulation-spaces', a lot of communication and 'business' occurs here. Just like streams, 'eddy-space' widenings *to the side of* main currents make still places, however frenetic the flow. Indoor plants, low furniture or bookcase screens can give semi-seclusion. Window seats, low windowsills, dwarf walls and other informal perches invite stopping.[32] Views of activities encourage lingering and brightness increases sociability.[33]

Outdoors, with varied sensory experience and interesting things to see, 165 feet (50 m) is a short path. Indoors, it's oppressively long. Non-straight passages restrict view – hence perceived

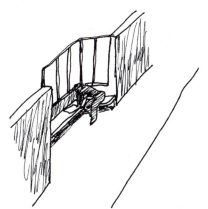 

Widenings as 'eddy-spaces', sitting bays and places with views

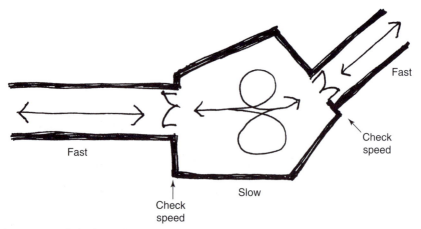

Fire-doors as speed-checks and 'place'-protectors

length – and make the unseen intriguingly inviting. Punctuation, such as swellings for sitting alcoves and constrictions at fire-doors, or bright light-wells and darker short 'tunnels' between distinct mood-zones, emphasize distinctions between stopping and movement places. The contrasting height makes places to pause in feel more 'at rest'. So does non-directional flooring after directional patterns. By dividing their length, passages feel less claustrophobic. With each part individualized, they're also more interesting to walk down.

Rooms on both sides of corridors mean that buildings can be smaller; cheaper to build and heat. But they cut us off from everything else, making places feel institutional. Single-sided passages allow views of the outer world and weather – orienting us in time and space. We aren't just at the mercy of the building. Being twice as long, however, they reduce chance meetings – invaluable for keeping teachers abreast of day-to-day issues. Mixing single- and

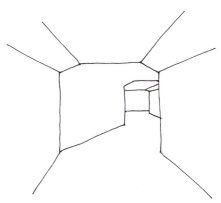

Non-straight passages prevent seeing everything at once, so always leave something new to look forward to

double-sided passages, with wider 'places' and narrower 'routes' can reconcile these conflicting mood and social needs.

Corridors aren't inevitable in schools. Short passages, interior 'streets' or 'courtyards', even rain-sheltered outdoor walkways often suffice. Interior courtyards linked to 'outdoor rooms' – such as hedged or walled gardens, paved sun-traps or under-pergola areas – feel more spacious, life-filled and spirit-freeing. Slide-away walls or roofs can convert winter conservatories into summer courtyards.

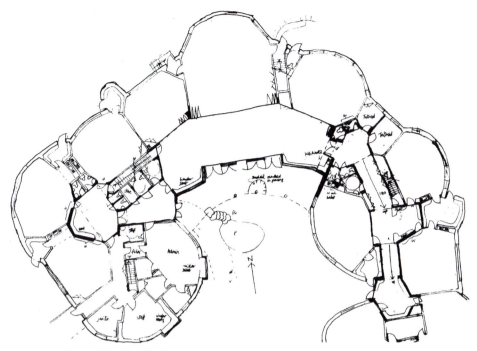

Mixing single- and double-sided passages

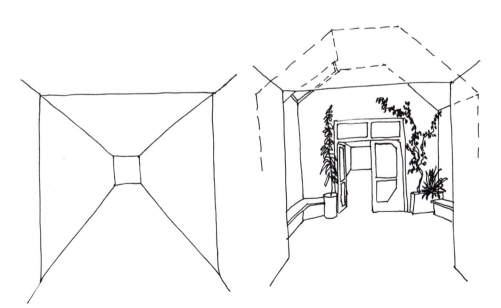

Re-enlivening corridors

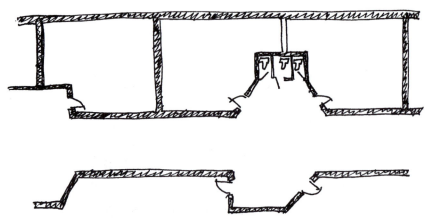

Internal street with bays

Boxes off long tubes say something about how their designers view their inhabitants. Corridor-related classrooms easily suggest factory conveyor-belt processing, but those opening off halls, courtyards or streets make schools feel like single social organisms. A courtyard or atrium at the *centre* of a school links everything practically, making the whole intelligible and placing community at its *heart*. To maximize *meeting*, Reggio Emilia preschools are arranged around piazzas – both internal and external. These range in mood from living room to village square. Unlike end-of-corridor hierarchies, this gives all rooms equal importance.[34]

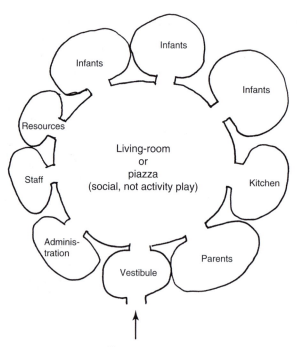

A common area at a child-centre's heart[35]

A Reggio Emilia piazza: half indoors, half outdoors

To feel spacious, indoor courtyards need height and light. If two-storey they're easily flooded with daylight. Balconies (wider than passages, for 'hanging-out') allow 'sidewalk-cafe' views of 'urban' life, socially linking different levels. Longer social views, however, mean children shout across to friends, making noise absorption essential.[36]

Two-storey courtyards are easily flooded with light. Balconies link levels socially

But what are indoor courtyards for? Are they for sociability, communal activities or – for infants – 'gross motor' play? Each requires a different mood and relationship to other spaces. For sociable lingering, courtyards need corner spaces and window bays clear from through-flow routes. Cross-flow – hence *diagonal* paths – increases *meetings*. *Gathering* or *play*, however, is disrupted by non-players passing through. It needs protected areas, hence *tangential* paths.[39] Also its noise and excitement compromise quieter activities in surrounding rooms, limiting timetable flexibility.[40]

School halls face similar dilemmas. Are they auditoria or courtyards for informal sociability? Slide-away seats allow both options, but will they always be slid away? Also, for a narrow range of activities and only a few hours use, halls are unduly expensive. Why not combine hall and gym? But do concerts and basketball have compatible requirements? Do floor markings, steel-mesh window-screens and impact-proof walls help concert mood? It's more mood-appropriate – and sometimes cheaper – to build separate spaces: one robust, spacious and unheated; the other, smaller and environmentally controlled.

In practice, halls are often too expensive for growing schools. Irkutsk Steiner School, Siberia, devised a novel solution: build classrooms in a circle. Within this, festivals, communal activities and school society could 'grow' this spirit. When eventually roofing, flooring and heating become affordable, the 'spirit-of-school' would already be present. As halls are usually primarily about *cultural spirit*, day-to-day sociability helps grow this without any expense.

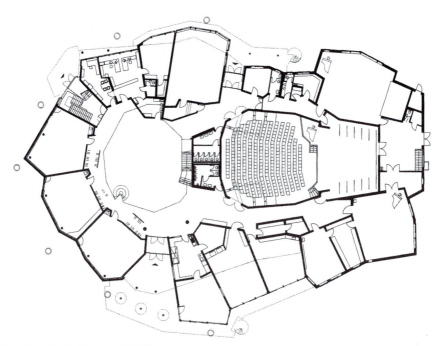

Chorweiler Waldorf School, Köln[37]

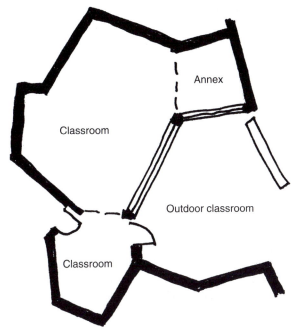

Geschwister School, Lünen[38]

Social identity and place

Big, homogeneous buildings aren't about class-sized groups, but about whole-institution 'community'. Identifying school 'neighbourhoods' by different colours, patterns or decorative motifs can't overcome *large-institution* feeling. By contrast, pavilion classrooms strengthen class identity and society, but their *form-based*, not *place-based* space-language brings suburban-dispersal associations. Between these extremes, courtyards keep whole-school identity, but humanize its scale by individualizing its parts. A central shade-tree, pool, basketball court, hopscotch markings or other activity-magnet, strengthens social focus. Children, however, often prefer to play round the back, out of teachers' view.[41] Oddly,

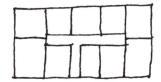

All activities in one building says 'institution'

All activities in separate buildings says 'suburbia'

teachers don't always want this. Fortunately, appropriately pruned shrubs and trees can give sufficient feeling of privacy without concealing mischief.

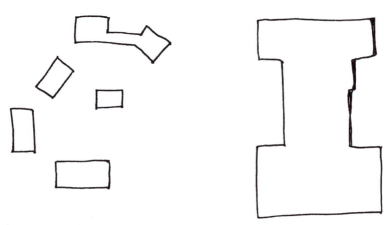

School plans can range from homogeneous blocks, through courtyard or clusters to pavilions

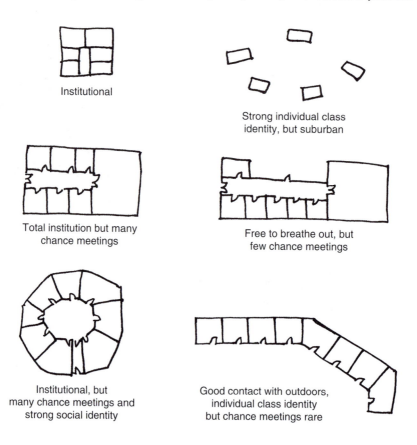

Institutional

Strong individual class
identity, but suburban

Total institution but many
chance meetings

Free to breathe out, but
few chance meetings

Institutional, but
many chance meetings and
strong social identity

Good contact with outdoors,
individual class identity
but chance meetings rare

'Village' layouts around 'greens' or semi-enclosed courts combine the social focusing of small courtyards with the freedom of more permeable edges. Around these, individual classroom 'front doors' and cloakrooms support class-group identity. Cloisters and arcades can visually link different rooms and make weather-buffered zones between

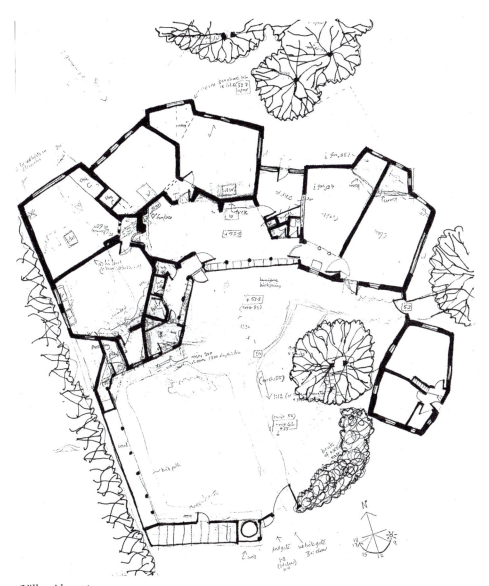

'Village' layout

North elevation

Classroom identity within a village whole

Cloister as an in-between realm

indoors and outdoors. If these go all around courts, they give a choice of route according to weather. Glazing ensures full weather-protection, but weakens 'front-doors' into 'corridor-doors'.

Central to kindergarten mood is 'family' atmosphere. For this, group individualization is essential. Down a passage in a larger school, kindergartens are no longer 'home households'. To feel a 'family', not 'just a part of a bigger school', each class needs its own kitchen 'heart', warm cloakroom and airy, non-institutional washroom and toilet – for easy supervision, perhaps opening directly from the classroom.[42] Pairs of classes can share cloakrooms, but individual ones better reinforce family identity.[43] In cloakrooms, children meet at both ends of the day. As much social life occurs here, there should be enough space for unpressured chatting; constriction brings squabbles. In cold climates, bulky winter clothes may require cloakrooms as big as classrooms.[44] This first stopping place on coming indoors also functions as a transition zone, helping quieten exuberant 'outdoorsy' vigour into more constrained indoor behaviour.[45]

Small primary schools, being more 'communities', can more easily share whole-community front doors. Cloakrooms and toilets, however, are better limited to single or groups of classes. Where these, and groups of classroom doors, open off social lobbies that invite lingering, group identity is reinforced.

For teenagers – already rebelling against perceived regimentation – such individualization is even more important. They, in particular, benefit by having individual class front doors. Courtyard layouts therefore suit them well. As they're more resilient, however, they can better cope with an unsatisfactory environment than can younger children. Unfortunately, they often have to. As anonymity is a form of disrespect – especially in our increasingly individualistic age – is this a factor in growing delinquency rates?

Teenagers need 'social rooms'. These can be compact. Proximity – as clubbers know – helps socializing. At Umeå Waldorf School, 15- to 18-year-olds' classrooms are grouped around a social-room/café. Teachers, instead of disappearing to a distant staff-room, share this. This lets teenage social life develop with vigour within the stabilizing context

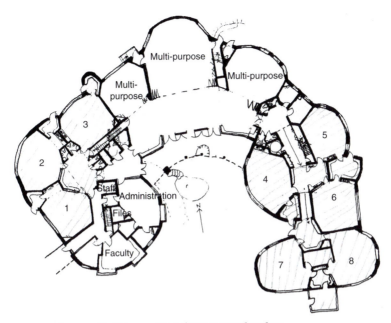

Classrooms grouped around lobbies, making distinct social realms

Light-flooded social lobby

Individualized class front doors

of a multi-age community.[46] Whereas teenagehood is often a period of alienation from the rest of society, such an approach develops social responsibilities. It also provides a rehearsal for inclusive cohesion – essential for social health.

Notes

1 Dudek, Mark (2000) *Architecture of Schools*. Architectural Press.
2 As at Umeå Waldorf School.
3 Bullying: 'a pattern of behaviour whereby one person with a lot of internal anger and consequent aggression and lacking interpersonal skills chooses to displace their aggression onto another person, chosen for their vulnerability' (*School Bullies and Bullying at School*, http://www.bullyonline.org/schoolbully/school.htm).
4 Maria Castella, teacher at South Devon Steiner School.
5 David Urieli, for college of teachers, Holywood Rudolf Steiner School, Northern Ireland.
6 William Golding, a teacher, so believed this, that it is the central theme of his book *Lord of the Flies*.
7 As per George Orwell's *Animal Farm* model.
8 Following the murder of a Nigerian child in London, West African relatives described Nigerian village children's play as *never* aggressive, *always* inclusive of all. (*Today* Programme, BBC Radio 4, April 2002.)
9 Ministry of Education (1952) *Moving And Growing*. HMSO.
10 Bidsrube, Vibeke (1993) *Children and Square Metres*. Paedagogisk Bogklub,

Copenhagen, cited in Dudek, Mark (1996) *Kindergarten Architecture*. Spon.
11 'Primary space' meaning space where children are active. Olds, Anita Rui (2001) *Child Care Design Guide*. McGraw Hill.
12 Dudek, Mark (2000) *ibid.*
13 Royal Institute of British Architects (2001) *A Sustainable School*. RIBA.
14 Robinson, F. (2005) Grounds for concern. *Learning through Landscapes*. Building Design, March.
15 Robinson, F. (2005) *op. cit.*
16 Robinson, F. (2005) *op. cit.*
17 Robinson, F. (2005) *op. cit.*
18 Robinson, F. (2005) *op. cit.*
19 Fenoughty, Susan (1997) *The Garden Classroom*. Unpublished Churchill Fellowship Report.
20 Robinson, F. (2005) *ibid.*
21 Svenshogskolan, Lund, Sweden, described by Fenoughty (1997) *ibid.*
22 Survey by Learning through Landscapes, cited by Robinson, F. (2005) *ibid.*
23 Olds, Anita Rui (2001) *ibid.*
24 We owe the accumulated wisdom, multigenerationally edited, of fairy-stories to this fireside tradition.
25 Crowhurst, S.H. and Lennard, H.L. (2004) *True Urbanism and the Healthy City*. IMCL Conference, 17 February 2005, Carmel CA, USA.

26 Lantz, H. (1956) Number of childhood friends as reported in a life histories group of 1000. In *Marriage and Family Life*, cited in Thomas, Derek (2002) *Architecture and the Urban Environment*. Architectural Press.

27 *Modern Barndom* No. 3 (1996). Reggio Emilia Institutet, Stockholm.

28 Marshall, Alan (1999) *Greener School Grounds*. Learning through Landscapes.

29 Research by Reggio Emilia preschool teachers. Ceppi, Guilio and Zini, Michele (1998) *Children, Spaces, Relations; Metaproject for an Environment for Young Children*. Reggio Children, Italy.

30 Bettleheim, Bruno (1950) *Love is Not Enough*. Macmillan, cited in Bayes, K. (1967) *The Therapeutic Effect of Environment on Emotionally Disturbed and Mentally Subnormal Children*. The Gresham Press.

31 van Eyck, A. (1962) (describing his Amsterdam children's home) *The Medicine of Recipricocity Tentatively Illustrated*. Architects' Year Book 10, quoted in Bayes, K. (1967) *op. cit.*

32 See, particularly, the work of Fielden, Clegg, Bradley, architects.

33 Dudek, Mark (2000) *ibid.*

34 Ceppi, Guilio and Zini, Michele (1998) *ibid.*

35 After Olds, Anita Rui (2001) *ibid.*

36 Olds, Anita Rui (2001) *Child Care Design Guide*. McGraw Hill.

37 Architect: Peter Hubner.

38 Architect: Hans Scharoun.

39 Olds, Anita Rui (2001) *ibid.*

40 Olds, Anita Rui (2001) *op. cit.*

41 An observation from Rex Raab, an experienced school architect.

42 Riscke, Elke-Maria (1985) Pedagogical aspects of kindergarten architecture. In Flinspach, Jürgen (1985) *Waldorfkindergärten Bauen*. Unpulished translation by Luborsky, Peter (1988).

43 Meyerkort, Margaret *Kindergarten Architecture and Equipment*. Unpublished. Compiled By Elvira Rychlak.

44 Thörn, Kerstin *Att bygga en skola*. Västerbotton, Västerbottons Museum.

45 Thörn, Kerstin, *op. cit.*

46 Thörn, Kerstin, *op. cit.*

CHAPTER 5

Issues of health

Dirt and hygiene: surfaces and textures

Are playgroups and schools good for health? Sometimes they seem infection factories. Colds, 'flu, tummy-bugs and childhood illnesses sweep through them. Part of this is inevitable when children meet other children. Is stricter hygiene the answer? Hygiene, however, like 'safety', has a deceptively simple ring, but different circumstances require different levels. While always wise, moderation is less neurotically tense – and often *healthier* than obsession. Visually, hygiene doesn't have to mean sterility. Plastic, though easily wiped clean, harbours bacteria in every minute scratch. Wood is often less smooth, but retains bactericidal properties from when it was a living tree, so is usually more hygienic.[1]

Is sharing germs entirely bad? The greater the exposure to others, the wider the anti-body range (hence broad-spectrum immunity) that children develop. Even the risk of leukaemia diminishes if children attended playgroups when small.[2] Moreover, as children excessively protected from dirt become more prone to Type 1 diabetes, eczema, asthma, allergies and other immune-system ailments in later life, scientific opinion is swinging away from excessive hygiene.[3] This highlights a dilemma: just as adventure causes accidents but circumvents worse ones, dirt causes illness – but how much future ill-health does it *save*? Just as vaccination and antibiotics work but diminish immunity-vigour,[4] how many things that we *don't* let our children do – for hygiene or safety – are, in fact, important to their healthy development?

Antibody acquisition is one thing, but illness? This starts with – but isn't limited to – dirt and bacteria. Bacteria mostly come from other children. But where does dirt come from?

Like 'weeds', 'dirt' is something in the wrong place. Outdoor mud is messy but harmless. Indoor dirt is barely visible, but often ends up in skin, eyes or lungs. However well cleaned, some buildings trap dirt. Inaccessible ledges and pipes hold dust. So do rough and absorbent textures. Absorbent materials retain dust and food smells. Fitted carpet is luxuriously soft, but virtually impossible to *completely* clean, so becomes a nice home for dust-mites – major asthma triggers.[5] With asthma affecting one child in five, this is a serious consideration.[6] (Also, as muddy feet aren't popular on carpets, complaints deter outdoor play. This means even less clean air for children!) Swedish schools, therefore, started to remove fitted carpets in the 1980s. Small mats are easier to beat out and air. (They're also good as mood and imagination changing props.)

Health and illness, however, isn't only about dirt and germs. There are many other physical, and even psychological, factors. Most of these are invisible.

Invisible factors

We don't live in a pure, unpolluted world. But pollution that is bearable by adults does more harm to children. They have proportionately less internal tissue to absorb pollutants and, with small and undeveloped livers, a lower ability to detoxify these. With bodies still forming and organs immature – even brains take up to two years to completely physically develop[7] – children are, therefore, particularly vulnerable to any influence that could distort healthy growth.

As microbes, chemical vapours, electricity and radiation are normal in life, every kind of building affects us chemically, electrically, microbially and radiologically. Mostly this is harmless, but some buildings – by their materials, heating and ventilation systems, equipment and contents – concentrate these to unhealthy levels. By World Health Organization estimates,[8] one in three buildings, both new and old,[9] is 'sick' – unhealthy to be in. Schools are no exception. In older schools, mould – affecting lungs, skin and allergy sensitivity – is common. Many newer ones have 'new office smell': chemical vapours from synthetic materials.

Air is typically ten times less clean indoors than outdoors. Indoor chemical pollution normally results from – in approximate order of magnitude – cleaning-products, paints, finishes, furnishings, furniture, building fabric, then outdoor air. Healthy schools involve, therefore, teachers, cleaners and governors, besides architects and builders. Fortunately, with even only basic understanding, indoor pollution is easily avoidable.

Materials and air quality

Visible in sunbeams, all air is full of dust. Noses are designed to filter most of this, but some small bits we breathe deep into the lungs. Sharp particles – such as glass-fibres – irritate the lung surface. Though most are eventually blunted by secretions, asbestos never is – that is why it's so dangerous. Most indoor pollution, however, is invisible – not dust but chemicals. We drink more than we eat, but we breathe vastly more than we drink. Lungs have a huge surface area, which exchanges chemicals directly to the blood. Any concern about how food-additives affect health and behaviour[10] must also apply to what children breathe. This makes *air quality* a primary health concern.

Everything around us is chemical. As almost all materials, natural, processed and synthetic, are on a chemical journey, they release small amounts of chemical vapour – smells. Some are good for us, some dangerous. How can we tell? What should we avoid? Things don't smell attractive or repulsive at random. A bad smell usually signals that something is harmful.[11]

Vapours *from life* are normally life-compatible,[12] hence we enjoy the scent of flowers.[13] But why should vapours from *industrially processed* products be? Many are toxic, some acutely so. Their cocktail combinations, though scarcely researched, are probably even more harmful. Although heavy-metals – often extremely toxic – are common in industry, most indoor pollution is from *organic* compounds. Organic chemicals – carbon-molecule-structured – originate in life. Plastics, for instance, are (mostly) made from oil – once living fern forest. Being close to body chemistry, organic chemicals are easily assimilated by the blood. Although heat accelerates vapour emission, this is primarily *age*-related: new buildings, paint, car interiors and plastic items – including toys – smell.

Urea-formaldehyde – common in industrial adhesives – emits formaldehyde. This is mutagenic and carcinogenic. As it's water-soluble, steamy conditions increase release. Glue-bonded carpeting, chipboard, MDF, laminates and internal-grade plywood aren't, therefore, wise in damp or warm rooms. (External boards, glued with phenol-formaldehyde, despite giving off some phenol, are safer.) Volatile organic solvents (VOCs) – mostly petroleum-based – are another major concern. Indoor sources include oil- and cellulose-based paints, cleaning materials, glues and even printing inks.

Plastics are made through a series of *synthesis* operations – making one compound from two or more ingredients. As *exact* ingredient quantity match is impossible, small amounts of unstable monomers remain. These slowly vaporize from finished polymers. Some, especially phthalate plasticizers, are of serious health concern. Flooring, upholstery, carpets, cushioning and foam-formed chairs are common sources.

Although some plants absorb air-borne chemicals, they are no substitute for toxic material removal. The next best remedy is generous ventilation. Sealing – by vapour-impermeable paint or pressed (not glued) overlay (such as bamboo board or linoleum) – also helps.

A century ago, most materials were natural. Those giving off toxic gasses hardly existed. Plastics and synthetic glues had not been invented. Even oil paint (though often containing lead!) was linseed-oil and wood-turpentine based. Natural alternatives to virtually every chemical product, including water-based or vegetable-oil solvents, still exist. Some are easily available, some not.[15] Pre-industrial materials such as lime plaster, stone, slate and unvarnished wood, or pre-petroleum ones such as linoleum, glass, fired-clay brick, pipe and tile, avoid most toxicity problems.[16] Ex-living materials, like wood and wool, have internal air-spaces that both buffer climate and absorb smells and air-borne toxins. Silk – spun as protection for moth 'babies' – does this particularly well. Clay and lime, though mineral, are close to life, so do this to some extent.[17]

Natural, minimally processed materials typically carry low pollution- and energy-costs. They're part of every local tradition, contributing to sense of place; part of every local economy, so socially supportive. Most are also attractive to eye, hand and nose, so approachable and appealing. This makes them good for the environment, for society, for health *and for children.*

Healthy materials	Unhealthy materials
Wood	Glued products
Clay products	Plastics
Natural fibres	Mineral fibres
Natural paints, water-based	Synthetic and VOC-based paints
Lime	Cement (climatically)

Indoor plants to detoxify air[14]

Plant species	Chemical absorbed		
	Formaldehyde From combustion (e.g. tobacco smoke), plywood, chipboard, MDF board, glued materials, cleaning materials	Benzene From combustion (e.g. tobacco), plywood chipboard adhesives, mastic, cosmetics, deodorizers	Trichloroethylene From paints, varnish, adhesive, mastic, cleaners, correction fluid
Aglaonema Silver Queen	✓	✓✓	
Azalea	✓✓		
Evergreen palm *Chamaedorea Selfritzii*	✓✓	✓✓	✓
Chrysanthemum *Morifolium*	✓✓	✓✓	✓
Dieffenbachia	✓✓		
Dragontrees *Dracaena deremensis Warnerkii*	✓✓	✓✓	✓
Dracaena marginata	✓✓	✓✓	✓✓
Dracaena massangeana	✓✓	✓	✓
Janet Craig	✓✓	✓✓	✓
Ficus benjamina	✓✓	✓✓	✓
Perennial Barberton daisy *Gerbera jonesonii*	✓✓	✓✓	✓✓
Goldheart ivy *Hedera helix*	✓✓	✓✓	✓
Elephant's ears *Philodendron domesticum*	✓✓		
Philodendron oxycardium	✓✓		
Philodendron selleum	✓✓		
Sansevieria laurentii	✓	✓✓	✓
Schidapsus aureus	✓	✓✓	✓✓
Peace Lily *Spathiphyllum*	✓	✓✓	✓✓

Indoor climate

Even with the healthiest materials, air quality isn't guaranteed. Oxygen is the 'fuel' for *life*, but breathing produces CO_2. Too much causes reduced alertness, lethargy, drowsiness and headaches. But 'too much' isn't much. Just 0.07 per cent (twice the normal 0.034 per cent) does this. In fact, as little as 5.4 per cent is fatal.[18]

Children breathe. Many children breathe – and sometimes sweat – a lot. This means a lot of moisture. Child-generated heat easily overheats rooms – but damply. Damp warm air makes us feel drowsy – not ideal for education! Classrooms, therefore, need to cope with rapid fluctuations in humidity. However harmless water vapour – from breath – sounds, in soft furnishings it encourages dust-mites and, on cold walls, means condensation – frequently a precursor to mould. (In fact, at 70 per cent relative humidity, mould can grow even without condensation.[19]) As most fungicides are toxic, many mercury-based,[20] it's healthier to control the cause: relative humidity. At between 40 per cent and 60 per cent relative humidity few pathogens survive. In much damper air, they flourish; drier air also suits some and additionally brings electrostatic problems.[21] Because the warmer air is the more water vapour it can hold, cool outdoor air – even if it feels damp – invariably contains less water than warm indoor air. The simplest way to dry rooms, therefore, is by ventilation. Humidity-stat controlled passive ventilation can remove damp air at source – but often lots more air is needed. Heating also reduces *relative* humidity. But heat and generous ventilation mean high CO_2 – and fuel bill – costs.

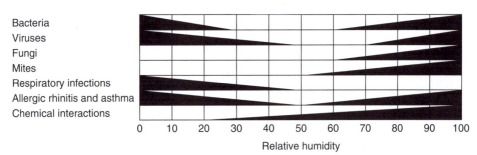

Relative humidity and pathogen growth[22]

The alternative is for buildings themselves to *buffer* humidity. Hydroscopic surface materials, such as wood, lime and, to a lesser extent, gypsum plaster and brickwork, buffer moisture – absorbing and releasing it. Most old buildings are built of these materials. As impervious paints or cement plasters seal surfaces, preventing air exchange, appropriately resurfacing old rooms can markedly improve indoor climate. Cement and concrete – common in newer buildings – are poor humidity-buffers; and glass, metal and plastic are impermeable. Sheep wool, cellulose-fibre, straw, hemp and cotton insulation perform well but, being located behind things, less quickly than *surface* materials. Clay – now available as plaster – and wood-fibre are quick-responding. Used for ceilings and pin-boards, they significantly improve humidity climate.

Although indoor plants and water features re-invigorate air, they can never substitute for clean outdoor air. 'Lots of outdoor air' brings up energy-conservation versus health issues. Heat-exchangers can retrieve up to half the heat lost by ventilation. This makes energy sense, but to preserve negative ions, exchange surfaces and inlet ducts can't be ferrous, nor can inlet-air be fan-driven. For air quality, it's better if a construction can 'breathe'. This lets fresh outdoor air replace stale indoor air even when windows are closed. Percolating slowly over a large area, there's no draught. As large molecules, typical of indoor pollutants, diffuse through porous insulation faster than oxygen or CO_2, walls that breathe act as gas- and particle-air-cleaners.[23] If air-pressure is lower indoors than outdoors, fresh air coming *in* through walls or ceilings gathers *outgoing* warmth on its way. This 'dynamic insulation' combination of high ventilation and minimum heat loss particularly suits humidity-generating spaces such as swimming pools and sports halls.[24]

Clean outdoor air is negative-ion rich. These air molecules, being an electron short, are 'hungry', so fasten onto small particles such as bacteria. Now heavy, they sink to earth where soil bacteria digest them – this is one reason why 'fresh air' feels fresh. Although healthy, fresh air is often too cold. Air-inlets behind radiators or between storm-panes and windows help pre-warm it. Piping through (large) underground clay ducts, raises – or, in summer, lowers – its temperature to near-annual average.

Different heating and cooling methods affect air quality differently. Each has mood, health, energy and energiz*ing* implications. What kind of warmth is best for children?

Air-conditioning makes the most comfortable climate (in theory – but its innate inflexibility can make some areas too hot or too cold). But it is hugely energy-expensive and old systems leak CFCs.[27] Also, as equipment typically costs 40 per cent of construction budget and only lasts for 15 years, it is capital-expensive.[28] Health-wise, recirculated air recycles everybody's bugs. Also, ducts are warm, moist and, with joints and bends forming eddy-traps, pathogen-friendly. Consequently, in mechanically ventilated buildings, bio-pathogens account for half of all building-related sickness. Forcing air through ducts also destroys bug-removing negative-ions, increases airborne particulates and causes noise and vibration.[29] Air-heating is associated with respiratory problems, headaches, irritability, weakened circulation and common colds.[30] All in all, this means sick children. By contrast, cool, fresh air aids deeper breathing – beneficial both

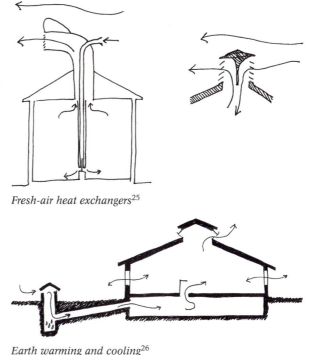

Fresh-air heat exchangers[25]

Earth warming and cooling[26]

for concentration and deep sleep.[31] Natural ventilation is healthy, cheap and easily adjustable. More flexible and locally responsive than air-conditioning, it lets *us* – not some invisible controlling machine – manage our needs. For health, there's no substitute.

Convection – using air to transport heat – is a common way of heating buildings. But the faster air moves, the

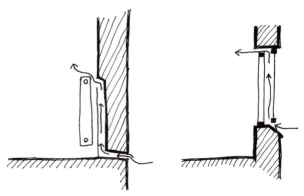

Air inlets behind radiators and between storm panes and windows

more dust it carries.[32] This we breathe. 'Radiators' actually convect. Even at 40°C, they produce dust-carrying convection currents. Hot ones carbonize the dust, making it sharper and harder – worse for lungs.

Convected air is often stratified: warm above but cooler at floor-level. Radiant heat isn't, but declines with distance from source. Thermal uniformity has a deadening effect on the body, dulling attentiveness, but thermal variety stimulates us. Passing between areas at different temperatures both invigorates us and emphasizes place differentiation – another alertness aid.[33] One aspect of this is *focal*-radiant warmth – particularly fireplace or stove, heart-*hearth* warmth. Warming more deeply, radiant heat allows lower air temperatures so higher – hence healthier – ventilation-rates without waste. Unlike drowsy-making and concentration-sapping warm air, cooler air is invigorating – and, as airborne dust, perspiration, VOCs and other such pollution is temperature-related, also fresher. Low surface temperatures require larger heating surfaces – such as floors or walls. To avoid 'heat-shading', heat best radiates from several directions. Like light, however, it 'bounces' around rooms – not by reflection, but by warming other surfaces. All this means that heat, which is more radiant than convective, is more pleasant, healthier and saves energy.

What about rooms with radiators sized for high surface temperatures? Lower flow temperatures (requiring longer heating periods) reduce airborne dust. Filling the open core of double radiators slows their heating and cooling, further lowering surface temperatures without reducing heat.

What is the best heat for children? Throughout evolution, we have been warmed by sunlight and fire. Our bodies, therefore, are adapted to radiant heat. Physically, a cool head aids concentration; warm heads bring headaches.[34] Cold feet are distractingly uncomfortable, but warm ones warm the whole body. A warm trunk is critical to comfort. This suggests warmer floors and body-zone but cooler air above us – thermal stratification opposite to that given by air heating. Radiant floors provide this, but radiant *walls* better expose the whole body, especially the trunk, to heat source. Does direction of radiant heat make much difference? Compare vertical and horizontal rain: 15 seconds of vertical rain wets head and shoulders only, but horizontal rain totally soaks us. Radiant walls warm us more deeply, but infants spend a lot of time on the floor, so lose – or gain – heat to or from it by *conduction*. Conduction is the most effective, and rapid, means of heat transfer. Bringing associations of snuggling up to mummy, conducted heat is deliciously warming. As underfloor heating provides both conductive and radiant heat, this is best for small children.

Forced-air heating:
Ducts trap microbial cultures
and blow out dust

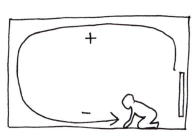

Radiators convect:
floor-level cool air – where children play – returning
to radiators

Radiant walls:
Balancing radiant 'heat-shade'.

Warm floors

Outdoor air

Fresh air isn't made indoors: only outdoors is it renewed. Plants absorb more carbon dioxide than oxygen, 'renewing' it.[35] They – and water – also 'recondition' air by holding particulates, absorbing toxins and odours, moderating temperature and humidity[36] and renewing negative ions.

Indoor air, therefore, needs constant replacement by clean outdoor air. But what about roadside buildings? Where can they get unpolluted air? The air from the roadside front is exhaust-laden – and noisy – but cleaner from the traffic-shielded rear or from roofs. Rear-inlet windows and vertical ('stack') ventilation is one option. As the higher the inlet, the fewer the airborne particulates, roof inlets access clean air, but need ducts (preferably clay) to convey this downstairs. Again, for negative-ion preservation, airflow should be driven by wind, not fans. As dust collects on bare surfaces, but vegetation anchors it, green-roofs provide less dusty air.

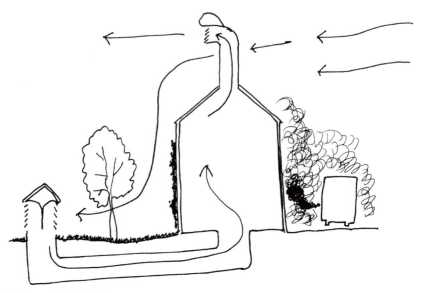

Roof ventilators with inlet air from rear

Vertical ventilation with green roof

Open-air play is healthy – but not all outdoor air is clean. For schools situated beside heavily trafficked roads, it definitely isn't. Fortunately, exhaust soot particles, being heavy, mostly don't travel far or high – so playground layouts that draw children away from road boundaries increase engine to lung distance. Cycle sheds, equipment stores and even climbing plants on boundary fences can make exhaust barriers. As tree-lined streets have up to one-tenth of the airborne dust of treeless ones,[37] the more greenery – grass, shrubs, trees, climbers on walls and roofs, even vegetated (or moss-covered) roofs – the better the air quality. Vegetation also quietens and makes welcoming playground and school mood. Such psychological benefits also contribute to health.

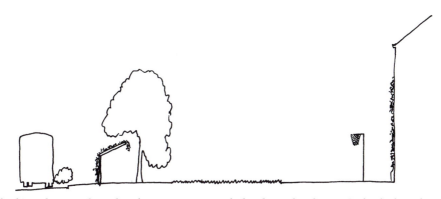

Climbing plants on boundary fences intercept and absorb much exhaust. Cycle-sheds and equip-ment stores make physical barriers, albeit only moderate in height. Playground layouts drawing children away from road boundaries increase engine to lung distance. Greenery – grass, shrubs, trees, climbers on walls and roof – cleans air

Electro-climate

Building-related sickness isn't only about chemicals, bugs and dust. Nor can our senses recognize every health-stressor. Radon and carbon monoxide, for instance, are invisible and odourless.[38] So is electricity. Apart from shocks or fires, how can this do any harm? Our bodies function through electrochemical processes. These can be disrupted by elec-tromagnetic fields (EMFs), stronger than the earth's – again, more dangerous to children than adults.[39] Fortunately, significant exposure is easy to avoid. Clearly, schools shouldn't be near power lines, transformers or microwave transmitter-receivers.[40] Nor should hous-ing, for children are at home nearly five times as much – and half of this asleep, their bod-ies in cellular-repair mode so particularly vulnerable. As EMFs reduce rapidly with distance, it's wise to keep most child-activities in the parts of buildings and land furthest away from such external sources – even smaller ones such as local transformers.

Most electro-pollution, however, comes from indoor sources. Virtually all (Western) buildings contain electrical appliances and cabling. Motors and transformers generate higher fields, but even cabling to inactive appliances produces some. Again utilizing dis-tance, careful appliance positioning and wiring layout can reduce these to the inconse-quential. In single-storey or corridor-layout schools, it's easy to route cables away from where children spend most of their time. Homes are more complicated, but an absolute first priority is to keep anything electrical 4 feet (1.2 m) from children's (and preferably anybody else's) *beds*. Instead of conventional bedside lamps, for instance, pull-switches distance wiring from beds without loss of convenience. As electromagnetism can also pass through walls and floors, cabling and appliances on the *other side* of these should also be distant.

Lifestyle exposure is harder to deal with. Many schools are committed to computer-aided learning. At home, many children spend hours playing computer-games or watching television. Often they're dangerously close to radiation-emitting cathode-ray screens. Like mobile-phone exposure, how much harm this does to health is disputed. But, as elec-tromagnetic bio-interference doesn't depend on crossing any threshold dose, it certainly doesn't do any good.

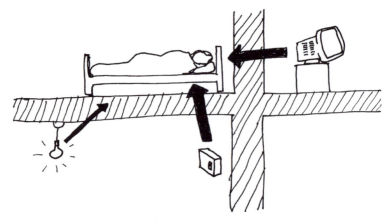

Electromagnetic field through wall and floor – distance to bed

Plastics are electrical insulators, so accumulate static electricity. Hence, plastic floors – whether, vinyl, nylon carpet or polyurethaned wood – electrostatically attract dust. (That's why they get dirty so quickly.) Small children play a lot on the floor, and so, if this is plastic, also accumulate static. This attracts dust to their skin and, when they rub them, their eyes. Exacerbated by ion-destroying fans and ducts, resulting rashes and eye problems forced the closure of many 1980s Scandinavian child-care centres.[41] Natural materials don't cause this problem, although in over-dry climates even they insulate.[42] Wood floors or linoleum[43] – not look-alike vinyl (PVC) – are better for lungs, eyes and skin. Cork (like wood, waxed, as plastic-varnish means all-plastic surface) is softer – more comfortable but less hard-wearing. Indoor water features can rehumidify – and give delight. Minimizing electro-pollution involves, therefore, heating and ventilation, materials, specification and design, as well as electric cable layout and appliance choice. Increasingly, however, its source is electronic appliances. Consequently, minimizing exposure depends on consciousness in use.

Geopathology

Although invisible, the earth beneath our feet emanates patterns of 'radiations'.[44] Long known to dowsers, these are subsensible, but discernible with instruments. Patterns crossing or intensified by geological disruption can concentrate these geoenergies to harmful levels. Do these matter? Opinions differ widely, but Käthe Bachler, an Austrian schools inspector, made an 11 000 case study correlating geopathological locations, serious illness and pupil problems in school.[45] She found that children's cots and beds placed over geopathological points always caused sleep disturbance; often serious health problems. School chairs placed over such points brought behavioural and learning difficulties. These findings, confirmed by other researchers, build on long-established folk-wisdom traditions.

Geopathological lines are narrow, so making crossing-points localized and therefore not too hard to avoid. For new buildings, geopathology surveys preceding design can ensure this. Whole buildings probably can't avoid all harmful points, but locating

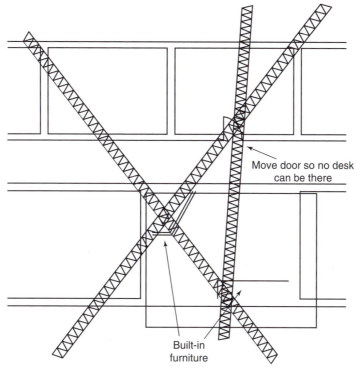

Passages, storerooms and built-in furniture to cover geopathological points

storerooms, passages or toilets over them eliminates problems. But what about buildings that already exist? They're too expensive to demolish. Moving beds and seats, however, is cheap. If better sleep or behaviour results, it is worth doing. If not, nothing lost! Building-in furniture over geopathological points prevents anyone sleeping or sitting there again.

Remedial action

Like 'super-bugs', most aspects of sick buildings are invisible, so easily alarming.[46] Geopathology, electromagnetism and ionizing-radiation leave (effectively) no sensory clues. Chemicals, moulds, heat, light, noise and vibration do. (In fact, the *Olf* system of measuring indoor pollution is based on smell.) Nonetheless, despite our senses being such good indicators, sick building syndrome can seem dauntingly complex and *some-one else's* fault – something we can't do anything about. In fact, however, most indoor pollution comes from things *used* in buildings: cleaning chemicals, photocopiers and suchlike; also from short-lived furnishings, such as carpets, chipboard furniture and paints. These are things *we* can do something about. With careful (multisensory) obser-vation and thought, commonsense measures – in most cases, straightforward and not unduly expensive – can remedy most problems.

After eliminating ongoing sources – such as replacing chemicals with natural products – ventilation deals with most indoor-air pollution. Ionizers, bacterial-grade vacuum cleaners, regularly cleaned forced-air filters, fitted-carpet removal and lower heater-surface temperatures (on longer, to compensate) cut airborne dust. Distance minimizes electromagnetism. Eliminating plastic surfaces reduces static electricity. And, for all routine replacements, using natural materials wherever possible nudges indoor climate towards the healthier. This indeed, is the golden rule: natural is healthiest – it's what humans, and all life, was designed for.

But beyond all these tangible things, what about architecture? Does this have anything to do with children's health? At one level, the right spirit in places supports harmony not conflict, encouraging care, empathy and good-will. At another, the moods that places induce affect psychosomatic tendencies toward health and sickness, hormonal balance and the vigour with which our bodies fight pathogens. This – called psychoneuro-immunology – is about how place-moods can nurture children. As place-moods are largely established by how sensory experience affects our feelings, 'sensory aesthetics' also have a significant bearing on health.

Notes

1 So long as the wood doesn't have cracks that defy cleaning!
2 BBC Radio 4, *Today* Programme, 8 May 2002.
3 BBC Radio 4, *Today* Programme, 9 August 2002.
4 Because of *how* they work, it's logical that they must.
5 There are others, notably vehicle exhaust fumes.
6 In Britain.
7 Venolia, Carol (1988) *Healing Environments*. Celestial Arts.
8 Holdsworth and Sealey (1992) *Healthy Buildings*. Longman
9 Braungat, Michael (2002) Beyond the limits of sustainable architecture. In Gissen, David, ed. (2002) *Big and Green*. Princeton Architectural Press.
10 Industrial levels of air-pollutants can be powerfully behaviour-altering. Solvent withdrawal symptoms, for instance, are associated with violence. Although there has been extensive research on health effects of prolonged low-level exposure, I'm not, however, aware of any on behaviour.
11 But the absence of smell doesn't guarantee non-toxicity – as carbon-monoxide and radon demonstrate.
12 A small number of people are allergic to some natural scents, such as turpene from softwood.
13 Some, of course, such as crysanthemum, are very mildly toxic, so are natural preservatives.
14 *Perspective* (1993) September/October; Curwell, March and Venables, eds, (1990) *Buildings and Health: The Rosehaugh Guide*. Royal Institute of British Architects Publications; and Planverkets Rapport 77 (1987) *Sunda och Sjuka Hus*. Statens Planverket.
15 For more on healthy building see, amongst others, Day, Christopher (2002) *Spirit and Place*. Architectural Press; and Mason-Hunter, Linda (1989) *The Healthy Home*. Pocket Books.
16 For more on a healthy indoor environment, see Day, Christopher (2002) *op. cit.*
17 Lime was once shellfish. Clay's colloidal structure exhibits life-*like* characteristics.
18 König, Holger (1989) *Wege Zum Gesunden Bauen*. Ökobuch.
19 Liddle, Howard (2005) in *Building for a Future* Spring, Association of Environmentally Conscious Builders, Llandysul.

20 Vinegar and borax makes a non-toxic fungicide. Mason-Hunter, Linda (1989) *ibid.*

21 May, Neil (2006) Green materials and energy efficiency – is there a conflict? In *AECB Yearbook 2006/7: The Sustainable Building Guide.* Association of Environmentally Conscious Builders.

22 After May, Neil (2006) *op. cit.*

23 Hinds, Jonathan (1996) Breathing walls. *Architects Journal* 26 January.

24 As pioneered by Gaia Architects.

25 After Bill Dunster.

26 Fredkulla School, Sweden.

27 Newer equipment uses non-CFC refrigerant.

28 Ford, Brian (1998) *Sustainable Urban Development through Design.* Royal Institute of British Architects CPD lecture at Cambridge University 12 February 1998.

29 For more on this, see Day, Christopher (2002) *ibid.*

30 Morgan, Chris (2006) Healthy heating. In *Building for a Future*, Autumn 2006, AECB.

31 Morgan, Chris, *op. cit.*

32 Snow-fences make this visible. Once wind is slowed, it drops its snow.

33 Morgan, Chris (2006) *ibid.*

34 Morgan, Chris, *op. cit.*

35 Indoor plants also do this, but to a limited extent. Only in exceptional cases (such as in 'tropical' greenhouses) can there ever be enough.

36 Water, however, never dries *damp* air.

37 There are 10 000–12 000 dust particles per litre in treeless streets, but only 1000–3000 in those with trees. *Building Green*, London Ecology Unit (1993).

38 For details on radon avoidance – both from ground and building materials, see Day, Christopher (2002) *ibid.*

39 As children's bodies are still forming, anything that distorts cellular development is particularly harmful. In fact, ionizing radiation is 20 times more damaging to children than to adults (Caldicott, Helen (2006) BBC World Service interview, 25 October).

40 Rule of thumb for power lines is at least 1 m distance per 1000 volts.

41 Fredholm, Kerstin, *Sjuk av Skolen.* Brevskolan.

42 As in desert-dry climates, arctic winters or some air-conditioning systems.

43 Real linoleum is made of linseed oil and hessian. Synthetic 'linoleum' is plastic (PVC).

44 Amongst many books, see, for instance Hall, Alan (1997) *Water, Electricity and Health.* Hawthorn Press; Underwood, Guy (2000) *The Pattern of the Past*; and Hagender, Fred (2000) *The Spirit of Trees.* Floris Books.

45 Bachler, Käthe (1989) *Earth Radiation.* Wordmasters.

46 Unscrupulous consultants (mercifully rare) trade on this to promote alarm – and hence their services.

PART III

Environment as an educational aid

CHAPTER 6

Our senses: meeting the world

From sensory experience to integrated thinking

We experience the world around us through our senses. This is our *only* contact with it. Adult *thinking*, however, is often only weakly linked to sensory impressions. Through past experience, imagination and assumptions, we make connections and form conceptions exceeding what we actually *perceive*. Watching (and hearing) films, for instance, we imagine whole realities without questioning the lack of other sensory information. In 'real' situations, many other senses complete the whole 'picture' – that multidimensional reality, which includes mood and meaning. Though we may concentrate on, notice or remember only one sensory aspect, others are always subliminally at work.

Children are less sophisticated (or less jaded and disinterested). For them the world is new – intriguing, exiting and challenging. Unable to separate out different sensory currents into selective aesthetics, music means movement, seeing invites touching, tasting (hence smelling), shaking and banging.[1] They need – and seek – to experience things with their *whole* bodies and through *all* their senses. Indeed, pre-verbal children communicate through many senses. To Loris Malaguzzi, children speak 'a hundred languages, but [are] deprived of ninety-nine'.[2]

As adults, we 'know' things by *making sense* of what we perceive. Optical-illusion pictures allow us different interpretations. We can switch from one to the other, but never 'see' both simultaneously. We can't *conceive* until we have *perceived*, but it's so hard to separate one from the other, we rarely distinguish perception from interpretation.[3] Small children, however, have insufficient experience to relate perceptions to an inventory of concepts – names of things. Very small children don't *think*. They *experience*. Without the protective filter of interpretation, sense-impressions go so deeply into their being that Steiner described 'the small child [as] entirely sense-organ'.[4] Thereafter, their thinking remains bound to the sense-perceptible world. Only when approaching puberty can children manage abstract thinking wholly independent from these.[5]

Without broad-spectrum sensory perceptions, it's easy to form premature conceptions. This is but a short step from shallow, simplistic, rigid thinking – opinionated and closed. Conception and perception need each other. In Western culture, however, they're rarely in balance – even in childhood. Although picture-making is natural to children, most Western children draw 'ideograms' – half picture, half words. These show isolated stereotypical images such as house, girl or swings, with speech-balloons and captions such as 'happiness', 'joy' or 'love' – abstract *thoughts* better described in words. In contrast, Sri Lankan and Korean pictures are richly evocative *pictorial experiences*. By conveying what they're about through colour and shape – direct sensory experience – these communicate qualitative *relationships* beyond verbal description.[6]

Although we're all born with senses, without sensory experience worth taking interest in, these don't develop. Much everyday experience is oversimplified, dull and disconnected. Much – like TV and video games – has been 'processed'. Does this matter? To medical doctor, Jeff Green, the senses 'are like a form of nutrition to the developing brain'.[7] Malaguzzi considered sensory *investigation* vital to child development: 'The environment must leave space for … connections of meaning made by [multisensory] "listening"'.[8] Reggio Emilia preschools, therefore, incorporate manipulative opportunities into architecture, furnishings and equipment. As our senses connect us to the soul of places, Steiner was even more emphatic: 'The real aesthetic attitude of man consists in the

What we see doesn't mean anything until we add conception to perception

Investigating light

sense-organs becoming vivified and the life-processes ensouled. Because in our materialistic age these things are not considered in accordance with reality, the significance of the change that takes place in man if he lives in an artistic element cannot be fully comprehended'.[9] If true a century ago, how much more so today! Sensory nourishment and *inspiration* by artistic experience is, therefore, central to Steiner education.

Sensory stimulus and attention

Sensory stimulus is also crucial to alertness and attention. Having evolved in a constantly changing world, noticing change was essential for survival. As stimulus-seeking organisms, we don't function at our best in unvarying environments.[10] In fact, without environmental variation, the brain looks for other ways to keep itself stimulated – such as action or introspection – or goes to sleep; concentration deteriorates, attention fluctuates and lapses. By contrast, changing sensory stimuli keep us aroused, awake.[11]

Although the dramatic increase of Hyperactivity and Attention Deficit Disorder is largely attributable to diet and video games, Kevin Nute contends that 'more varying interior environments, particularly for developing children, might also have a useful role to play in ameliorating what are essentially *stimulus-seeking behaviours*'.[12]

What sensory stimulus vivifies attention without distracting? Attention Restorative Theory suggests the gentle movements of familiar natural phenomena – such as re-forming clouds, waving grass, settling snowflakes or lapping water – as they demand little or no conscious effort to process, are especially effective in delaying the onset of mental fatigue.[13] Sensory experience *always* brings deeper understanding.[14] This is essential to interest – another factor affecting attention. We engage, enthuse and learn so much from direct experience. Videos are no substitute. Experience is the key to meaningful learning.

Our many senses

Beyond the five conventional senses: sight, touch, hearing, smell and taste, most scientists add movement, balance and warmth, but are there more?[15] Are there senses of danger and divinity? Do we have an intuitive sense of truth? Why do we recognize that the nature-created world is true in spirit, but much in the made world – such as Barbie-dolls – despite naturalistic *appearance,* isn't? How do we recognize what someone means, even if we don't understand their words?

To accurately, meaningfully and holistically assess the world around us, Steiner considered we need twelve forms of information: four will-oriented, four feeling-oriented and four cognitive senses. As cognitive senses, he added language, thought (or concept) and individual-spirit recognition to hearing.[16] These access the spirit-essence of whatever we meet. So does sound – when tapped, things reveal their integrity: solid or hollow, 'sound' or cracked.[17] In contrast, our will-oriented senses – balance, movement, well-being (or health) and touch are essentially body-bound. Between higher (spirit) and lower (bodily) senses are those most linked with feeling and mood: smell, taste, sight and warmth.[18] Mood-of-place depends particularly on these.

The physical senses

The body- and feeling-bound senses have obvious implications for our *physical* environment. Each works on us in a different way. Some, like touch, we're doing all the time, so are rarely aware of.[19] Others, particularly sight, are much more conscious – we choose what to look at. Touch, movement, balance, taste and smell tell how things affect us;[20]

hearing, sight and warmth, more about the nature of those things. Its warmth instantly communicates whether a bowl is china, metal or plastic. Some senses are more about sequential comparison (particularly in time). Whether things feel warm or cool is largely comparative. After icy water, even cool air feels warm! Similarly, after being in a 'warm' light, neutral grey looks bluish. Other senses are more about fixed state.[21] Whether in vases or outside chemical factories, roses smell the same.

Information about our surroundings usually depends on several senses. Besides seeing space, we also hear it, so hard or soft materials affect qualitative impressions of spaciousness. As well as temperature, colour and material affect how warm or cold we feel. Warm-coloured rooms actually *feel* warmer.[22] Multisensory investigation establishes, therefore, *multimodal* relationships with things. Just looking at, measuring or reading about them, can't do this.

Scent

Scents have ill-defined boundaries, fading gradually; they vary with wind-direction, temperature and humidity. They're non-directional, hard to describe in words (namely categorized concepts). We can distinguish about 10 000 aroma nuances.[23] Dogs recognize some half a million.[24] Smell powerfully induces emotion, largely at a pre-cultural level. Accessing instinctual memory, it's possibly our oldest sense. (Warmth and touch are other contenders.) It speaks to us deeply enough to trigger memories – even from childhood – we didn't know we had. Smell-induced memories can be strong enough to produce psychosomatic reactions such as stomach-pain or constricted breathing.

All senses fade without renewed stimulation, but olfactory awareness declines with constant familiarity. Other people's cars – or houses – smell; ours 'don't'. And we ourselves *never* have body odour or bad breath. Though we scarcely notice it, every place, every person, has a unique scent – one layer of their identity. Subliminal or conscious, this very much affects us – making houses near sewage works sell cheaply, but perfume manufacture a multimillion dollar industry.

Smells aren't only 'good' and 'bad', 'nice' and 'nasty'. They convey information about the *essence* of things and how we *relate* to them. As well as affecting how we feel, smellscape helps us navigate and place ourselves in time. Different parts of gardens, of buildings, smell differently. What they're made of and how they're used affect this. Some rooms, such as kitchens, smell differently at different times of day. Some smells are transitory, such as cigarette-smoke or exhaust; absorbed into fabric, however, many persist as background odour. Others, such as cooking, are associated with a time of day; or with a season, such as damp earth or moulding leaves. To raise children's awareness, Reggio Emilia preschools use plants, also building and furnishing materials to deliberately orchestrate 'smellscapes'.[25]

Though rarely designed to smell, *all* buildings do – usually subtly, sometimes strongly. We expect this in flower-gardens and toilets, not elsewhere. But, as virtually all building and furnishing materials have an odour, this is inevitable. Unsealed wood, fresh paint, synthetic carpet, even new paper, smell distinctively. In many institutions, cleaning materials drown all other smells. Smell is an indicator of the chemicals, benign and harmful, children are exposed to. So, if buildings or their contents, even toys, smell unpleasant, this is usually a health-warning![26]

How buildings smell also subliminally affects mood. Steiner Schools, Swedish 'Nature-Schools' and other eco-schools, committed to natural, eco-friendly (hence healthy) materials, typically use water-based (or low solvent content) natural paints, cleaning products and suchlike. Of natural origin, these have attractive plant-based scents, 'colouring' the whole building mood.

Touch

Touch is another early sense. Mother's touch is our first nourishing sensory contact with the external world. Babies explore the world by touching and tasting. For children under three years of age, or with special needs, touch is the most critical sense – making touch-friendly materials, furnishings and toys particularly important.[27] 'Touch-friendly' means much more to them than brightly coloured; soft dolls more than hard plastic ones; soft cushions and bean-bags more than play-furniture or patterned flooring. In fact, they're invariably drawn away from visually stimulating things to those worth *touching*.[28]

Touch is sensed by the skin, our largest organ. It links us to feeling – hence we use the same word for tactile and emotional feeling. Hands give more 'feeling' than eyes, making tactile experience more important to our *inner* being.[29] For children, touching is so essential to learning about the world that 'can I see?' usually means 'can I touch?' Touch also conveys how people are feeling. Unfortunately, touch-aversion is common in modern society. More pathologically, some children are 'tactile defensive' – frightened of being touched.[30] If deprived of loving parental touch in infancy, and with few chances to touch natural, especially living, things, children develop a disturbed sense of touch. In adolescence, this manifests as low awareness of other people's boundaries – leading to violence and aggression.[31] As the centre of the palm (where we *do* things) seems linked to the heart (where we *feel* things), Ruskin Mill, a centre for socially disturbed adolescents, uses felt-making as therapy. By rolling felt in the palm, teenagers experience the therapeutic touch their parents never gave.[32]

We learn something of the essence of things from how they *feel*. Being closely related to warmth and humidity exchange, touch tells us how things are to live *with*. It readily communicates welcome or revulsion; comfort or discomfort; richness or sterility. A whole world of 'feeling' lies in texture – tactility intertwined with mood. Multiple materials may offer tactile stimulation, but can be confusing or overly 'busy'. More important is that those things with which children are in physical contact, such as floors and lower wall surfaces, invite touch. Wooden handles feel more 'hand-friendly' than aluminium or plastic; textured walls (rough-cast excepted!) than smooth; soft floors than hard. Once we think 'touch', manifold possibilities for tactile place-identity emerge: smooth and rough, hard and soft places; rigid and flexible surfaces; complex, directional and even-textured ones. Even inexpensive, everyday materials – such as brick, tile, linoleum, cork or carpet flooring; smooth or hand-textured plaster; planed or sawn[33] timber walls; solid, slatted or fabric ceilings – make experientially rich tools for establishing place-identity. Outdoor texturescape offers even broader tactile and mood possibilities. How do moss, dry leaves, sand, hard paving or bouncy plywood, feel (and sound and smell) to walk on? How do they make *us* feel?

Living materials record their growth (as directionality) and history (as irregularities). Industrial ones, being produced by uniform processes, are uniformly textured. Unlike clay, stone and wood, manufactured materials – such as plastic, concrete, chipboard and MDF – feel dull to touch and lifeless to work. However inviting they *look*, they never *feel* it. Concrete crawling-pipes are hard, abrasive and repellent to touch – depressingly grey and unexciting to play in. Mass-production, standardization and hygiene-obsession favour industrial materials with little tactile appeal. However clean and tranquil, hygienic and practical or robust and inexpensive, if unwelcoming to touch, we can't feel at home with them. Although common in institutional buildings, they're the opposite of what children need!

Warmth

Warmth is yet another early sense. Baby animals, snuggling to their mother's warmth, can be enticed away by heating lamps.[34] Warmth – human, social, physical and mood – helps us feel comfortable, at home. Places reveal life-compatibility – or hostility – through warmth. So do the materials they're made of. Ex-living materials have internal cells to interchange warmth and moisture with their environment. Industrial ones don't. Hence steel handrails are cold – or burn in sun; plastic, sweaty to hold; but wooden ones comfortably, comfortingly, hand-warm. Polyurethane lacquer retains wood's *appearance*, but denies its *feel* – no moisture exchange with the skin, no internal-air thermal-buffer, no subtle pressure-absorbing elasticity, just a hard glossy barrier.

Metabolism produces heat. We must lose this or overheat and die. How fast we cool affects whether we feel cold or warm. Air *temperature* is only one warmth factor. Humidity accelerates heat flow, but reduces perspiration-evaporation so we easily feel too hot or cold, rarely comfortable. In dry air we can tolerate a much wider temperature range. Hydroscopic materials absorb moisture. (Wool actually warms (slightly) when doing so.) This dries indoor air so that, at the same temperature, we feel warmer – one reason why wood and clay buildings feel more cosy than concrete, brick or stone ones.

We also exchange heat with our surroundings by radiation. We lose it to anything – such as room surfaces – below 37°C (body temperature). Temperature-difference, surface-area, distance and the absorption rates of different materials determine how fast. White clouds or trees suck less heat than night-black clear sky; wood less than masonry. Wooden walls – or body-high wainscoting – are therefore warmer, more cosy. We also lose heat by conduction, again at different rates. For kneeling children, cork is – and even *sounds* – warmer than tile. In cool climates, there's nothing like warmth to make us feel at home; in hot ones, coolness to refresh us.

Sound

What we hear isn't bound to what we see. Sound goes round corners. Tone of voice, laughter or crying instantly tells how someone – even if they are out-of-sight – feels. All sounds influence us, affect our mood. Much like smell, there are some we're aware of, even focus on, and background ones we're barely conscious of, but which are just as potent. Just as invisible music practice enriches a school, the moods of gurgling streams, roaring winter wind or word-indistinguishable swearing enter into us – even without conscious listening.

The sounds of use are distinctive: footfall crunches gravel; it's silent on deep-pile carpet, sounds hard on tile and hollow on planks. There are also breeze sounds, such as rustling leaves or beaded-curtain rattle. Things that 'speak' are more fun than silent ones: clunking door-latches, creaking hinges and stair-treads, trundling sash-windows and sliding insulated shutters make us more aware of otherwise semi-conscious actions. Children enjoy out-of-the-ordinary sounding places such as tunnels, caves, echoing walls, bridge-arches, mufflingly silent spaces or pipes to speak down. Reggio Emilia preschools consciously design such sound effects into places.[35]

Size, shape and proportions also affect sound. Sound is bound up with space – cavernous or cosy, open or enclosed. Large rooms increase the interval between origin sound and echo – good for chanting, but not speech. The confusing acoustics reduce children's understanding and attention. Circular rooms, often desirable socially, focus sound as they do people! Breaking the enclosure and geometry, sloping walls outward to bring focus-point above head height and acoustically absorbent wall-hangings can counteract this.

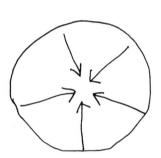

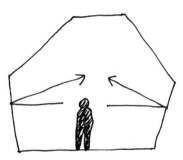

Circular rooms focus sound

Sloping walls outwards brings focus-point above head height

Places have individual acoustic identities. Some rooms listen outward, others are inward-focused, protected. Hygienic places sound different to comfortable ones. Soft-furnished, lived-in rooms sound softer, more welcoming, than hard, smooth-surfaced, empty ones. Amongst masonry materials, concrete and cement plasters are hardest. Lime retains subsurface elasticity: a 'life' critical to Gothic cathedral acoustics. Brick texture slightly breaks up sound. Wood reverberates in a living way, its tonal warmth – utilized in musical instruments – differing with species.

Although crucial to place identity,[36] soundscape is rarely fixed. Just as concert halls have acoustic absorbent material under flip-up seats, hard rooms filled with soft things sound softer. The sounds of life – natural and human – vary with season and time of day. Outdoor sounds tell us about weather, life and what's happening outside. Furnishing rooms differently, opening windows, drawing curtains or even filling shelves changes sound-mood.

Unwanted, intrusive sounds we call noise. This is a major source of social friction. Loud noise always *used to* mean danger. Although commonplace nowadays, we can't shed aeons of adrenalin-triggering response, so it unavoidably stresses us, increases error and accidents,[37] and can even precipitate physical illness. Physiologically, it causes tensed muscles, fatigue, diminished reflexes, and long-term exposure is linked with high blood-pressure and heart disease; effects that can persist for many years after moving to somewhere quieter.[38] In schools, it reduces reading ability, concentration and attention-span, induces depression and triggers violence.[39] As external noise – particularly road and railway – fosters aggression and behavioural problems,[40] acoustically double-glazed windows (draught-sealed, and with noise-attenuating ventilators) easily pay their way.

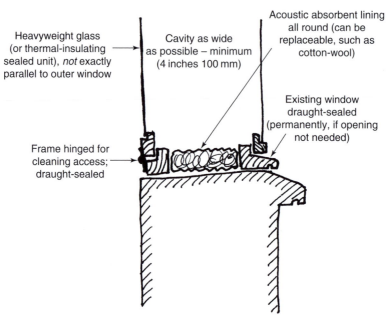

Heavyweight glass (or thermal-insulating sealed unit), *not* exactly parallel to outer window

Cavity as wide as possible – minimum (4 inches 100 mm)

Acoustic absorbent lining all round (can be replaceable, such as cotton-wool)

Existing window draught-sealed (permanently, if opening not needed)

Frame hinged for cleaning access; draught-sealed

Inexpensive anti-noise glazing

Against traffic noise, sound-barriers – preferably multiple – such as mounds, willow-earth walls or noise-tolerant buildings such as sheds, gymnasia or workshops work well. Even imperforate plank fences help. Vegetation – trees, climbing plants or hedges – adds absorbency, reducing echo. While sounds carry clearly over still water or tarmac – which 'reflect' them – over grass they're so sucked from the air that lectures are inaudible. Space for non-noise-sensitive activities – such as parking – increases road-to-ear distance. Doubling distance quarters noise. Tinkling water or rustling leaves help mask it.

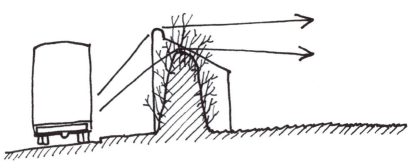

Sheds and willow-earth walls as noise-screens

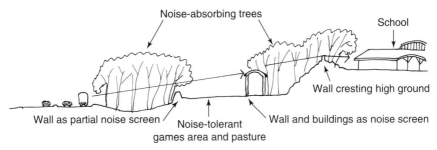

Noise shielding

What about indoor noise? Buildings themselves produce some. Plumbing knock is easily remedied, but fluorescent buzz and air-duct hum indicate things so unhealthy they shouldn't be near children.[41] Carpet, rubber or cork flooring dampen footsteps at source. Some noises, however (such as impacts from ball games and amplifier-boom), reverberate through structure – particularly 'drum-skin' walls and floors. Structure-borne noise usually needs expensive *structural* measures to remedy.

Most room-to-room noise (such as voices), however, is airborne. Noise-zoning (in space or time) eliminates most problems. Noiseproof fold-away walls are usually too expensive to be practical, but there are many easy, albeit disruptive, retrofit measures. These include: blocking *all* cracks and holes; replacing lightweight doors with heavy, draught-proofed ones; lengthening sound paths by locating doors so that they are not opposite one another; absorbent-surfaced 'air-locks' (as are common outside auditoria); storerooms and built-in cupboards as noise screens; increasing the weight of walls and floors and adding absorbent-lined reverberation voids.

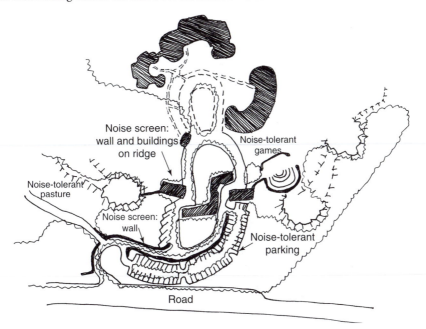

School: buildings as noise screen

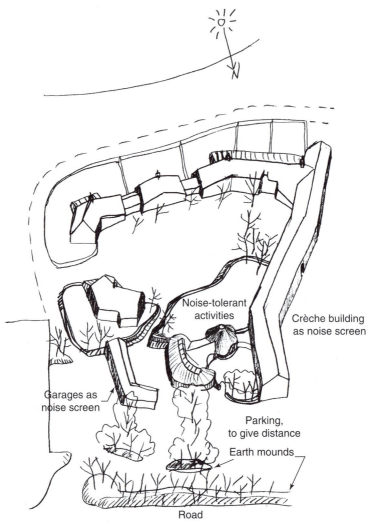

Multiple barriers; noise-tolerant activities

Noise-tolerant activities

Crèche building as noise screen

Garages as noise screen

Parking, to give distance

Earth mounds

Road

Many layers of noise protection: barrier, absorption, distance, masking, double-glazing, ventilation from quiet side (or noise-attenuated)

The source of most noise is children themselves – the smaller and more excited, the louder. Absorbent materials, such as cushions, carpets, pin-boards, wall-hangings, cork internal window-shutters or heavy curtains, upholstered furniture, leafy plants or even coats on chair-backs dampen this. As small children can only reach low things, high ceilings increase space without acoustically absorbent furnishings and people, so reflect more noise.[42] For quiet activities, therefore, Olds considers rooms shouldn't be higher than 7 feet (2.15 m).[43] Ceiling acoustic tiles are effective, but their removable access panels suggest 'something' scary hiding up there. Acoustic plasters, soft-board, wood-wool panels or open slatting over sheep's wool are less ugly. Cloth ceilings can conceal generous absorbent material and be shaped for scale and texture. In such ways, noise-control has visual and mood implications.

Noise-screening built-in cupboards

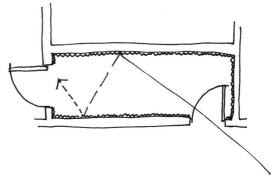

Absorbent-surfaced 'air-locks'

Sight

Sight is our most precise sense. The optic nerve is huge compared with that from any other sense organ. Being so informational, it's bound up with thought. While what we see profoundly influences how we feel, sight only shows the *outside* of things – so lacks the emotional immediacy of smell, taste or hearing.

Sight isn't as simple as it seems. Whether we focus on shapes or colours depends on age. As colour is principally *experience*, children up to about two years of age recognize it better than form. Thereafter, as shape becomes more easily *interpreted*, this dominates recognition, although colour has more effect on women than men.[44] (Also colour-blindness is rarer in women than in men.) We passively absorb colour into our emotions. Shape recognition is more active: it requires eye movement.

Although our culture is visually led, emotionally, we 'hear' what we see. The first sounds we hear are mother's heartbeat, reassuringly regular, varying but slightly. This rhythm benchmarks all music. Slow tempos are peaceful; fast are agitating. Over 80 beats per minute physically stresses the heart muscles.[45] Similarly, eye movement powerfully influences soul-state. 'Acoustic' qualities, such as visual tempo and loudness, cacophonic or calm shape-relationships, powerful or gentle colour, dramatic or subtle lighting, abrupt or flowing direction changes, induce how we feel from what we *see*. As its mood-influences range through calming, soporific and rousing to aggressive, architecture is sometimes called 'frozen music'.

While what we *see* is only shapes, colours and their meetings, conceptual associations also influence our responses. We normally talk about what things look *like*. Not what we actually *see* – unselectively and without conceptualizing. We so bond conception to perception that we rarely objectively see. Interpretation leaves room for wide divergences. This is why witnesses typically 'see' different versions of the same event.

Nonetheless, we all see the same thing – or do we? Even after babies have learnt to focus their eyes, do they see what adults do? Faces grow slowly, but eyeballs fast; for five-year-olds, eyeballs are almost adult-sized, but without full muscular control for binocular vision. Three-year-olds are inept ball-catchers, but even at six, only one in three children has normal mature vision, and few can sustain the optic muscular effort of near-vision tasks, such as reading, for long.[46] (Is early reading and TV the reason why there are so many opticians on the high street?) This slow development of vision affects movement and dexterity – one reason children seek other sensory reinforcement to whatever they 'look' at. This is one reason why *visual* design needs *multisensory* support.

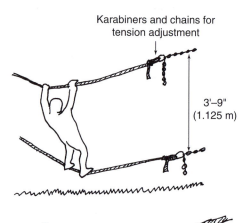

Karabiners and chains for tension adjustment

3'–9" (1.125 m)

Balance

Through balance we resolve opposing one-sided forces. Lateral balance becomes established around the age of seven. Balance *challenges*, however, continue to appeal into adulthood, stimulating health and alertness, physical and mental development. Children don't only need equipment, such as trampolines and stilts. They also appreciate balance-challenging opportunities, such as walls or trees to climb, tree-trunks to walk along and boulders to hop between. Felled (or uprooted) trees (trimmed to prevent rolling) make imagination-stimulating – and inexpensive – climbing frames. For safety, grooving offers grip when wet and bark-stripping prevents hand-hold-detachment surprises.[47]

Balance-stimulating equipment

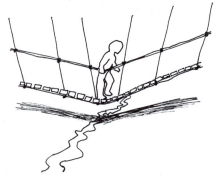

Suspension bridge

Good for chasing games[48]

Twirling, swinging and bouncing

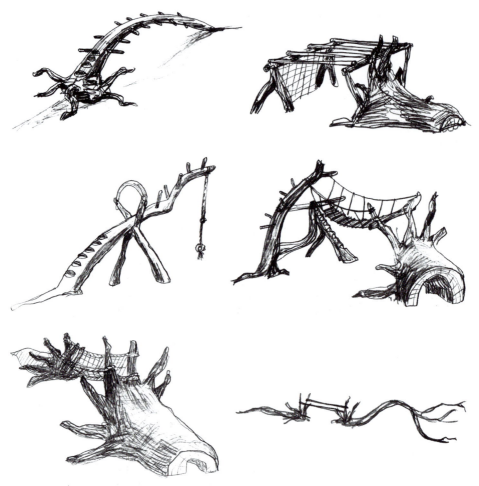

Lots can be done with tree-trunks, rope and netting[49]

Balance lets us find our equilibrium in space. As Green describes, 'this sense gives us the possibility of a "point of view". This is the basis of attention, [and lets us] see the world in a unique and particular way'. It is thus connected to our individual identity.[50] Bodily balance practice also develops mental and moral balance,[51] and mitigates balance-related learning difficulties such as dyslexia.[52] Dyspraxic children, lacking spatial and perspective awareness, particularly need balanced *surroundings*.[53] Architectural balance – or its lack – has an inductive effect on posture. Like all environmental patterns, it also influences how we think. In rigidly zoned surroundings, it's easier to hold black-and-white views than where all forces interweave in dynamic balance. Living amongst force-resolved buildings we start from a baseline of dynamic stability; amongst de-constructivist ones apparently falling apart, we rely on *invisible* structure being stronger than apparent *de*-construction.

Balance doesn't necessarily mean symmetry. All living things have symmetrical *organizing principles*, but one side always differs from the other. As manual-work declines, our left and right hand sizes diverge less, but we still have doing and giving, supporting and receiving sides. Print a portrait photograph the wrong way round and it looks strange – the subtle asymmetries are part of our character. Symmetry has a non-living quality. Balance is alive. In nature, archetypes (such as trees) are symmetrical, but environmental pressures (such as wind and sun) are asymmetrical. All living forms resolve – balance – these opposing pressures. Similarly, living, balanced architecture induces living, balanced soul-moods.

Movement

Movement is one of our languages of expression. It both expresses and induces mood, and reveals our character. For small children, movement and feeling are inseparable; they can't help expressing what they feel through their bodies. 'A child "moved", is literally "moved" [by emotion]; he leaps in the air, jumps for joy, shouts and laughs, or, if the experience is unpleasant, he may cry or beat the table with his fists, and kick'.[54]

Small children copy the movements around them – including those of machines. Machines start, run, change gear, speed-up, slow down and stop. Their movement quality is even, repetitive, but with sudden mode-changes. The movements of living things have living variety and are feedback-controlled, and so, like nature's cycles, 'breathe' from one state to another. Their mode-switches grow out of each other – as when horses 'change gear' from trot to canter. Some attribute children's increasing lack of self-willed control and attention-deficit to the start-stop, non-'self-controlled' nature of mechanical movement.[55]

As, for every infant, verbal language develops from gesture, movement fluency is important to its mastery.[56] Movement and posture develop spatial orientation, a prerequisite for engaging with symbols: reading. The writing hand's movement *quality*, and the mood this brings, help internalize the *quality* of each letter. As it also helps children recognize boundaries, stimulates exploration and brings separated things into relationship, Olds describes movement as 'the bedrock of all intellectual development'.[57]

Movement quality reinforces make-believe, intensifying characters and stories. When acting, every role requires a different character of movement – and speech. Reciprocally, by extending children's powers of expression, this deepens their capacity for growth.[58] Different movements induce different moods.[59] Children's movement is full of variety: from crawling and rolling to hopping, skipping and running.[60] Only with pre-teen lassitude does walking – actually shuffling – predominate. From babies pulling themselves up, through toddlers climbing better than walking, to older children with full physical abilities, the movement challenges they seek out are 'both a means towards, and a reflection of, maturity'.[61]

Physical activity stimulates blood circulation and oxygenation, encouraging alertness and reducing proneness to infection. Movement, by changing our relationship to things, ensures the sensory variation necessary to keep the brain awake. Immobility is a basic precondition for boredom.[62] Children – especially 11- to 14-year-old boys – prevented from moving, switch off. Consequently, movement activities – particularly dance – besides fostering a team-based approach to work, bring dramatic improvements in academic learning.[63]

Although movement is an educational necessity, TV and video games make children increasingly inactive.[64] Many can't even walk 550 yards (500 m).[65] Meyerkort and Lissau note that 'in the age of intellectualism and technology it is not easy ... to offer young children opportunities whereby they can develop the fine and gross movements which are intelligence-forming, the basis for creative thinking in adulthood'.[66]

Nowadays play is less spontaneous than even one generation ago; it often needs to be encouraged. Equipment increases fun. Joined-up activity opportunities – as when slides or rope-bridges aren't just dead ends but lead on to other things – allow flow *between* activities. This encourages free play, exploration, decision-making, attention-span development and spatial awareness.[67]

Olds recommends that young children's environments stimulate the widest range of movement for body- and object-control, and self-in-space experience.[68] Surfaces, textures and ambience, which encourage sitting, swaying, crawling, wriggling, rolling, bouncing, running, grasping, bending and throwing, encourage a full range of exploratory movement. So do lofts, platforms, slides, fireman's poles, nets, ladders and bouncy surfaces.[69] (Platforms are safer than sunken 'caves' as children push more on the way in – when they're still near the ground – than on the way out – which starts high above it. Pushing-off risk increases when some children are big, some little.) As hills and slopes suit rolling, sliding and running down, 'king of the castle' and similar games, Olds suggests child-care centres have at least two, four to five feet high slopes with 1:3 to 1:5 gradients.[70] High/Scope gardens routinely include 'hills', swings, see-saws, rocking things and play-structures.[71] Besides being fun, such facilities are tools for *mental* as well as physical development.

Children also enjoy *being moved*. Slides, swings, bouncy bridges, aerial-runways and rocking boats do this. Movement helps disturbed children find ways to reconnect to the world.[72] Distressed children often rock themselves. As rocking absorbs excess energy, an adult's lap in a rocking chair is calming and deeply therapeutic.[73] Not coincidentally are the words motion and emotion similar. For treating mild depression, Green finds exercise – and especially 'joyful' movements, such as dance – often as effective as anti-depressant drugs.[74]

Movement, whether of body or eye, powerfully influences state-of-soul. Both our movement through space, and how that space itself flows, mutates and breathes can soothe, calm, entrance, tense, thrill or challenge. Fluid or harsh movements, awakening or relaxing ones affect us accordingly. As building-, room- and place-gestures resonate as inner mood experience, this gives architecture, furnishing and landscaping child-developmental responsibilities.

The finer senses

Without the senses of well-being, language, thought and individual spirit, we can't be environmentally aware, socially responsible or insightfully engaged. The 'higher', spirit-revealing, senses – sound-music, language-meaning, thoughts-and-concepts, and individual-essence – build human wholeness. Their *development*, however, depends on the cultivation of the 'lower', more will-bound senses – balance, movement, well-being and touch – which tell about our *own* state. In the first seven years, nourishment – or its lack – from these senses also affects brain development.[75] Educator Per Ahlbom, therefore, stresses how important it is that infants' environment cultivates these lower senses. *Balance*, like hearing, takes place in the ear; clear hearing distinguishes individual sounds from ambient background. Likewise, it's the *movement* patterns of sounds that form language. *Well-being* – or its lack – shapes those earliest, but unvoiced, concepts such as contentment, hunger, discomfort, insecurity, long before infants can verbalize them. Through *touch*, we physically 'meet' things. It tells us about form, texture, resistance and interpenetration (both into us by sharp things, and into them if they're soft). Although we only touch the *outside* of things, we experience how they impress themselves on *us*. Hence touching something else makes us more aware of ourselves – linking touch to our sense of individual identity.[76]

Environmentally, besides letting us *feel* hungry, ill or tired, our sense of well-being, warns us when buildings are making us sick. Our sense of thought affects how we understand the clarity of functional intention and organizing ideas of places. Our language sense relates to places' legibility and their 'languages' – of form, space, scale, colour, structure and materials. And with our individual-spirit sense we hear how places speak of their underlying values – their 'spirit-of-place'.

If it's true we have a sense (or intuition) of divinity 'hard-wired' into the brain – as neuroscientific research increasingly concludes[77] – this has major implications for children. Agnostic adults are able to over-ride this. Children can't. Nor, worldwide, do a majority of adults, for all religions hold special places sacred. Anyway, whatever our views, we have no right to disabuse children. Both for them and the world we live in, the environment we provide for them should support, not counter, such an attitude.

The senses and thinking

Sensory delight sustains a large consumer market: sound fidelity, comfort, holidays – and sex. As, nowadays, we have enough *things*, it's 'the sizzle, not the steak' that sells. We *choose* coffee for *flavour*; for hit, we merely drink more. Just as deliciousness improves digestibility, and light nourishes both soul and body, material and sensory nourishment reinforce each other.

We increasingly trust knowledge *about* things. This *concept*-based knowledge, though abstract, we regard as 'objective'. Hence book-knowledge is widely valued, but direct response to sensory experience considered 'subjective'. Effective action, however, *always* depends on *fully* understanding situations, so must include what we learn from our senses. As the senses' job is to tell us about the world around us, they're essentially *grounding*. In fact, as NASA experiments showed, sensory deprivation quickly brings distorted perceptions of reality, hallucinations and panic.[78] Whereas *thinking* easily leads to abstract, unworkable ideas, sense-experience-based observation doesn't. It anchors us in reality.

Each sense has different boundaries, tells us a different aspect of the world and brings us into a different relationship with it. Multilayer information rounds-out understanding. Multisensory awareness encourages multifaceted, trans-category, feeling-related thinking. Monosensory 'knowledge' supports monotrack thinking. Dogs, led by smell, tangle leads round trees. Human monothinkers can be exceedingly clever, but never wise. Single-track thinking (correctly) views nuclear power as economic defence against political instability in oil-producing states. But it's not broad enough to recognize that this same political instability also brings nuclear terrorism!

Relating senses to each other is the basis of relationship thinking. Rich sensory experience helps children relate perception to conception, and feeling to meaning. This keeps thinking alive, not category-bound. Multisensory information reveals the essence of things, and shifts focus from *thing* to *relationship*. By multidimensionalizing our understanding, this opens creative channels we didn't know existed. As preparation for socially and ecologically responsible adulthood, sensory nourishment in childhood is indispensible. Unfortunately, this doesn't just happen. It needs conscious design.

Notes

1 Ceppi, Guilio and Zini, Michele (1998) *Children, Spaces, Relations; Metaproject for an Environment for Young Children*. Reggio Children.
2 Malaguzzi, Loris, the former director of Reggio Emilia municipality and founder of the 'Reggio Emilia' approach to preschool education.
3 See Lindström, Berefelt and Wik-Thorsell's concern for perception–conception balance.
4 Aepli, Willi (1955) *The Care and Development of the Human Senses*. Steiner Schools Fellowship of Great Britain.
5 Between the ages of eight and ten. Aepli, Willi *op. cit.*
6 This study compared American and Swedish children with Sri Lankan and Korean ones. Lindström, Sylvia, Berefelt, Gunnar and Wik-Thorsell, Anna Lena *Livets träd: Världen genom barnets ögen*. Rabén & Sjögren.
7 Green, Jeff (2006) Sensing the world and ourselves. In *New View*, Autumn.
8 Ceppi, Guilio and Zini, Michele (1998) *ibid*.
9 Steiner, Rudolf *Riddle of Man, his earthly and his cosmic origin*. Lecture 9, cited in Aepli, Willi *ibid*.
10 Nute, Kevin (2006) *The architecture of here and now: natural change in built spaces*. Proposal for The Architectural Press.
11 Vernon, M.D. (1962) *The Psychology of Perception*.
12 Nute, Kevin (2006) *ibid*. My italics.
13 Kaplan, S. (1995) The restorative benefits of nature: toward an integrative framework. *Journal of Environmental Psychology* 15,; and Kaplan, R. and Kaplan, S. (1989) *The Experience of Nature: A Psychological Perspective*. Cambridge University Press, cited in Nute, Kevin (2006) *op. cit.*
14 Szczepanski, Anders, director of Environmental and Outdoor Education at Linköping University. Quoted in Fenoughty, Susan (1997) *The garden classroom*. Unpublished Churchill Fellowship report.
15 In 2005, the *New Scientist* listed ten generally accepted senses, with 11 more as possibilities. Some researchers, however, list 40 or more – which raises the question: when is a perceptive ability a sense?
16 Steiner, Rudolf (1996) *The Foundations of Human Experience*. (1919 lectures) Anthroposophic Press.
17 Aepli, Willi (1955) *ibid*. and Steiner, Rudolf (1996) *op. cit.*
18 Steiner, Rudolf, *op. cit.*
19 We have more senses than the purely physical. As long ago as 1916, for instance, Steiner identified twelve. Steiner, Rudolf (1916) The twelve senses and the seven life-processes in man. In Davy and Bittleston, eds, (1975) *The Golden Blade*. Rudolf Steiner Press.
20 And what Steiner called the sense of life: about health and physical well-being – whether we feel well or ill,

hungry or sated. Mostly we're only aware of this sense when things *aren't* right. (See Steiner, Rudolf (1916) in Davy and Bittleston, eds (1975) *ibid*.

21 Davy, John (1975) On coming to our senses. In Davy and Bittleston, eds (1975) *op. cit*.

22 The extent to which this is psychological or physiological is open to question. Traditionally, red winter underwear was considered warmer, and some consider red simulates molecular excitation.

23 At least, non-smokers can!

24 Humans have 5 000 000 olfactory cells compared with a dog's 220 000 000. Ceppi, Guilio and Zini, Michele (1998) *ibid*.

25 Ceppi, Guilio and Zini, Michele (1998) *op. cit*.

26 But if something *manufactured* smells *nice*, read the contents to see if scent was added!

27 Montagu, A. (1971) *Touching: The Human Significance of the Skin*. Harper & Row, cited in Olds, Anita Rui (2001) *Child Care Design Guide*. McGraw Hill; and Kuhfuss, Werner (1979) *Evoloution genom Lek*. Järna Trykeri.

28 Green, Jeff (2006) *ibid*.

29 Matti Bergstrom, quoted in Lundahl, Gunilla, ed. (1995) *Hus och Rum för Små Barn*. Arkus.

30 Green, Jeff (2006) *ibid*.

31 Gordon, Aenghus (2003) Lecture at *On the Edge of Landscape* conference, Pishwanton, Scotland.

32 Gordon, Aenghus (2003) *op. cit*.

33 Sawn wood should be sanded to prevent splinters.

34 This is routine for piglets to protect them from accidental crushing by their mother.

35 Ceppi, Guilio and Zini, Michele (1998) *ibid*.

36 The concept of 'soundscape' was developed by Murray Schaeffer in the 1980s. *The Sound Hunter,* BBC Radio 4, 11 February 2006.

37 *International Archives of Occupational and Environmental Health,* cited in Dudek, Mark (2000) *Architecture of Schools*. Architectural Press.

38 Jarvie, Catherine (2003) Noises off. *Observer Magazine* 27 April 2003.

39 Jarvie, Catherine, *op. cit*.

40 Research in Austria, cited in *Today* Programme, BBC Radio 4, 29 May 2002.

41 See Day, Christopher (2002) *Spirit and Place*. Architectural Press, for some five to ten reasons why they're rarely necessary.

42 Olds, Anita Rui (2001) *ibid*.

43 Olds, Anita Rui, *op. cit*.

44 There is, however a blip, as colour is more dominant at around four and a half years of age. See Bayes, K. (1967) *The Therapeutic Effect of Environment on Emotionally Disturbed and Mentally Subnormal Children*. The Gresham Press.

45 *Today* Programme, BBC Radio 4, 28 May 2002.

46 Ministry of Education (1952) *Moving and Growing*. HMSO.

47 Marshall, Alan (1999) *Greener School Grounds*. Learning through Landscapes.

48 Recommended by Soo Hutchinson, Loopy Soo play leader.

49 After David Nash.

50 Green, Jeff (2006) *ibid*.

51 Steiner, Rudolf (1916) The sense organs and aesthetic experience. In Davy and Bittleston, ed. (1975) *ibid*.

52 Information from teacher, Dr Maria Castella. Dyselexia affects about one child in fifteen. Confirmation by new research, BBC Radio 4, *Today* Programme, 30 October 2006.

53 Dr Maria Castella *op. cit*.

54 Ministry of Education (1952) *ibid*.

55 Aepli, Willi (1955) *ibid*. If this was true in 1955, how much more so today!

56 Meyrkort, Magaret and Lissau, Rudi (2000) *The Challenge of the Will*. Rudolf Steiner College Press.

57 Olds, Anita Rui (2001) *ibid*.

58 Ministry of Education (1952) *ibid*.

59 Ministry of Education, *op. cit*.

60 Ministry of Education, *op. cit*.

61 Ministry of Education, *op. cit*.

62 Nute, Kevin (2006) *ibid*.

63 Interview with a headteacher of a secondary school in Southampton, England: *The Learning Curve*, BBC, 10 June 2003.

64 Amongst Europeans, British children especially. London School of Economics Survey of 1000 youngsters 1999, quoted in Fenoughty, Susan (2001) *The Landscape of the School Grounds.* Comenius.

65 Some 10–15 per cent of Polish ten-year-olds can't: Kaczmarek, Aleksandra (2004), teacher. Unpublished interview.

66 Meyerkort, Margret and Lissau, Rudi (2000) *ibid.*

67 Olds, Anita Rui (2001) *ibid.*

68 Olds, Anita Rui, *op. cit.*

69 Quoted in Dudek, Mark (1996) *Kindergarten Architecture.* Spon.

70 Olds, Anita Rui (2001) *ibid.*

71 High/Scope is a nursery school curriculum developed in the USA.

72 Kuhfuss, Werner (1979) *Evoloution genom Lek.* Järna Trykeri.

73 Kuhfuss Werner, *op. cit.*

74 Green, Jeff (2006) *ibid.*

75 Green, Jeff (2006), *op. cit.*

76 Bochemühl, Jochen (2003) Lecture at the *On the Edge of Landscape* conference, Pishwanton.

77 Tulley, Mark (2006) *Something Understood.* BBC Radio 4, 11 June 2006.

78 Davy, John (1975) On coming to our senses. In Davy and Bittleston, eds (1975) *ibid.*

CHAPTER 7

Light and darkness: age and situation

Light and health

Light is essential to life. All biological energy depends on photosynthesis. For *health*, however, we don't just need light – but the *right* light. Not surprisingly, as humankind grew up outdoors, we need more light than is normal indoors, and the nearer its spectrum is to sunlight, the better. Can we get by with less light, or with a restricted spectrum? In the nineteenth century, people had to. Urban smoke so blocked sunlight that rickets (from vitamin D deficiency) was widespread. With the current 'indoor-generation' children, this is re-emerging, leading to calls for vitamin D to be added to milk and food products.[1] Also, an excessively indoor life brings 'light jet-lag' – poor sleep at night but no full wakefulness by day. Even for babies, who can't tolerate excessive brightness, inadequate full-spectrum light increases risk of jaundice.[2] Sunlight – moderated for their sensitive skins and unselective eyes – ameliorates this.[3]

Sunlight is bactericidal – particularly effective against tuberculosis.[4] It's vital for calcium assimilation, vitamin D production and liver processes,[5] accelerates toxin elimination,[6] and nourishes hormone-regulating organs (pituitary, pineal and hypothalamus) affecting melatonin, growth and balance.[7] But light – amount and quality – doesn't only have biological and photochemical effects; it also affects how we relate to the world.

Thinking and dreaming: openness and security

Humans are photo-centric beings – drawn towards light. It enlivens, invigorates us. Light illumines – it makes things clear. It also aids mental clarity to the extent that students in well-daylit classrooms typically progress 20 per cent faster in maths and 26 per cent faster in reading.[8] It's no coincidence that we talk about 'the clear light of thinking' and 'I see' means 'I understand'.

By helping us be alertly awake, fully present, light has an *incarnating influence*. In semi-darkness, seeing less clearly, we must fill in knowledge-gaps with imagination: less fact, more fantasy. For different ages of children – from dreamy babyhood to intellectual, material-fact-based 'reality' – different levels of awakefulness or dreaming, intellect or imagination, objectivity or fantasy, are appropriate.

Some things need lots of light; for others it's too much. Light energizes – good for running-around play. It's hard even to *feel* like watching television in freshly glittering sunlight; it's too activity inducing. Half-light is more passive-state: better suited to daydreaming, resting or sucking a security blanket – 'ruminating' with inwardly focused attention. Archetypically, shade feels more secure: protective-enclosure shades, also we're less visible, less exposed. Small children like to snuggle up in *darker* – protective – places. At home, they

Quiet light for resting

make burrows behind cross-corner sofas, beneath blanket-draped tables or in under-stair cupboards. Recognizing this need, Reggio Emilia preschools provide 'burrow'-

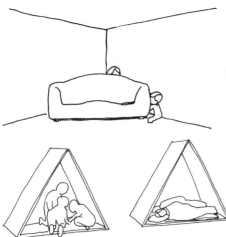

making props, such as roll-up mats and triangular tubes;[9] and Waldorf kindergartens typically have clothes-horse-like frames and coloured veils for children to make filtered-light 'nests'.

It's generally assumed that bright light is a 'good thing'. Bright interiors help us feel awake, mentally alert. Good for intellectual work, they're essential for teenagers. Small children, however, aren't ready to be woken

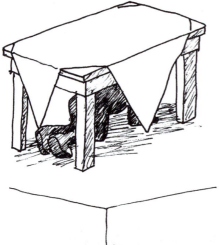

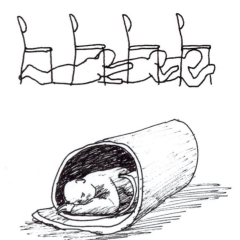

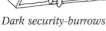

Dark security-burrows

from their dreamy, fantasy-rich in-between world. For healthy development, they need to spend part of their time in an imagination world. This – like dreaming – lets them assimilate their many experiences and build them into a coherent whole. Like Trolls, fantasy-worlds and daydreams easily turn to stone in the full light of the sun. These need magic mood – twilight *quality*, though not as dark. For joyous atmosphere, kindergartens need to be cheerily lit, but they also need dreamily darkish bits. Because room centres are active, these should be brighter, but play corners make better imagination-retreats if darker.[10]

Shadow exploration

None of this implies gloom. Sunlight is essential for health, also to lift spirits. But access to the magically dark is as important as the upliftingly bright. Indoor lives – and gloomy climates – make us so crave brightness, this counter need is easily forgotten. (To remedy light-deficiency, outdoor play is far more effective.)

In hot or harsh light, we seek relief in dark interiors and shade oases. Darkness has as many qualitative variations as light. These induce wide-ranging moods. Dens under spring birch leaves feel light, spirit-levitating; under thick rhododendrons they feel dark, heavy, even sinister – elvin and dwarfish moods.

Dark secret places

Spring birch leaves or thick rhododendrons: elven or dwarfish moods

Daylight

Without light and shadow, we can't see form. Different light directions change shadows, affecting what we see and how this feels. Towards the poles, low sun, casting long, soft shadows, is very welcome. In the tropics, high sun is something to shelter from. Its shadows are short and hard. (In southern countries, shade-casting moulding and deep apertures often dramatize these.) High and low light, and soft and hard shadows are, therefore, bound up with gentle welcome and harsh drama.

Until recent times, light direction always meant something. Archetypically, light from above only occurs outdoors or underground. Indoors – or in a cave – it's from the side. Rooms lit solely from above can feel as if they are underground – especially with dramatic light in an otherwise dark room. In human experience-archetype, shafts, trenches and crypts are about hiding, hibernation and earth-mysteries. Such light brings, therefore, protective, inward-focused, dramatic or even ritual-evocative mood.[11]

Principal light from below is unnatural; objects appear weightless, conferring unreality, strangeness. While shade is often underlit by reflected light – windows, for instance, brighten ceilings, and water and snow reflect sparkle-filled light – its source in overhead daylight is always visually apparent. This isn't so with artificial light, hence its potential for magical unreality. Along with colour, hardness, focus and intensity, theatres use light *direction* to create mood. Like all stage-managed drama, light from below can be exiting, fun. Too much, however, creates too strong a mood-world that doesn't exist. For children, this can be disorientating.

Light direction affects mood

Light reflected off ceilings brightens rooms. Dark ceilings drink up light. Higher ceilings allow light to shine down onto work-surfaces. Low ones reflect at shallower angles, so obstructions – such as beams – cast more shade. Higher ceilings therefore need less electric light than low. In classrooms, daylight from the left avoids shading writing.[12] But what about left-handed children? These – one in fifteen – need light from the right. As there are already enough factors determining who should sit where, the more locations that suit either hand, the freer the choice. Light from two directions provides this – and much more!

In nature, light comes from *all* sky directions. Even cloudless sky is never uniform – nor fixed. Although rarely noticed, daylight – and consequently, shadow – varies in colour, direction, inclination and intensity. Light from differently coloured sky directions, or reflected off coloured *things* – even loose rugs – brings different moods. Orientation and fenestration can, therefore, make rooms liberatingly or stuffily lit, cold and gloomy or warm and invigorating.

Monodirectional windows, however, bring monomood. They also maximize gloom–glare contrast with uncompromising silhouettes. Glare–gloom is soporific: slide lectures, though more interesting than unillustrated ones, send more students to sleep. Hence, southwest-facing windows induce yawns and sleep towards winter sunset.

Our eyes can cope with brilliance up to three times that of ambient background. Anything brighter is glaring. For windows, deep, splayed reveals intercede middle tones between bright sky and darker room interior. If textured, these scatter and enliven light. Shiny materials, such as gloss paint or varnished floors, reflect glare into the eyes. Reflection can also render blackboards and computer screens illegible. Will it? In theory, diagrams can predict this, but light 'bounces' everywhere, and reflects off unplanned things, such as white shirts. Mock-up models help, but it is safest to design for several layout options.

Windows from several directions soften both light and form-modelling. By eliminating gloom, they overcome glare. Placed in three walls, they flood rooms with light and, by letting us experience the sun's movement, bring a mood-palette wholeness to the day.

Daylight subtly changes in brightness, colour and directional balance from minute to minute. Even light from sun-pipes, light-shafts and atria reflected-sunlight has some of this living quality. Electric light doesn't. Constantly varying light quality nourishes both eyes and light-sensitive organs – essential for healthy child development. Consequently, rooms lit from more than one direction are more interesting, more visually 'alive' and healthier, than monodirectionally lit ones.

Educationally, this constant subtle variety keeps the brain awake.[13] Without this, children don't remain alert for long. (This is one reason – amongst several – why fluorescent-lit environments are so fatiguing and attention-deficiency is so common.) The play of moving lights and shadows fascinate children. As ambient, non-attention-demanding background, however, such visual

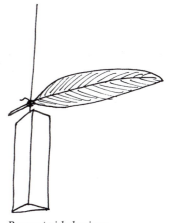

Breeze-twirled prisms

stimuli help children remain attentive. Breeze-stirred shades vary in translucency as they gently move. Sunlight reflected from rippling water or refracted through breeze-twirled prisms is enlivened with rainbow colours, always moving. Wind-stirred leaves set high-light-pattern and light-scatter in motion. They dance in a restful, visually undemanding, way – each species differently: aspen almost always aflutter, horse-chestnut more sluggish. Trailing plants over windows swing and caress; vine-leaves on pergolas ripple. Such movement qualities work into us.

Windows

Windows aren't just necessary for light. They also have developmental and educational implications. In particular, they affect children's attention and feelings of security. A major consideration is: what should they look out at? View-less rooms feel traps, but seeing things *going on* – especially others playing – pulls children's attention *out*, compromising their concentration. Victorian schools overcame this with windowsills so high that even adults couldn't see out. Effective for disciplining attention, these made good educational sense, but were dauntingly institutional! What views don't distract? Fluttering leaves or drifting clouds rest the eye. Though high-level views, these needn't preclude low glazing.

For focused kindergarten activities, too much glass – even without views – is 'fly-away' distracting. What about roof lights? These only show non-distracting sky. But for young children, focus flies up and away through this hole in their enclosing-gestured, mood-protective sheath. Even doors that have their lower parts glazed draw children's attention out. Likewise, windows opposite one another – or opposite entrance doors – feel as though something has driven through the room, carrying away children's attention.[14] See-through also increases the risk of bird-strikes.

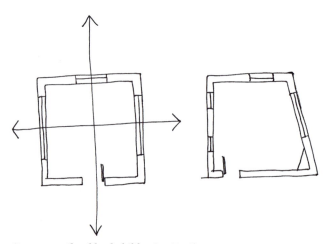

Windows opposite one another bleed children's attention

Window walls connect outdoors and indoors, but only visually; our other senses say they're different places. Confusion about what is what disorientates small children. What's outside, what inside? Is this somewhere to stop in or to travel through? Floor to ceiling windows lack containing-gestures. This further weakens the distinction between inside and out.[15] Indeed, unless prevented by visual 'barriers', children can run into them. (Also, warm room air convects behind pelmet-less curtains – a thermal reason why window-heads should be a little below ceilings.) Large windows are in any case too exposed for children's needs. They offer no psychological protection whatever. Children can't 'hide behind mother', but constantly feel 'on display'.

Do high windowsills make children feel more secure? Or do they just feel trapped? Low sills allow us to 'breathe-out' of rooms. Refreshing, but neither reassuringly protective nor attention-focusing. Traditionally, windows rarely exposed the lower body, so rooms felt securely 'holding'.[16] To keep children's attention indoors, some kindergarten teachers therefore feel windowsills must reach 2 feet 8 inches (800 mm).[17] Others prefer all windowsills to be *below* child eye-level. These opinions reflect educational approach. Distraction barely compromises unstructured play, but focused activities need children's attention kept 'in'. Window size also affects this. Tiny windows at kneeling eye-level don't compromise secure enclosure, but large ones need higher sills. High sills can seem imprisoning, but window seats can make them feel accessibly low.

Freedom from nostalgic associations made undivided glass a signature of modernist architecture. For teenagers, this enthusiasm to leave the cluttered past behind is still relevant. Also, such windows have the clear simplicity and liberating openness they need. But for small children, they're *too* open. Subdivided windows – even large ones – feel more 'protectively' enclosing. Conveniently, these also increase ventilation options. Windows divided above children's eye level can give light without distracting views. With a light-shelf division – shaped or high enough to avoid dazzling adult eyes – the upper section can flood the room with light. Below this, translucent pictures, curtains, coloured veils, pot-plants or climbing plants can obscure child view, allowing invitingly low windowsills. Alternatives for this lower section include water sluicing over glass, or mini-greenhouses – foliage filled most of the year but, in winter, sprayed or steamed for frost patterning.

 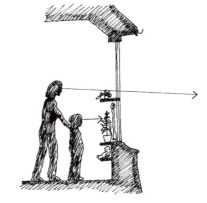

Light without distraction

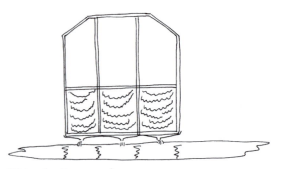

Water sheeting over glass

Mini-greenhouses

How should be windows divided? Two parts have a bi-polar oppositional quality; three, a moderating balance; four is a quadriform Cartesian-axis number; five, alive and not quite definable. For us world-weary adults, three often feels *too* perfect – a cliché for balance. But for small children, uncritically new to the world, it's 'just right'[18] – like the third brother in fairy-tales, third bear in Goldilocks. Four is too firmly material; five a little 'big'.

How large – or small – should windows be? What if rooms change function? Can we transform brilliant light – suiting intellectual clarity – into the dreamily magic, luminous glow kindergarten children need? While easy to darken an over-bright room, it's hard to (naturally) brighten one too dark. Light-shelves reflect sunlight deeper indoors. Reflection from pale colours, white floors, and clearing windows of overlapping curtains and ornaments increase light – but only so much. Slightly oversizing windows (or – as high windows cast light further – raising window-heads) is safer. Window size has heat-loss implications, but as the school-day is limited to the warmest quarter, moveable insulation can minimize this. For mood, coloured veils, curtains, translucent pictures or leaf foliage easily reduce – and texture – light. Like Japanese paper screens and Indonesian shadow-puppets, things

Moderating overbright windows

behind translucent screens cast intriguing shadows. Translucent materials can glow soul-warmingly. Traditional Indian and Arabic perforated screens obstruct direct sunlight but radiate its glow. Such techniques can softly en-magic overbright glazing.

Artificial light

In sunlight-enlivened places we're aware of weather, season and time of day. In windowless, electrically lit places we aren't. But what do windowless schools actually *teach*? They lead children to assume that dependence on artificial light, ventilation and temperature-control is normal. Worse, by totally disconnecting everything indoors from the outer world, they imply that education has nothing to do with anything beyond the classroom, has no connection with the *real* world. This does nothing for interest, motivation, flexible thinking, pattern-recognition and relationship-consciousness – essential for any ecologically responsible action.

In the 1960s research found children in windowless schools – with nothing to look at but blackboards – 'more intelligent'. Current research, understanding intelligence more broadly, finds the reverse![19] In windowless cages, laboratory rats attack each other or damage themselves. Could children ever behave like rats? Could violence in such environments be related? Hormonal imbalance, sensory monotony, social claustrophobia and feelings of imprisonment suggest it could indeed be.

A major culprit is fluorescent lighting. Its light is flat, even and dead. The lack of varied visual stimulus fosters distraction; next comes stimulus-seeking behaviour. Worse, it causes increased levels of cortisol (stress hormone) and ACTH (growth hormone and source of adrenaline), agitating children's behaviour and distorting normal healthy development. The 120 flashes per second of fluorescent lighting can induce hyperactivity and trigger epileptic seizures.[20] There are also health concerns related to restricted light-spectrum, electro-magnetism and, until recently, PCB-leakage. Typically, fluorescent tube lighting layout is regimented: it neither individualizes parts of space nor gives any appearance of respecting individual occupants. Not surprisingly, children taught under full spectrum light[21] are less stressed, moody, hyperactive, attention-deficient and fatigued, and absent only one-third as often as those taught under fluorescents.[22] Fluorescents have no place near children.

Electric light is expensive. Even more expensively, its warmth adds to buildings' cooling loads. This is the argument in favour of fluorescent tubes. But there are other ways. Compact fluorescent bulbs give a healthier and less flat light; light-tubes can bring daylight into deeply internal spaces, and switching lights off makes huge savings. With everyone too busy to think about this, most lights in most schools are on all day – unhealthy, expensive and causing pollution (especially CO_2). Fortunately, occupancy- and photo-sensors can easily turn off unnecessary lighting.

Electric light frees us from the constraining rhythms of time. Outdoors, it changes spatial boundaries; we only see lit areas; the dark beyond is unknown. Light pollution often overwhelms starlight. To minimize 'spillage', low-level path-lights and down-lighters can limit illumination to specific places. Indoors, merely switching some lights on, others off, can dramatically change room-mood and how children use places.

'Christmas-tree' strings of tiny coloured bulbs bring festive or magical atmosphere. Soft wall-lights gently illuminate the whole space, whereas hard spot-lights focus interest, usually on objects. Central lights 'centre' our attention. As on the stage, pools of light surrounded by darkness make *places* – dramatic for play – within larger spaces. Ambient light over a large area encourages group activity. Directional lights – single or overlapping – and dramatic shadow-casts increase mood range. Coloured light – and shade – adds a further dimension. Multiple power- and lighting-points maximize lightscape and mood-change opportunities. With such varied qualities, electric lighting is an emerging art form.[23]

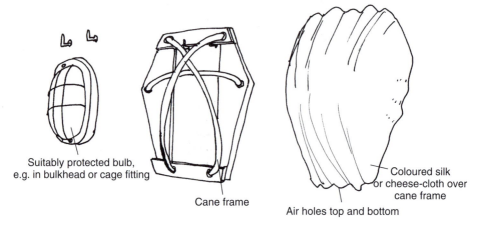

Suitably protected bulb, e.g. in bulkhead or cage fitting

Cane frame

Air holes top and bottom

Coloured silk or cheese-cloth over cane frame

Wall-light for gentle light

Electric light is measured in candle equivalents – but candlelight feels incomparably different. Unlike electric lighting's unvarying lifelessness, its spectrum – near sunlight's – and constant variation nourishes our light-related hormone-regulating organs. Entrancing and magical, it intensifies the celebratory mood of dark seasons. Candlelight-festivals, such as Santa Lucia, Advent and Christmas, redeem winter darkness. Are there fire-risks? Candle-lanterns or night-lights floating in water – above child-reach – minimize, though can't eliminate these. Mouse-gnawed electric cables or self-combusting linseed-oil rags, however, burn down more schools than do candles. The issue is less about safety – manageable with care – and heat (candles are typically used at cool times of year) but about *quality*. There are always utilitarian requirements to light, but light always brings *mood*. Without compromising its functional aspects, what moods do we want? What moods are appropriate, when?

Light and mood

Light powerfully affects mood. Brightness brings joy, levity. Gloom feels burdensomely heavy – 'gloomy'. Inadequate light – of strength, spectrum and duration – is depressing, causing Seasonal Affective Disorder. Indoor light is typically only one-tenth of out-doors. But how much light do we need? Varying with climate and culture, there's no one 'ideal' level. British gloom and long, dark Scandinavian winters cause light craving. Americans, valuing intellectual vigour, demand big windows, lots of light, even in sub-tropical regions. Other hot countries – whose building traditions and lifestyle long pre-ceded air-conditioning – prefer dark interiors to escape summer glare and heat. As

Studios need big windows

different activities, different rooms and parts of rooms need different moods, uni-form lighting is unsuitable, deadening. By varying in brightness, warmth, texture and quality, light can bring another level of mood-richness to places.

The *quality* of light depends largely on its dialogue with matter. Contrast sun stroking textured walls or glinting off shiny cars. Sun in a concrete yard doesn't feel the same as on a grass lawn. Sunlight through open windows feels fresh; through dusty glass or scratched acrylic, claustrophobic. Quality is key to mood. But what quality, what brightness, what window-design is *appropriate* depends on age.

Play nooks need tiny windows

Living in an 'inner' world	*protective, dreamy*	*twilight*
↓	*imagination world*	↓
↓	*interesting, inspiring world*	↓
↓	*effective, practical*	↓
Fully incarnated into the 'real' world	*awake*	*bright, clear light*

Notes

1 Vitamin D deficiency leading to weak and distorted bones.

2 Venolia, Carol (1988) *Healing Environments*. Celestial Arts.

3 Hobday, Richard (2000) The healing sun. In *Building for a Future* vol 10, N. 1 Association of Environmentally Conscious Builders, Llandysul.

4 In 1890, Koch proved that sunlight killed tuberculosis bacteria.

5 Gapell, Millicent Sensual interior design. In *Building with Nature*. Also Daniels, Robin (1999) Depression – a healing approach. In *New View*, 4th quarter, London.

6 Hobday, Richard (2000) *ibid*.

7 Gapell, Millicent, *ibid*. Also Daniels, Robin (1999) *ibid*.

8 Studies in the USA by Heschong Mahone Consulting Group, cited by Monodraught in *What's New in Building*, September (2004), London.

9 Ceppi, Guilio and Zini, Michele (1998) *Children, Spaces, Relations; Metaproject for an Environment for Young Children*. Reggio Children.

10 Source: kindergarten teacher Elvira Rychlak.

11 Ceppi, Guilio and Zini, Michele (1998) *ibid*.

12 For European scripts. Hebrew is written from right to left.

13 Nute, Kevin (2006) *The Architecture of Here and Now: Natural Change in Built Spaces*. (Proposal for The Architectural Press).

14 Riscke, Elke-Maria (1985) Pedagogical aspects of kindergarten architecture. In Flinspach, Jürgen (1985) *Waldorfkindergärten Bauen*. Unpublished translation by Luborsky, Peter (1988). Also, Meyerkort, Margaret, briefing notes on kindergarten design. Unpublished.

15 This brings up climatic, cultural and pedagogical differences. In warm-climate Italy, life tends to flow without barrier from indoors to outdoors. Reggio Emilia preschools utilize ceiling height windows for an 'osmotic' relationship between school and protected gardens. Ceppi, Guilio and Zini, Michele (1998) *ibid*.

16 Rennnert, Klaus (1985) Evaluating the material collected from the kindergartens; an attempt to summarize. In Flinspach, Jürgen (1985) *ibid*.

17 Rennnert, Klaus (1985) *op. cit.*

18 Riscke, Elke-Maria (1985) *ibid*.

19 Also, we now recognize more kinds of intelligence than just intellectual: emotional intelligence, social intelligence, spiritual intelligence,

humour intelligence, wisdom intelligence and so on.

20 Olds, Anita Rui (2001) *Child Care Design Guide*. McGraw Hill.

21 The non-visible spectrum components of full-spectrum electric lights tend to have a short life. Even daylight spectrum, however, is limited through most glass. For health, we need full spectrum, natural, light.

22 Health news, *Higher Nature*, Summer 2001(?).

23 There are even electric lighting festivals. The one at Alingsås, Sweden, annually transforms the town's spaces and moods.

CHAPTER 8

Colour and children

Colour: what is it?

What is colour? Simple; everyone knows. But colours change in different lights. Not everyone sees the same red. Indeed, do any of us? Some people can't distinguish red from green. Some can't see any colours. Animals don't. (Allegedly. But have any ever said so?) Scientists talk of split light and vibrations, but we – and even they – experience moods and sometimes even transcendent beauty. Does colour have an objective reality? Or do we create it in the eye?

There's something magic about colour. It *only* exists where light and substance meet – nowhere else. Opaque matter shows no colour within its depth – only at the surface is this visible. Night is dark and colourless, but the moment sunlight appears, even air acquires beautiful colour. Both materially and symbolically, colour lives *between* heaven and earth. Different hues, pigments, media and techniques tend more to the ethereal or the substantial. Its effects can be magically entrancing. Perhaps colour *is* magic. Certainly, its influence on mood is inescapable.

But what is it scientifically? Newton thought colours were fragments split from white light. Attempting to follow his research, Goethe looked through a prism at a white wall, but couldn't find any colours! He did, however, find them at *edges* wherever dark *met* light,[1] so concluded that colours appear *between* light and darkness.[2] He also observed that the eye, striving to maintain balance, 'creates' complementary colours. These persist as after-images. Researching colour's effects on mood and state-of-soul for 40 years, Goethe has been called 'the first environmental psychologist'.[3] Printing and stage-lights use Newtonian theory to make any colour from any three others (equally spaced around the colour circle). In 1957, however, Edwin Land (the inventor of Polaroid photography) demonstrated that only *two* colours were necessary – practical confirmation of Goethe's theory.[4]

From an artistic standpoint, Kandinsky considered that colours have associative meanings – such as red with fire – and 'tastes'. Resonating within us like musical instruments, these can be orchestrated. Like Goethe and Steiner, he considered that colours exhibit 'inner movements': expanding in yellow and orange, contracting in blue and violet, and powerfully latent in red but inactive in green.[5] Colours also have spatial implications – but these defy simple formulae. Conventionally, blue recedes and red advances. Certainly, the atmosphere makes distance look more blue.[6] Some blues, however, are so dense that they seem close, and dilute reds and violets can feel cold – difficult to locate spatially.

Approaching colour from the point of view of physics, as meaning-association or as fashion, obstructs direct feeling experience. Analysing a picture that speaks to us makes its 'voice' fade. When entering a coloured room, we don't *think* about it in words, but *experience* it. Colour as an orchestral instrument, a weaver between polarities, as a complementary balance-inducer – all help us understand how it affects us – but more important is how does it make us *feel*. In particular, what colour-moods do children need?

Physiological and mood effects

Everything we see is coloured. *Nothing* visible is free of colour. This has profound consequences, for colour affects the autonomic nervous system, muscle tension, cortical activity, enzymatic and hormonal secretions.[7] Blood-pressure, breathing rate, reaction time and eye blinks respond measurably. Colour affects mental abilities: red, for instance, reducing ability to judge weight, size and time. It's also thought to influence intellectual development and even character.[8]

Mood-wise, colours are classified as rich, fresh, warm and calm. Rich colours are the most saturated, strong and intense. Fresh colours contain no black, so feel pure, clean. Warm ones are soft and gentle – easy on the eye. Calm are understated, grey-muted off-shades.[9] *Mood effects* are culturally, often universally, shared. Are these predictable?[10] Psychologists think so.[11] Warm colour is more active, drawing visual, emotional and social interest outward. Cool, soft colour, more passive, encourages concentration.[12] 'Active' hues – yellows, oranges and reds – energize, excite; 'passive' ones – blues and greens – calm, quieten. Related to this, colour can even affect how *physically* warm we feel. Between these simple poles – active–passive, warm–cool – lies an infinite range of subtle qualities.

Summarizing extensive research, Bayes describes reds and oranges as active and warm, even aggressive. Red is exciting, stimulating, defiant, contrary, hostile, active, hot, passionate, fierce, intense;[13] orange: welcoming, jovial, energetic, forceful, exuberant, hilarious; yellow: cheerful, joyful, inspiring, vital. (Light) yellows bring 'light' mood. Browns feel cosy-passive, 'earthing'. Tonally and warmth-wise, aged dark wood feels more 'indoorsy' – hence cosier (or gloomier) – than cream new wood. Green is calm, peaceful, serene, quiet, refreshing; blue: calm, peaceful, soothing, tender, secure, comfortable; but also melancholy, contemplative, subduing. Purple is stately, dignified, also mournful, mystical; black: despondent, dejected, ominous, unhappy, but also strong, powerful, defiant, hostile. White is youthful, pure, clean, frank.[14] Bayes therefore suggests orange for welcoming entrance halls and yellow to invigorate gymnasia.[15]

There is a strong alignment between 'inner movements', physiological effects and mood induction. As different times and circumstances crave different moods, this leads to colour fashions. Colour *preferences*, however, are individual. Curiously, they're also time-related. Research has found that children prefer red desks early (in terms of the morning and week), but yellow, blue and green later on. This shouldn't be surprising: in mood terms, they favour an activity boost to start, then mood-levity – or de-stressing – later.[16]

Beyond personal preference, colour has sufficient physiological and psychological effects to give it powerful therapeutic potential. Pioneering colour therapy for special-needs children, Michael Wilson trapped coloured light underwater. As children moved in the pool, their limbs would splash either red or blue. Red helped activate the autistic ones, bringing them more out of themselves. Blue calmed the hyperactive ones.[17] Similarly, colour can influence behaviour, even dramatically: 'bubble-gum pink' subdues violent prisoners within seconds.[18] Painting toilets red prevents dawdling.[19] But what is mood-reinforcement and what behaviour-manipulation? When does therapy become control?

Colour experience

We experience colour as *ambience* and as *relationships*. Psychological tests use small colour samples. These show preference, but for full immersion in its mood, colour must fill our visual field. When close to Marc Rothko paintings, their colour fields' soft vibrating edges invite us to meditatively 'enter' them. Postcards can't do this. Barnet Newman, another 'field' painter, even fixed a notice, telling viewers to stand close.[20]

Tone and intensity, especially red and blue, affect the apparent proportions of rooms. Walls that are darker below, lighter above, emphasize height. If darker above – especially with dark ceilings – rooms feel lower and more enclosed. Whether oppressive or cosy depends on whether this complements or counters space-quality and activity-mood.

White (or bright) areas seem larger than dark ones. Tranquillity feels spacious; simplicity makes spaces feel bigger than those with complicated patterned surfaces. Minimally furnished rooms, softly shaped with gentle plane-meetings and light textures (such as hand-finished plaster) calm us. Whites, greens, blues and life-filled pale greys also do. It takes skill, however, to prevent white rooms feeling harsh and lifeless; blue ones, chilly; grey ones, gloomy; green, heavy, cloying – and reflecting the colour of a sick complexion. Colour areas fading into one another unify, so quieten. Those bound to forms or planes feel more meaningfully located, but emphasize separateness over unity.

Do colour *relationships* harmonize or contrast? Fight, enliven, enrich? Might room colour clash with children's clothes and playthings? Or would it be safer a little subdued? Every colour – not just the primaries – has its complementary colour. These bring life – but if equal in weight and area, they fight. Like life, absence of contrasts is dull, but excess is exhausting. Do colours accentuate each other: dark ones making light ones glow; quiet ones letting bright colours flame; bright 'accents' enlivening duller ones? Do they balance one-sided moods? Or are they too exciting – initially stimulating, fun, but soon feeling discordantly unsettling? What harmony or contrast, calm or stimulation, suits what situation?

So powerfully do they influence *mood*, and such potential do their *relationships* have for harmony or discord, spirit-uplifting beauty or teeth-gritting ugliness, that colours are too important just to leave to fashion or dramatic whim.

Outdoor colour

What does colour say *on* buildings? Traditionally, most buildings were either made of self-coloured earth, stone or timber – part of the landscape – or were painted with local earth or mineral-oxide colours. Unconsciously, but unavoidably, they respected their context. Their fabrics, likewise, were coloured with plant dye, so connecting with nature. A few, more expensive, buildings used imported materials and pigments. This emphasized their specialness. Nowadays, though no longer compelled by poverty, paints from locally dug coloured earths establish a distinctively local palette – anchoring buildings in place. (These pigments can be used with easy-to-make home-made binders – such as lime-milk or egg-oil.[21])

We're accustomed to permanent colour paints, but most fade in sunlight, and the colours of lime-based paints deepen when wet, even in humid air. Amongst non-painted things, leaves and flowers dramatically change colour-mood from month to month; also with light and weather. Even roads change colour as they dry. Such temporal elements in 'colourscaping', make colour an agent of life and time as well as of mood.

Light, substance and colour

Some colour is surface-bound, like paint; some intrinsic, like wood or brick; some impregnated, like colour-stain; some floats, like Lazure. And some is just light – invisible until it illuminates something. Painting is embellishment. Someone has added (usually joyous, sometimes celebratory) mood. Occasionally, however, surface colour feels 'superficial'. Intrinsic colours, appearing to go the whole way through, feel 'honest', anchoring. Stains, though only penetrating a few millimetres, are no longer 'on' the surface, so *feel* intrinsic.

Colour, surface-texture and light affect each other. Different light directions enrich, shade or flatten colour on textured surfaces. Coloured light favours, reduces or eliminates some parts of the spectrum, altering the colour we *see* in pigments. Hence, risking the attention of the store detective, some shoppers take clothing to shop-door daylight before purchasing. Coloured glass, translucent fabric veils, light-bulbs and lampshades colour light. Interacting coloured light is ethereally entrancing. In the theatre, it's part of creating a world beyond the real world. Differently coloured windows or veils, for

Interactive colour from two differently coloured windows

example, blue – making orange-brown shadows – and red – with blue-green shadows – create magical effects. Not surprisingly, colour therapy principally uses *light*, not pigment.

Although painted surfaces reflect coloured light, their coloured *surface* is visually dominant. In Lazure painting, several thin transparent veils (usually different colours) are washed over a textured white ground. Light passing through these colours is scattered by the texture and reflected back through them, so is gently variegated, and changes subtly with changing light and eye movement. Even if only in small ways, such non-assertive brain stimulation helps counter attention deficit. Lazuring can use pigment so gently that we're barely aware of colour *surfaces*, so they feel less space-bounding. Although using pigment, this technique colours *light*, so confers a 'living' quality and lets the colour's mood permeate our whole being. It has the potential for deeply soothing beauty.

Colour for children

What colours should be around children? Small children love – and instinctively paint with – bright colours. Toy manufacturers, viewing childhood as all about active 'fun', use strong primaries – mostly in the active-colour range. These sell well but their appeal doesn't always last. In the 1960s, some educationalists thought children *only* recognized primary colours.[22] Nowadays, however, these are considered *over*-stimulating.[23] In small spaces, such as play-cupboard interiors, or on small areas, such as door-surrounds, strong colours can be exciting. But larger areas, for example in whole rooms where we find ourselves for hours, need gentler stimulation and more mood-balance.

Up to about six years of age, children usually favour clear, warm colours (reds, yellows, oranges) – no surprise; at this age, they're activity-led, not feeling- or thought-led. Boys tend to keep a preference for red longer than girls – again, this conforms with behaviour. Older children prefer blues.[24] Unless anxious, children use little black except for outlines.[25] Birren considered that red displays uninhibited love of life; but, used defiantly, hostility or affection-seeking. Orange shows 'good adaptation to life and society' but yellow, timidity. He found children who prefer cool colours to be more deliberate, less impetuous – blue often indicating conformity and obedience; green, balance but emotion suppression.

This active–passive progression has age implications: blue night-lights, filters or curtains help hyped-up infants sleep. For older children, blue surroundings calm their mindless bodily activity, 'waking-up' their thinking concentration. Tonally, small children, still 'descending' into their material bodies, need to be drawn down; rooms brighter below, darker above.[25] Adults, already journeying from bodily to spiritual growth, need the reverse: lighter above, darker below.

According to Steiner, small children experience colour differently to adults. To them, soul warmth and invisible goodness mean more than physical appearance. As, until about seven years of age, children experience their inner world at least as vividly as their material surroundings, 'inner colours' – complementary after-images – often have stronger influence on mood.[26] Hence, while rose-pink kindergartens are warm and secure, colour-reversal imparts calm.[27] (As violence implies difficulties in relating one's inner desire world with outer social reality, could this be why pink quietens violent prisoners?) Once sense-impressions over-ride inner pictures, however, blue is more calming.

Ages and colour moods

0–6	Cosy, secure – magic
7–12	Active, alert – balance
12–14	Black and white polarities
14–17	Romantic

Steiner school classrooms are coloured in a deliberate sequence, matched to age. Each new colour marks a step on the staircase of developmental growth and achievement.[28] Kindergartens are pink, dreamy, only semi-earthly. As children become increasingly 'in' their bodies, colours progress from activity to joy: red, orange, then yellow – regal, child-valuing, hues. After a balance point of green, quiet, inwardly reflective, mentally awakening colours (blues[29]) stabilize adolescent emotional swings and support intellectual awakening.[30] Reddish violet for 14-year-olds brings a new balance. Corresponding to the completion of childhood, it completes the colour circle.[31]

Just as 'primitive' artists express emotional complexities, subtleties, paradoxes and multiple layers of meaning in ways that are impossible verbally,[32] children, not yet fluent in words, express themselves through art.[33] As Birren observes: 'Color more than any single aspect of painting has been of particular value in offering clues to the nature and the degree of children's emotional life'.[34] Colour being so meaningful for emotional *expression*, the colours children *absorb* influence how they feel.

Children don't need the same mood-environment all the time. They do endlessly different things: investigate, adventure, imagine, create and destroy; withdraw, sulk, run-around, chat, collaborate and fight. To suit, balance or heal state and activity, they need a palette of mood-places: darker and lighter, warmer and cooler, active and dreamy. Different ages, times-of-day, seasons and weather bring different activity – hence mood – emphasis.[35]

While general ambience needs to respond to climate and – particularly – age, room-moods don't have to be fixed. Hooks, beams and rails allow dramatic mood change. Coloured cloth, paper, plants and lighting can even transform colour, light and space from 'Rembrandt' to 'Van Gogh' mood.[36] Tunnels under tables or between cloth-draped shelves can link different 'mood-rooms'. Coloured curtains, translucent screens and veils, and fabric on light-reflecting surfaces – tables, windowsills and light-shelves – are simple and effective mood-changers. Multiple layers allow colour and darkness to change as needed: brighter and warmer for active play, darker and bluer for rest times. Such simple devices give many possibilities to adjust space-mood as required.

Helping places support their many mood-needs is what colour for children is about.

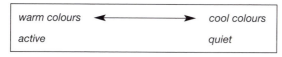

warm colours ⟷ cool colours

active   quiet

Notes

1 Zajonc, Arthur (1993) *Catching the Light*. Bantam Books.
2 Goethe, Johan Wolfgang von (1810) *Zur Farbenlehre*. Translated as Rupprecht, M. (1971) Goethe's Colour Theory, Van Nostrand Reinhold.
3 He called these the 'moral effects' of colour.
4 Zajonc, Arthur (1993) *ibid.*
5 Kandinsky, Wassili *Concerning the Spiritual in Art*. Or *Om det andliga i konsten*. Konstakademien (1970).

6 Goethe demonstrated how illuminated matter emerges from black into the blue end of the spectrum; and darkened light recedes from white into the yellow, then red end.

7 Olds, Anita Rui (2001) *Child Care Design Guide*. McGraw Hill.

8 Küller, Rikard (1974) Arkitekturpsykologisk forskning. In Acking, Carl-Axel (1974) *Bygg mänsligt*. Askild and Kärnekull Förlag; cited in Farnestam, Sandra (2001) *Arkitektur i skolan*. Unpublished dissertation, Umeå University.

9 Dulux advertisement, *Architecture Today*, September 2005.

10 These are 'shared to a significant extent by members of the same culture' (R.M. Gerard).

11 Gerard, R.M. (1958) *Differential Effects of Colored Lights on Psychosociological Functions*. University of California, quoted in Bayes, K. (1967) *The Therapeutic Effect of Environment on Emotionally Disturbed and Mentally Subnormal Children*. The Gresham Press.

12 Enns, Cherie C. (2005) *Places for Children*. University College of the Fraser Valley.

13 At least, for Europeans.

14 Bayes, Kenneth (1967) *ibid*.

15 Bayes, Kenneth (1967) *op. cit*.

16 Simmonds, E. (1962) Furniture and equipment for maladjusted children. Thesis, cited in Bayes, Kenneth (1867) *op. cit*.

17 At Sunfield Children's Home, Clent, UK, as long ago as the 1960s.

18 Olds, Anita Rui (2001) *ibid*.

19 Simmonds, E. (1962) *ibid*.

20 *Who's afraid of red yellow and blue?* Tate Modern catalogue (2002).

21 Nant-y-Cwm Steiner school, Wales, was painted like this; the ochre dug from within a few hundred metres. Lime-milk is lime, water and a little urine, milk-thin, made at least a week before use. Egg-oil emulsion is equal parts of egg, boiled linseed oil and water, with a splash of peppermint oil to prevent the egg from rotting. See Day, Christopher (1998) *A Haven for Childhood*. Starborn Books.

22 Karl Luscher (of Luscher Test fame) found children had a colour preference scale, from red, yellow, orange to purple-grey and dark colours. I question the validity of all tests based on isolated samples, also on de-contextualized 'preference'. Other research, such as that in Reggio Emilia preschools, shows broader and more variable preferences. Ceppi, Guilio and Zini, Michele (1998) *Children, Spaces, Relations; Metaproject for an Environment for Young Children*. Reggio Children.

23 Dudek, Mark (1996) *Kindergarten Architecture*. Spon.

24 Bayes, Kenneth (1967) *ibid*.

25 Birren, Faber (1978) *Color and Human Response*. Van Nostrand Reinhold. These conclusions are widely, but not universally agreed.

26 Riscke, Elke-Maria (1985) Pedagogical aspects of kindergarten architecture. In Flinspach, Jürgen (1985) *Waldorfkindergärten Bauen*. Unpublished translation by Luborsky, Peter (1988).

27 Patten, Angela, *New View*.

28 Thörn, Kerstin *Att bygga en skol*. Västerbotton, Västerbottons Museum.

29 Thörn, Kerstin *op. cit*.

30 The colours Steiner himself recommended differ for different schools. He emphasized that colouring shouldn't be by dogmatic formula but should respond to the particular situation: light quality and direction, geographical and cultural location, as well as children's ages.

31 Riscke, Elke-Maria (1985) *ibid*.

32 Early twentieth century discovery of African art introduced European artists to a hitherto unimaginable power.

33 Birren, Faber (1978) *ibid*.

34 Alschuler, Rose H. and Hattwick, La Berta Weiss (1947) *Painting and Personality*. Quoted in Birren, Faber (1978) *op. cit*.

35 Bayes, Kenneth (1967) *ibid*.

36 As in Anita Midbjer's work at Umeå University.

CHAPTER 9

Space: shape and quality

Response to space

Why do we feel at ease in some rooms, uncomfortable in others? Although materials, textures, colour, light, furnishings, acoustics and heating all play a part, the *shape* of space is a major factor. This is partly about proportions. We can't feel cosy or homely in somewhere too vertical; nor free, at ease, in somewhere proportionally low – even with ceilings well above head level. Scale – how things compare to *our own* size and eye level – differs for children and adults. Children easily feel daunted in high rooms. They're more relaxed in child-scaled ones.

Gesture also plays a part. By mimicking building gestures ourselves we learn a lot about how places will make occupants feel. Conversely, what gestures do *we* make to stop, condemn, welcome or soothe people? Can confronting planes welcome? Often they're too aggressive for children.[1] To welcome, don't we more usually beckon or embrace? Can dynamic diagonals create tranquillity? Aren't horizontals more effective here? What about alertness: do we lie down or sit up? Is this better served by horizontality or verticality? Like a calm sea, horizontality is visually 'quiet', relaxing. Externally, it makes buildings modest and undemanding. What about entry gestures? Wall-undulations can form sun-trap bays or, under wall-brushing trees, shade oases. Deep roof overhangs shelter. Flat roofs and walls neither shelter nor gesture invitation. Building body-language is as fluently expressive as the human version.

Indoors, mood is largely about spatial *quality*. What happens when planes meet? Right-angled corners bring planes into collision, conflict. Acute-angled external corners aggressively arrow at us. Internally, they're cramping, trapping. Obtuse-angled ones are more welcomingly gestured. Externally, they feel gentler, less abrupt. Curves bring planes into more gentle meetings with each other. Domed ceilings and arched openings feel less severe than flat ones. Facetted curves have similar gesture qualities: they're less restful but firmer. Curves, therefore, suit younger – more dreamy – children; facets, older – more awake – ones.

Space-language: from life-energy to thought

Dead buildings say life is dull – not a good message for children. They need life. Nothing alive is ever fixed; *all* living things are always changing. Buddhist sand-mandalas, intricately

Sheltering building edge[2]

built grain by grain then ritually swirled into dust, or Joseph Beuys' sculptures using fat and honey, are metaphors of this transformation principle. This doesn't mean dissolving buildings, but creating ones whose mood responds to – instead of dominating – life, season and weather.

Energy doesn't mean disordered or unstably dramatic spaces. Despite adventures and emotional outbursts, children crave harmony, balance and security in their lives. As they're on their way to adult, rational, consciousness, to thinking – remembering and anticipating – before doing, their drawings, initially just energy 'scribbles', work towards a two-axis framework and strive towards balance – the bringing of opposites (right and left, above and below) into harmony.[3] Reciprocally, this progression from energy-shaped to ordered drawings reflects children's environmental needs as they grow. Their buildings need to follow a similar development.

Free lines are about uncontrolled life. But we can easily feel *too* free, unanchored, to be practical. How organized can places for children be before becoming deadening and institutional? How free before feeling chaotic? These principles – life-energy and ordered organization – are manifestations of totally opposite form-giving powers: nature and thought.

Neither unrelieved clarity nor exuberant complexity feels comfortable. One is boring, life-inimical; the other, chaotic, insecure. Optimum balance varies according to age, activity, culture and circumstance. Even weather affects this: hot climates make us crave calm quietness; cold ones, cosy activity. Many children find lack of sensory stimulus so boring that their attention wanders. For them, any kind of jolt relieves monotony. Those with Asperger's Syndrome, however, are easily overburdened by discordant sense impressions; they need simple, calming rooms – gentle but not dull.

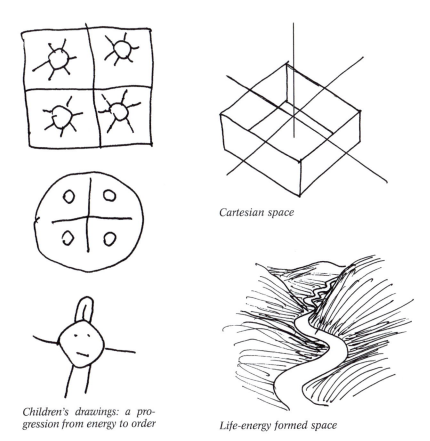

Cartesian space

*Children's drawings: a pro-
gression from energy to order*

Life-energy formed space

This touches on another polarity: rectangularity and organic curves. Curves are the shapes – and movements – of all *living* things; the shapes of *nature*. But thought, especially consequential logic, also 'thought-up' movements such as up, down, right, left, are essentially straight. Rectangles are shapes formed by human *thought*. Again, neither extreme suits us. Lifeless thought is arid. Thoughtless life-vigour, too unfocused. Yet again the balance point depends on many factors, especially age. Small children live in activity; teenagers more in thought. With 'gestures' appropriate to age – from dreamy, fluidly soft, to hard and thought-organizing – rooms can support the developmental stages through which every child goes.

Function and space-mood

Despite mood being central to architecture, we're only recently emerging from Le Corbusier's dictum that 'a house is a machine for living'. Time-saving efficiency eases life, but no-one enjoys feeling like a cog in a machine. Some parts of buildings don't work unless shaped by order and organization. But others are more about life, so – without compromising efficiency – need to prioritize mood qualities. For every room, therefore, we need to ask: is it principally for *things* or for *life*? As storage is about organizing *things*, rectangular rooms work best. But life, its movements and human bodies aren't rectangular, so non-rectangular spaces better suit most other purposes.

Dedicating rooms, buildings and areas to single functions may seem logical, but it is an essentially modern concept. Traditional village schools comprised just two multiyear rooms. Until eighteenth-century industrialization, few house rooms had fixed functions. Artisans, shopkeepers and professionals worked from home, making towns, though wealth- and trade-zoned, completely mixed use.[4] Nowadays, as adults we use rooms for clearly distinguished purposes, but that's not natural to children – one reason they're not always popular in adult workplaces! As Herman Hertzberger observes, although clarity of function adds efficiency, something 'exclusively made for one purpose, suppresses the individual because it tells him exactly how it is to be used. If the object provokes a person to determine in what way he wants to use it, it will strengthen his self-identity'.[5] Stimulation is what children need, not assembly-line thinking.

Room function suggests mood and behaviour parameters. Kitchens are warm, homely and tolerate messy play. Although good for water-play, the echoing hardness of bathrooms doesn't feel welcoming. Living-rooms, though soft, can be constrainingly formal; also television-focus inhibits imagination. Bedrooms are personal realms – free to establish long-term mood. Attics, cellars, storerooms and garden sheds are full of mysterious (often tantalizingly forbidden) things to stimulate inventive play, but have very different moods. Cellars are *underground*. Cave-like, they invoke archetypal roots, a magical but

Nest-nooks

disquieting past, and subhuman monsters. They're usually dark, cold and musty – a climate independent of weather. In contrast, attics amplify it: heat or rain-beat on roof, frost and draught, sunlight chinks or bare bulbs and deep shadows. Though full of past clutter, they're *above* the world – places from which imagination can fly.[6] From such an attic, C.S. Lewis' world of Narnia opened.[7] But imagination-nurturing rooms needn't be forgotten and chaotic. As Bartlett writes, if built for children's needs, houses 'would be all attic and eaves, huge closets and little doors, cubbies and alcoves and dark shadowy places, laundry chutes, dumb waiters, settings for mystery and exploration'.[8]

Old buildings are full of redundant spaces for children to explore. They're rich in creativity-stimulating settings for fantasy play. 'Well-designed' buildings aren't. These work efficiently. Few modern homes have attics or cellars. Many aren't even houses. Consequently, for children's needs, newer, more 'rational' and 'space-efficient' buildings need mood-evocative spaces for *non-predicted* uses deliberately designed – or furnished – in.

These don't have to be irrational, whimsy or useless spaces. Alcove-niches and semi-defined *places*, from ledges and landings to deep windowsills, serve this purpose. Domestic nest-nook opportunities include curtain-fronted cupboards, behind-furniture and under-stair spaces. Such places make ideal play-nests: child-scaled, (almost) adult inaccessible, dark and a bit magic, but in the middle of domestic life. Windows, however tiny, emphasize territorial identity, making these into miniature 'houses'. Separate windows transform bunk-beds from mere sibling-stacks to distinct private realms. Sleeping lofts in roof-spaces both make good nests and liberate such floor space that even cramped box rooms become spacious playrooms. Such places make children feel special, confirming that they're at the centre of adults' value.

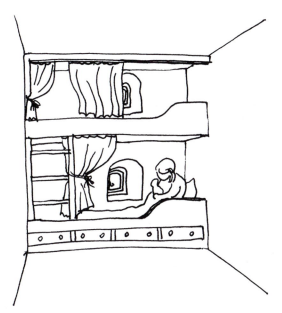

Two bunks, two windows, two complete realms

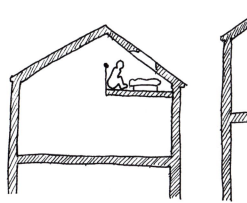
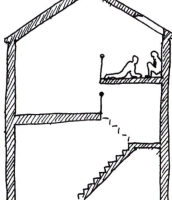

Private realms

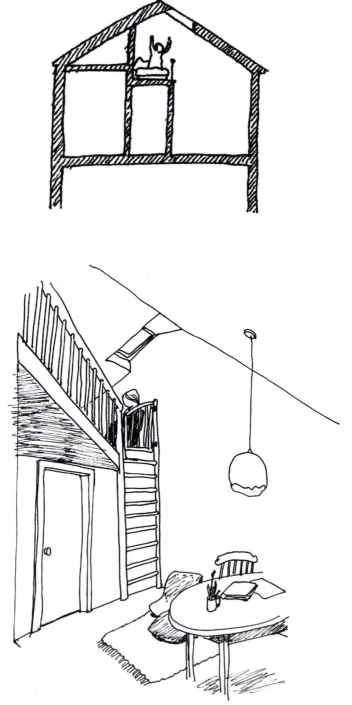

Even in small houses with low roofs, space for sleeping (or play) lofts can usually be found. Children love these

Continued

Usability and space

How rooms are used depends, in large part, on where doors are. Tight in corners, they sterilize wall space – no room for shelves or furniture. But doors do more than this. Two doors in a room create a path. In play spaces crossed by paths, small children wonder who will suddenly appear. This makes them feel insecure. Always having half an ear cocked, they're easily distracted, so can't fully commit themselves to play. In rooms with too many doors, movement flow so dominates protected corners that these cease to be 'places'. Indeed, for all ages, this makes small rooms virtually useless.

Imaginative play flourishes best in 'protected regions'. As mid-floor is generally too exposed, this makes corners the highest value parts of rooms, too valuable for doorways. Non-rectangular rooms or those with alcoves and niches have more corners. Modifying child-care rooms, Olds would always first identify potential protected regions – ideally, each big enough for about four children – then relocate doorways, or

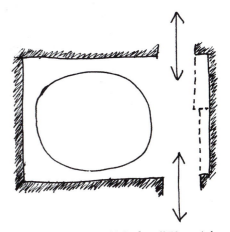

Door near corners: 10 inches (250 mm) for shelves, 20–24 inches (500–600 mm) for furniture 6–10 feet (1850–3000 mm) protected area for play

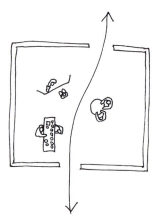

Pathway-edge areas suit furniture-based play, but not floor-play

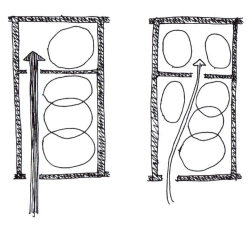

Moving a doorway increases usable space[10]

use furniture, to redirect paths *tangentially* not *across* them.[9] As infants often play on the floor – and once down usually stay put, not run about – protected regions become floor level 'territories'. Differing floor or ceiling levels, open post frameworks, space-dividing shelving or even just overhead beams can strengthen their spatial definition. Changes in flooring, materials, textures, acoustics, colour or lighting do as well. The better protected these subplaces are, the better they're more 'used'.

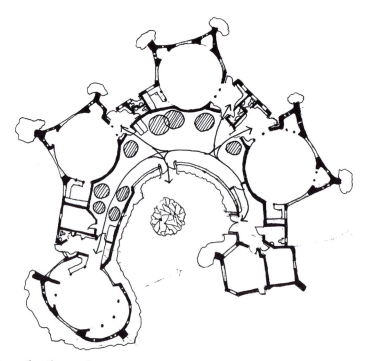

A corner is worth a thousand routes

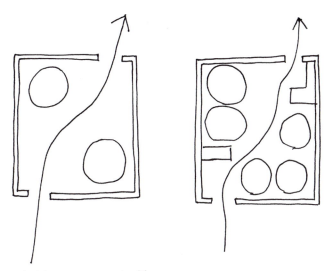

Kindergarten: maximizing corner opportunities

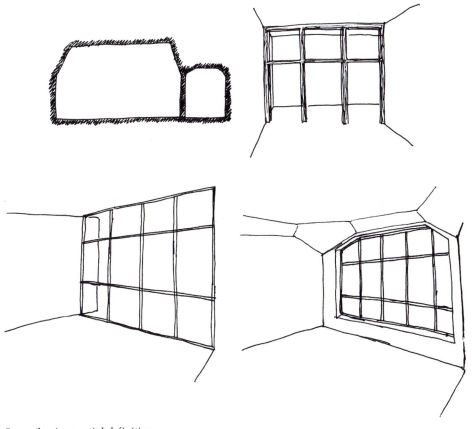

Strengthening spatial definition

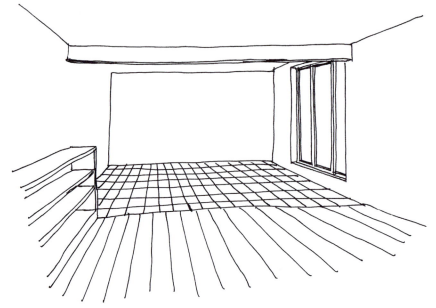

Strengthening spatial definition

Classrooms

Traditionally, classrooms are rectangular. But should they be? Does classroom shape have educational implications? Researching this, James Dyck found shape has 'considerable effect on learning outcomes'. He observed that classrooms need to be compact for whole-group activities, but also offer separated spaces for study. Rectangles keep groups together, but leave study-groups too much in each other's space. He concluded that these conflicting demands are better served by short, fat L-shaped rooms.[11] For one teacher to keep a whole class in view, 'arms' must be short or angles obtuse. Uneven length 'arms' make rooms both feel less formal and, by increasing the difference between their parts, extend the range of uses they suit – making them much more flexible

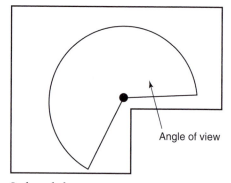

Angle of view

L-shaped classrooms

than rectangular ones. But does making classrooms into (effectively) dual spaces compromise unified group identity? Opinions are divided. But, if nothing else, this strengthens the case for alcoves.

Alcoves can clearly differentiate wet and dry, messy and clean areas. Active and quiet, public and semi-private realms, such as areas for study, group-work, displays and specialist equipment also benefit from spatial differentiation. Some alcoves can be formed simply with furniture. In all cases, different flooring – such as changing from wood to tiles or cork – and beam 'thresholds' or lower ceilings reinforce the distinctiveness of different realms. Some, such as snack-kitchenettes (with kettle, cooker, fridge and sink), need plumbing. Kitchenettes are particularly reassuring for phlegmatic children, for whom food is a security magnet. Educationally, they introduce the concept of responsibility. Who cleans, washes-up, puts food away? How are rotas and tasks decided?[12] Such simple facilities bring early lessons in cooperative management. But for wet and dry conflict, counters work adequately alongside any wall, but kitchenette *alcoves* transform classrooms into sociable 'home' bases.

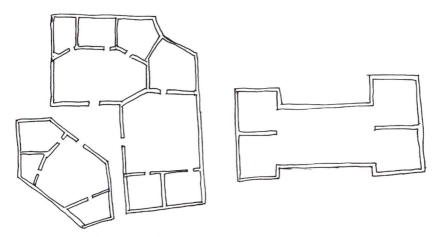

Group rooms and study corners or sub-rooms

Mood-wise, rectangles are uncompromisingly abrupt. Their planes collide. For younger children, they're also insufficiently embracing. Concave plans are more protectively gestured. Round spaces, from woodland clearings to rooms, and round centres of attention, such as tables, lawns, fire-pits, encourage sociability. Their very geometry makes circles group-focused, innately egalitarian. Using a string and two nails to scratch a circle makes visible the (literal) tie between circumference and centre. Sitting in a circle, we're social equals, sharing a centre – whether conversation or spectacle. Merlin wasn't stupid when he seated King Arthur's warring knights at a round table. Not surprisingly, many children's games are ring games. Like community dances, these express, and encourage, community. Centrally focused spaces direct attention to the

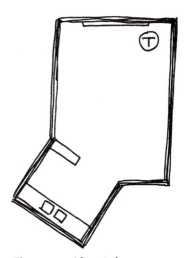

Classroom with wet alcove

shared centre. Cross-corner furniture or centralizing focus – as achieved by light – can give a 'circular gesture' to square, or even oblong, rooms.

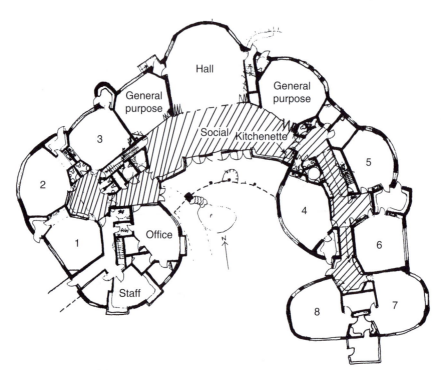

School with alcoved classrooms

Desk layout has social implications. Circles are egalitarian. Straight rows are about hierarchical formality: listeners and lecturer. Curved ones, while still teacher-focused, have less rigidly disciplinarian overtones. Length and breadth emphasize directional focus or group interaction. Central tables unify focus. Scattered ones are about separate work-groups, with little relationship to each other. Normally, room shape implies layout, and this establishes hierarchical and social relationships. It makes more sense, however, to choose our preferred relationships and shape rooms accordingly.

Things and spaces

As children play with *things*, not with buildings, does it matter if rooms are dull? But rooms are where things happen, where imagination scenarios are played out. Dull rooms, therefore, increase dependence on *things*. As thing-dependence is hardly sustainable, it's better if rooms *themselves* stimulate imagination. Rooms specifically designed for this need very little in the way of consumerist 'props'.[13] Interest and variety – textures to feel, light to lick with your eyes, colour to taste, or strange acoustics, such as sounding deep underground or lost in the clouds – encourage fantasy to flower. Even how shelves and hooks display and make available playthings or household utensils help set room mood and play directions. In such ways, even small changes affect the mood of rooms, how children feel in them, how they think and behave, and even how they feel that they themselves are thought of.

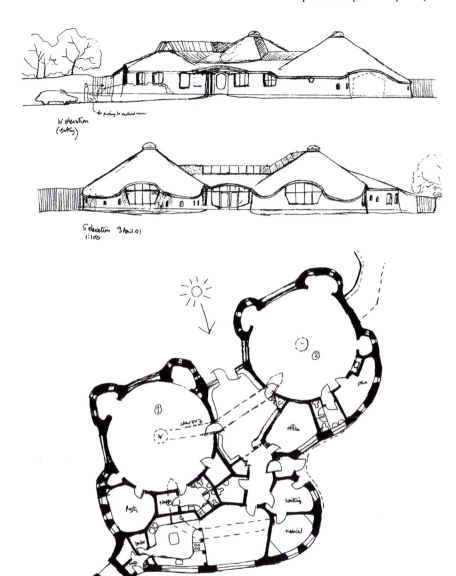

Crèche

Notes

1 Olds, Anita Rui (2001) *Child Care Design Guide*. McGraw Hill.
2 Hampshire County Council primary school.
3 Kellog, Rhoda (1970) *Analyzing Children's Art*. Mayfield Publishing; and Goodnow, Jacqueline (1977) *Children's Drawing*. Fontana/Open books.
4 Aries, Philippe (2000) *Centuries of Childhood*. Quoted in Dudek, Mark (2000) *Architecture of Schools*. Architectural Press.
5 Hertzberger, Herman (1969) *Harvard Educational Review: Architecture and Education* 39, quoted in Dudek, Mark (2000) *op. cit.*

6 Bachelard, Gaston *The Poetics of Space.*

7 In C.S. Lewis' novels; not in the film made from them.

8 Bartlett, S. et al. (1999) *Cities for Children: Children's Rights, Poverty and Urban Management.* Earthscan and UNICEF, quoted in Enns, Cherie C. (2005) *Places for Children.* University College of the Fraser Valley.

9 Olds, Anita Rui (2001) *Child Care Design Guide.* McGraw Hill.

10 After Olds, Anita Rui (2001) *op. cit.*

11 Dyck, James A. (1994) The case for an L-shaped classroom. *Principal* November, cited in Dudek, Mark (2000) *ibid.*

12 Castella, Maria (Waldorf teacher) (2002) unpublished interview.

13 This, at least, has been the experience of Nant-y-Cwm Steiner Kindergarten, Wales: more or less the same, few, contents over 15 years are fully adequate (source: Anita de Vries and Fran Creighton, teachers).

Places for children

CHAPTER 10

What *places* teach: silent lessons

Silent lessons

Children are born to learn. Not necessarily what adults *want* them to learn, but learn they will – from every experience. We expect children to learn things *in* school, but what do schools *themselves* – buildings, playgrounds, rooms and corridors – teach? What social patterns, habits and expectations do children learn?[1] Place-messages aren't only visual. What does the smell of disinfectant say: loving place-care or desperate bug-extermination? Or what about buzzer-bells: are they about valuing individuals or forcing conformity? Both of these are so practical we rarely even question what unconscious attitudes lie buried in them. As such messages strongly influence children's feelings, values, attitudes and behaviour, the environment is sometimes called a 'hidden curriculum'. Being hidden, it's hard to identify direct causal links, but its impact is nevertheless profound.[2]

As our environment becomes the 'normality' we're used to, its subliminal messages and imprinted values become embedded in *us* – the longer the exposure, the more deeply they do so. Even adults rarely notice these, but children, being less conscious, have almost no filters. Fortunately, adults are both a little aware of what's happening and come with pre-established values. Children, however, aren't and don't. Moreover, still forming their individuality, they're more malleable. Unfortunately, advertisers know this well.

Environment influences *everybody's* behaviour. Gloomy gravity subdues us; boisterous colours and sparkling light energize. Bright paint can levitate gloom – but only so much. Moreover, joyful surface doesn't convince unless it's meant. Indeed, deceit sows mistrust. Appearance speaks of underlying *values* – both good and bad. So clearly do these speak that it's hard to refute Olds' assertion that 'raising children in concrete boxes without much sensory variation or relationship to nature suggests we believe sterility will not hurt them and that nature is not very important'.[3]

Such messages we read from the very outset. First impressions bias how we 'read' places – and their occupants. But first impressions are superficial – or are they? When we visit someone's home, its furnishings, contents and *mood* – from how it's lived in – reveal lots about the householder's character. Somehow we intuitively glimpse the underlying values that have shaped the surface.

What do places say to children? Do they sing in the soul? Or curse? As Cherie Enns observes, 'If children see their environment as a portrait of themselves, we might ask ourselves what our local environments tell them. If children learn by observing and participating, what does their daily routine teach them about the adult world? Our current built form may leave children and youth wondering if they are wanted in most public places'.[4]

Can we be surprised that disenchantment and cynicism is so widespread amongst young people?

Materials and mood

Place-mood isn't just about nice or tasteless surroundings. There are invisible factors such as warmth, smell and sound, and intangible ones, such as homeliness. Mood may vary with light, seasons, weather, but there's a permanent underlying spirit reflecting what its *really* about. This in turn signals how we should behave. Children haven't yet learnt places' behavioural expectations. Without adult restraint, their life-vigour lets them run in church, howl in hushed libraries and giggle in serious lessons. Their mood leads their behaviour – place-mood significantly influences this.

A large part of place-mood is what places are *made of*. Some places seek to defy aging. Like people, the harder they try, the more lifeless they look. Nor is this sustainable. Glossily perfect synthetic materials are ruined by scratches, crazing or discolouration – the wear-and-tear of life. Less industrially processed ones become texturally richer with age. They mature. Living plants change from day to day, but lawns and evergreens provide (almost) changeless environments – the outdoor equivalent of constantly electric-lit interiors. While it's physically possible to live in such unvarying places, it's a lifeless, boring and temporally disconnected experience. Nor do such places offer any lessons on maturation, aging and rebirth. More significantly, what does disrespect for aging say? These messages have social and self-image implications. Environmentally, accepting only the new and perfect means lots of mature things are thrown away.

Materials speak strongly. There are worlds of difference between tarmac or grass, bush and tree playgrounds; between concrete panels and timber boarding. Generally, masonry buildings are protectively enclosing, durable and rooted in place; predominately glass ones, more open, expansive and light – in illumination, weight and mood. (But, like hilltop buildings, with view comes exposure.) As masonry buildings suggest a past-to-present time-continuum, stone, brick and earth have 'old' associations. Industrial-material ones look to the future, making glass, steel, aluminium and plastic feel 'new'.[5] Timber is somewhere in between – lighter, newer, but rooted in nature.

Small children need protective, durable surroundings for security. For teenagers optimism about the future is inspiring – whatever *our* worries, it's vital we never deflate this. Being more open to the world and intellectually alert, glass buildings' openness and light suit them (but not their concentration) better. High-technology buildings and industrial materials, however, incur huge environmental costs – both in manufacture and thermal performance. Also, cold, hard materials, such as steel or large sheets of glass, make buildings feel unfriendly; they're products of machines, not life. Moreover, regardless of how attractive such buildings may be, they aren't easy to adapt. They therefore inevitably say: 'As *we* won't change, *you* must conform!' Wood is touch-friendly, warm and alteration-tolerant. It permits wide mood range, from cosy enclosure to extensively glazed openness. Masonry is in-between. Though cold and hard, it's visually and texturally warm, and not too difficult to alter.

Earth-based security for young children: clay walls, clay-straw ceiling[6]

What about buildings constructed of materials that are mismatched to children's age? To 'lighten' and open-up buildings with a mood that is too heavy, whitewash or pale surfaces increase light reflection, making them feel more spacious. For overglazed rooms, glazing-bars, light-shelves or shading slats moderate unprotected openness, and deep mullions give more substantiality. Porches and verandas allow windows to open into darker, semi-protected buffer zones, not directly into bright, expansive space. Greenery softens industrial, unfriendly or domineering materials, making them more approachable. In such ways we can modify how apparently unsuitable buildings 'speak'.

Appearance messages

Many old schools were built in Gothic style to impress Christian 'values' (such as beating?) into children. Many newer ones, because 'modern' symbolized 'best', are in modernist – but now somewhat dated – buildings. Others again are in former stately homes – graceful, but redolent of squire-archical values. What style best suits children?

Styles are shaped by fashion; they're unconcerned about what buildings *say*. Fashion is their priority. Art historians, however, relate styles to contemporary attitudes, values and consciousness. Neoclassicism and neovernacular speak of nostalgia; high-technology of industro-technical optimism; postmodernism, the drama of force; deconstructivism, nihilist disconnection; new baroque – like old baroque – of power. Although such styles have produced some striking, even beautiful, buildings, they utter no words of love, encouragement or stimulation to growth. No food for children's souls.

Another aspect is what things look *like*. This brings *associated* values. Should schools look like houses, offices or factories? Homes, ideally, have a protective aura; work-places a practical one. But schools? Schools *aren't* homes. But nor should they be insti-tutional. Institutions require individuals to conform. Education is about developing individual potential. These are opposite approaches.

Institutional and residential scales are markedly different. Civic scale, though imposing and dra-matic, tells children we care more for prestige than for them. To maxi-mize grandeur, many older schools have entrance-doors twice adult height, often atop imposing stairs.[7] But educational buildings can't feel child-welcoming, child-*valuing*, without homely scale.

Similarly scaled things feel dif-ferent if man-made or made of natural materials: 10-foot (3 m) walls or 50-foot (15 m) buildings are daunting; hedges or cliffs those sizes are small. They 'say' different things. Hence, vegetated walls or buildings beside larger trees feel smaller. Even on larger buildings, enriched texture, detail and delight at low level draws our attention down, reducing *experi-enced* scale. Ways to reduce scale include extending eaves to make

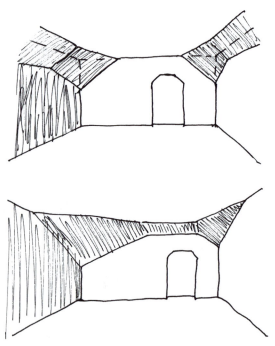

Reducing perceived scale by shaping ceilings down to walls. Doors and windows need 7 foot (2 m) height, but corners can come right down

them low, showing more roof than wall, earth-berming walls, building into slopes and siting buildings beside large trees or in hollows.

Two- or three-storey schools say different things than single-storey ones. Their smaller footprint speaks of valuing land – but why: for cost-economy or nature conservation? Does the second storey repeat the first? This is about fitting in numbers – box-packaging children. Or does it celebrate the greater light, air and privacy? This is about offering varied environmental delight – valuing them.

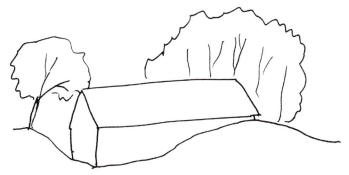

Reducing building scale: low eaves, more roof than wall, earth-bermed walls, buildings built into the ground, in hollows, beside larger trees; enriched visual interest at low level

Extended (single storey) eaves make buildings look lower

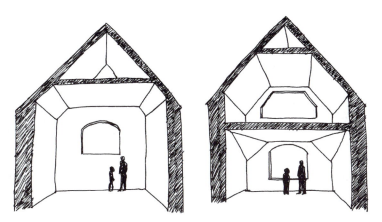

Reducing scale, before and after

Single or repeated storeys say different things

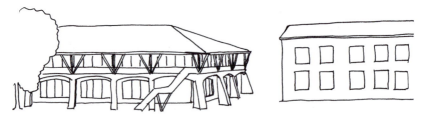

Same sized buildings, but storey differentiation gives a different message

Permeability and opacity

Are buildings domestic-welcoming or institutional-controlling? The more flexible are movement patterns, room-activities and public–private choice, the less institutional do buildings feel. In houses, you can wander between rooms, their functions mostly fairly elastic. Spontaneous activity and self-chosen privacy are reasonably easy. In institutions, corridors dictate orderly movement, and rooms are dedicated to specific compartmentalized activities. Homes have private toilets and family-scaled cloakrooms. Institutions have toilet

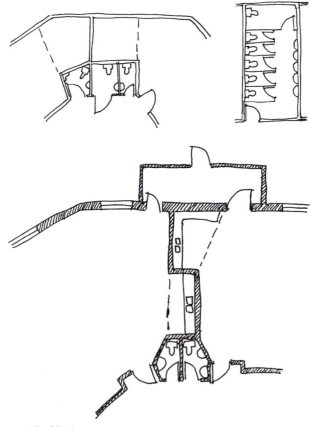

Single toilets versus toilet blocks

blocks and huge cloakrooms – for the herd. Not surprisingly, this promotes herd behaviour, especially in pre- and early adolescents. Single toilets respect individuals, both by granting privacy and projecting expectations of responsible behaviour. Although they cost more, it's increasingly recognized that this expense is soon recouped by decreased 'trouble'.

Institutions are typically 'opaque' – focused on what goes on *inside* them and disinterested in anything outside. Is disregard of context the right lesson for environmental responsibility? But how should schools relate to their surroundings? Should they socially or visually enmesh? Or should they withdraw, be insular? Should there be strong barriers or progressive layers of privacy and protection? Generally, pedagogy sets the attitude, but social and environmental context establishes the form, giving city and village schools very different risks and social roles. Pedagogically, Reggio Emilia favour 'osmotic' relationships.[8] Other approaches regard the 'child world' as a fragile island to be protected by walls and gates, or perhaps many screening layers – from porches and 'buffer-spaces' to arrival–departure courtyards and privacy-landscaping. Others again are only concerned with *physical* security. For this, wire-mesh fences suffice. This school-to-surroundings relationship is the first layer of message.

'Attuning' building to fixed and seasonal views

Place messages

Usually the first thing we see when we approach an 'owned' place are the fences enclosing it: barriers. What do barriers say? Most are *intended* to deny us freedom – but their messages need not be so oppressive. Razor wire says 'I hate you. I am a vicious guard'. But even walls say 'Keep out'. Walls for ball-bouncing, climbing, displays or murals, however, shift focus from obstruction to *use*. Wire fences, by keeping what we see inaccessible, sometimes feel more imprisoning than impermeable walls. If, however, they're overgrown with climbing plants (roses increase security), these become hedges, which now say 'Look at me'. Their flowers, leaves and songbirds bring delight. As we don't question that buildings – even greenhouses and cycle-sheds – must be there, these rarely feel imprisoning. Hard surfaces, however, make enclosures feel more entrapping.

Grass, bushes, shade-trees and vines on walls moderate this. Other non-offensive barriers include water, 'ha-has', plant-pocketed 'green walls' (overhung at the top) and netted tennis-courts. Barriers are often unavoidable. But do they rebuff or welcome us? This depends only partly on design. Their message depends on attitude. A silk glove never convincingly disguises an iron fist, nor calloused skin a warmly helping hand.

Equal barriers, but different messages

Wall as a fence and a ball-bouncing wall   *How can noise-barrier walls avoid saying 'keep out!'?*

Imprinted values

Buildings are designed for efficiency and appearance – within price parameters. But they're unavoidably imprinted with values: how the people who designed, built, administer and maintain them view their inhabitants. One manifestation of this is buildings that look expensive but are, in fact, cheap. They feel flimsy, deteriorate rapidly in use, and clearly say that we're too stupid to notice the deception. Another is how they're *organized*. In some schools, for instance, classroom sequences are hierarchically graduated. Such age or activity groupings are organizationally logical, but need care. On the one hand, they reinforce group identity or mood zones, but on the other, what does grouping low-ability classes, or putting workshops at the refuse-skip end say?[9] The reasons may be solely practical, but it's easy to infer judgement. People who feel to be judged as inferior shut off.

Before

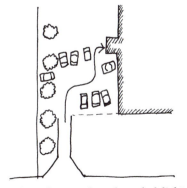

After

Before

After

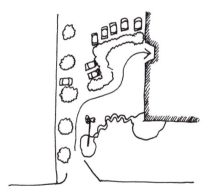

Entry through car park or through delight

While part of every place has been consciously organized and designed on a basis of *unconscious* values, there are usually also parts where things have been put there just because it was the easiest thing to do. Often, nobody has ever thought about these – they just 'happened'. Some schools, for instance, are entered though a car park – the first thing children meet. Obviously, this is convenient, but what *priorities* does it imply?

Maintenance is another – often unconscious – priority issue. It says a lot about how places – and by implication, their inhabitants – are cared for. As Fenoughty observes, schools that don't value and care for their grounds, 'can hardly expect … pupils to grow up with the caring attitudes needed in society'.[10] Not surprisingly, portable, isolated and vandalized buildings emanate uncared-for, out-of sight, out-of-mind messages. Run-down places sap morale and attract graffiti and vandalism. This often progresses to antisocial behaviour and crime. Prompt repair of minor damage shows that somebody cares. This, in turn, reduces vandalism. A headteacher described reversing a notorious 'sink' school's decline: within twelve months' of overpainting graffiti, repairing damage and making minor improvements, 'the smashing of windows, which had been a nightly problem, totally ceased. Something made the kids think before picking up that brick and throwing it. It's about pride. Having a school that looks good is about telling children they're worth something'.[11] Conversely, how we're valued affects whether *we* value and care for things. As the head of another vandalism-bedevilled school observed: 'If you don't respect each other, you won't respect the environment'.[12] This is reciprocal.

Maintenance is about everyday care. Design is about underlying values. Both reflect on us, and how *we* are valued. The moment we enter any building, or even its grounds, we sense these hidden, usually unconsidered, messages. *Every* place communicates these. Subliminally, we *always* understand these[13] – and behave accordingly.[14] But how often do we address this consciously?

What *should* schools say? Designing schools, we always ask teachers this exact question. In my last two projects, answers have included:

> I'm welcoming to parents, strangers, but still a school.
> The school is worthy of professional respect.
> I respect each stage of a child's growth.
> Growing up is fun.
> Children's work and play is as important as adults.[15]

Or, more place-specifically:

> I am magically intriguing, secure – but community-enmeshed.
> I will lead you from imagination to inspiration.
> I am multilayered, from community-welcoming and active to protected, enchanted
>   and reverently sacred.
> I rise to an island of magic, lovingly valued.[16]

Although these answers appear to range widely, they share underlying core values.

Place-messages also reflect how we value culture and heritage. Are the imagery, implied values and technological standard something we're connected to or, however appealing, something from another place, time, culture or social stratum? Children from different backgrounds bring cultural expectations with them, feel at home with different things. Culturally, one size never fits all. It's all too easy to imply that local culture and traditions are worthless. This isn't just about what European-style buildings say to African schoolchildren, or city-centre technical sophistication says to low-income rural communities. Nor is it answered by Islamic mud-styled concrete or folksy neovernacular nostalgia. School and church used to be at the centre of social life. Fittingly, they were 'special' buildings – of similar materials to neighbouring houses and shops, but different in scale and form. Nowadays, many school buildings so differ in materials and construction, they're not linked to the local cultural continuum. If sufficiently inspiring, they can say: 'for you children alone – not anyone else – we offer something special'. Unfortunately, however, it's much more likely they'll just appear arrogantly disrespectful. Instead of supporting their cultural context, such buildings feel imposed obligations. To children, they say: 'however little you enjoy it, you *have to* go to school'.

Invisible education

Children don't become environmentally responsible, socially empathetic, balanced, self-motivated individuals overnight. It's a process of *development*. From *all* places, we *absorb* lessons. Some are deliberate: labelled cluster-bins, for instance, encourage waste separation. Some are unconsidered: overflowing litter-bins encourage dumping. Less conscious lessons include those about values, self-worth, behaviour expectations and responsibilities. *All* buildings, *all* places, teach. But few have been planned with lessons in mind. Some devalue, demoralize us, some enrich and inspire.

This raises the question: what are we teaching children all the time we're not teaching them? What will their everyday environment teach? This is no small matter, for the values and attitudes they absorb will shape the whole of their adult lives.

What do schools, playgrounds, flats and houses say about the value of each individual child? Do they confirm that children are respected, loved? If not, why did we build them? And what sort of people do we expect these children to become?

Notes

1 Löwenhielm, Gunnar (1999) *Rum för en ny skola*. ARKUS 33, *Arkitektur och skola: om planera ett skolhus*. Byggförlaget, cited in Farnestam, Sandra (2001) Arkitektur i skolan. Unpublished dissertation, Umeå University.

2 Marshall, Alan (1999) *Greener School Grounds*. Learning Through Landscapes.

3 Olds, Anita Rui (2001) *Child Care Design Guide*. McGraw Hill.

4 Enns, Cherie C. (2005) *Places for Children*. University College of the Fraser Valley.

5 There are, of course, 100-year-old glass buildings, and ultra-modern clay ones.

6 Nibble School, Järna, Sweden. Designer and builder: teacher, Per Ahlbom.

7 Sometimes there were two entrances: one for boys, one for girls. Or big and little children might have separate entrances.

8 Ceppi, Guilio and Zini, Michele (1998) *Children, Spaces, Relations; Metaproject for an Environment for Young Children*. Reggio Children.

9 Blundell-Jones, Peter (1996) Foreword. In Dudek, Mark (1996) *Kindergarten Architecture*. Spon.

10 Fenoughty, Susan (2001) *The Landscape of the School Grounds*. Comenius.

11 Hampton Geoff, quoted in Dudek, Mark (2000) *Architecture of Schools*. Architctural Press.

12 Hemmälin Rita, headteacher of Baggermossen School, Stockholm, quoted in *Dagens Nyheter,* 1 September 2001.

13 For more on this see Day, Christopher (2002) *Spirit and Place*. Architectural Press, and Day, Christopher (2002) *Consensus Design*. Architectural Press.

14 Values are potent. The World Trade Center was attacked *solely* for the values it symbolized. Farnestam, Sandra (2001).

15 Meadowbrook Waldorf School teachers.

16 Mendocino Waldorf School teachers.

Welcoming arrival

The journey experience

How we journey to, then meet, places has a major influence on how we subsequently experience, respond to and behave in them. But adults and children experience journeys differently. For infants there are two distinct places, barely related to each other: where they are now, and the heart-centre of things – home and mother. To adults, the journey between these is a 'link', but for children, it's a 'barrier'. They need a 'causeway' to link these two 'islands'. If they walk or cycle, they 'know' the way through bodily experience, so can always get back home. Driven, they neither build body-memory nor are they in navigational control, so they don't have a link, can't get back. Additionally, vehicular travel is sensorially dysfunctional; visual overstimulation unlinked to other sensory information, and speed unrelated to children's tactile experience. In consequence, children travelling by bus to school are typically more anxious and aggressive than those who walk.[1] Walking to school with a parent also links school and route to family, freeing children to enjoy the journey's views, sounds, scents and events. In this way, they learn the details, sensory identities and inter-relationships of their neighbourhoods – a first geography lesson. Knowing where *we* are in it, the world makes sense. This builds relaxing confidence. Bus or car journeys can't offer this.

Arrival: meeting a place

Few children actually *want* to go to school. They *have* to. Fortunately, the whole issue of schools in the community is opening up. The more that schools, and their outdoor facilities, are community resources – social, cultural and recreational as well as educational – the more attractive they are for parents and older siblings. This brings them closer to being places where children actually *want* to go. Out-of-hours use, however, raises security issues. Separate entries – from either school or street – eases these. As these entries invite different groups and numbers, they need different facilities, notice-board information, scale, atmosphere and, particularly, different *approach journeys*.

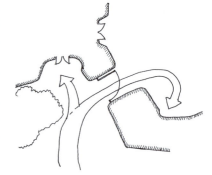

Dual approaches: hall and school

a) Entrance for outsiders

b) Entrance for residents

Special needs school

Gloomy, sunken entrance – or moss and fern garden?

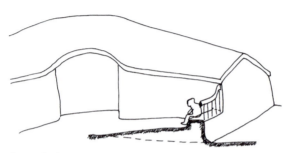

Courts higher than street-level feel safer

Magic doesn't need lots of light, but coloured jewels of light

As we approach buildings, we get initial clues of what they value – or don't.[4] Do materials, shapes, colours and ground-surfaces respect – or disregard – their context? Are they inviting, welcoming – or unapproachably anti-human, soul-less? How do their gestures greet us? Meeting someone with outstretched arms, our gesture and subsequent hug is not symmetrical, confronting and entrapping, but enfolds in a free way. Similarly, buildings approached a little obliquely feel less confrontational: their entrances *invite* us. Likewise, frontal entrance-staircases give a sense of haughty monumentality, but steps *alongside* walls are much less formal.

The front door is a key destination. Does it welcome us? What do its proportion, portal-quality, entrance and doorway shape say? The vestibule continues this greeting – or its lack. Indoor plants soften even the hardest rooms. Residential furnishings give child-care centres a domestic mood. Seeing other children playing can even make playgroup look fun enough to over-ride parting from parents. An entry route leading past semi-supervisory rooms with warm presence, such as office or kitchen, establishes a homely mood immediately on arrival.

A hug isn't symmetrical and confronting, but enfolds in a free, not entrapping way

a) Entrance for outsiders

b) Entrance for residents

Special needs school

For children, the most important thing about going to school is meeting friends – a purely social issue. But environmental experiences on the journey there also colour their mood. To make school more appealing, therefore, it's worth tracing children's arrival journeys. What experiences do they pass through? What do they see? How do they arrive? How do they meet people and things? What are children's first impressions?[2]

Though journeys start with the thought of going somewhere, the closing sequence – when we feel the destination's 'presence' – most colours our response. For schools, this typically is: gate, grounds, path, school building, entrance doorway, passage, then class-room door. Path and passage – influencing how we move – are phases of mood-progression. Gate and doorways – about how we meet things – are thresholds. The quality, character and messages we encounter on this journey influence how we interpret all subsequent experiences.

Arriving at school means leaving a 'free' world behind and entering a 'structured' one; perhaps also parting from parents. This is a significant point. What does the entrance say? Does it welcome you – perhaps with an archway – or is it just a gap in a security barrier? Is there shelter nearby? Somewhere to leave bags when playing, or to wait for a bus in rain?

The school gate is also where parents wait for children. But do they just stand around or do they meet? What would increase conviviality? Is there a shade-tree, notice-board and/or seats or low sitting-wall? What about toddler entertainment: is there a sandpit or play-equipment?[3] Or, more substantially, is there a café, shop, reception-office or craft-workshop? These provide both a social nucleus and gate-keep the entrance.

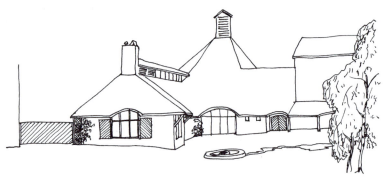

Café and hall as a link between a special needs school and the surrounding community (Czech Republic)

The journey from gate to door, however short, establishes the mood of arrival. Is it a con-frontationally frontal approach? Or an informally indirect one? Frontal geometry is such as routes focused down straight avenues, *compel*, don't invite us; we don't feel free to choose. But intriguingly unfolding to a not-yet-visible destination makes us *want*, not *have*, to go somewhere. As only small deflections block through-views, path realignment can usually achieve this. If bends don't 'make sense', however, they'll feel randomly imposed, need-lessly obstructed. Also, if turns and corners aren't protected by substantial obstacles such as trees, bushes, boulders or water, short-cuts quickly trample grass to dust or mud.

Is the route clear, confusing or chaotic? Complications, such as reversing direction or squeezing between other buildings, add confusion – causing insecurity stress. Is it across weather-exposed tarmac, sun-fried, rain-lashed or icy-wind-bitten? Or is it sheltered beneath overhanging tree arches, vaults of interlaced willow or planted trellis? Are there aromatic flowers to brush, sudden openings to views and sunlight? Tunnels of blossoming vegetation (intermingled species extend flowering season) add aroma and microclimatic change to reinforce welcome. Such delight-rich paths cost little to create, but transform how it feels to come to school.

Dense cities rarely allow any approach-journey space. As 'place-for-kids' markers, play-centres opening straight off pavements often utilize colourful façades,

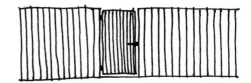

Minimal changes to gate and fence can transform the entry experience

flashing lights or huge window-display teddies. These are unequivocal signals, but do nothing *for* children, nothing soul-nourishing, nothing to make them feel special. Even just a floral archway around the door helps. An inviting, sunny entry raises the spirits. An ugly, awkward or gloomy one subdues and burdens. A walled courtyard, solid-gated, can shield traffic noise and enclose 'child-mood', separating it from the hectic city all around. While bare walls are acoustically reflective and feel imprisoning, cloaking with vegetation can create a 'woodland clearing' mood. If overshadowed by buildings, however, flowers won't grow well. But – as in forests – moss and ferns can thrive. For kindergarten children arriving early in the morning, play equipment here increases welcome.

Inexpensive welcome

Gate to walled courtyard

Welcome!

Gloomy, sunken entrance – or moss and fern garden?

Courts higher than street-level feel safer

Magic doesn't need lots of light, but coloured jewels of light

As we approach buildings, we get initial clues of what they value – or don't.[4] Do materials, shapes, colours and ground-surfaces respect – or disregard – their context? Are they inviting, welcoming – or unapproachably anti-human, soul-less? How do their gestures greet us? Meeting someone with out-stretched arms, our gesture and subsequent hug is not symmetrical, confronting and entrapping, but enfolds in a free way. Similarly, buildings approached a little obliquely feel less confrontational: their entrances *invite* us. Likewise, frontal entrance-stair-cases give a sense of haughty monumentality, but steps *alongside* walls are much less formal.

The front door is a key destination. Does it wel-come us? What do its proportion, portal-quality, entrance and doorway shape say? The vestibule con-tinues this greeting – or its lack. Indoor plants soften even the hardest rooms. Residential furnishings give child-care centres a domestic mood. Seeing other children playing can even make playgroup look fun enough to over-ride parting from parents. An entry route leading past semi-supervisory rooms with warm presence, such as office or kitchen, establishes a homely mood immediately on arrival.

A hug isn't symmetrical and confronting, but enfolds in a free, not entrapping way

Monumentality: frontal staircase versus steps alongside the wall

Welcoming porch

Welcoming and unwelcoming corners

Entrance to convey welcome

Being there

When first left at playgroup or kindergarten, infants can feel 'abandoned' – a frightening experience. But when parents hang around instead of rushing off, insecure children feel much safer. Lingering space by the entrance encourages this; a parent's room even more. It's also somewhere to informally meet teachers, and helps involvement in school life. As parents of small children are often socially isolated, its community-building and friend-making role is also important.

Where should this room be? Down a passage or upstairs, parents are – from a child's point of view – barely half there. Astride or opening off the entry route, it's easily accessible;

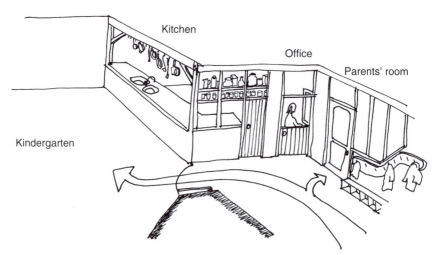

Parents' room as eddy off entry route. Office and kitchen are also nearby havens. Homely sounds and smells (such as conversation and coffee)

| Parent's room astride entry route | ← ─────────────────→ | distant parent's room |
| children feel secure | | lets children feel fully present |

Parental proximity: what balance does the situation require?

by the entrance it both welcomes and informally supervises. A parents' room feeling like a home-from-home, *from which* playgroup or kindergarten opens, feels a secure base for infants to sally forth from. Parental proximity makes children feel secure – but if *too* easy to flee to mummy, it doesn't help them fully *be* in kindergarten. Between sufficient security to allow children to dare independence and so much that they aren't free, is a fine balance.

As small children aren't ready to cope with the insecurities of the wider world, they need protective surroundings. In cities and harsh climates, this psychological – and perhaps physical – protection needs to be stronger than in countryside and gentle climates.

Strong thresholds and predominantly solid entrance doors increase this 'insulation'. All-glass ones weaken it.[5] (Doors for teenagers, not needing to be protective, can be more transparent.) While the security of parent accessibility eases arrival, thereafter the kindergarten suite needs undistracted internal focus. This is a progression from permeability (parent within reach) to protective enclosure.

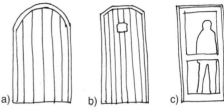

(a) Secure door; (b) Secure door with tiny window so it isn't 'shut in your face'; this also lets visitors choose non-disruptive moments to enter (c) Insecure, attention-distracting door

Indoor journeys

Outdoor principles – directional clarity, but intriguing invitation – also apply indoors. Passages that lead to light draw us on. Clarity as to where to go (hence how to get back home) increases children's confidence.[6] Routes that aren't *obvious* easily disorientate small children, burdening them with worry. For infants, choosing between left and right is a prematurely awakening, sometimes stressful, decision. Their route, therefore, should *lead*, never *turn aside*.[7] But what about old buildings with tee-junction corridors? Flooring materials or pattern, ceiling heights, spatial constrictions, colour and light can clearly distinguish side from main routes – even round corners.

Children feel more securely in control of an unfamiliar world if able to survey rooms at a glance immediately upon entry. For longitudinal rooms, this implies end-, not side-, entry.[8] Similarly, stepping (or ramping) *down* into rooms allows

Stepping down into a room allows a view down into it

commanding view into them. Moreover, as such rooms can't exude 'superiority', we more readily feel 'at home' in them.

Inner and outer journeys

To be in harmony with what we're doing, we need to be in the right mood for the job. Different activities – such as cooking, reading or games – induce very different moods. Whenever progressing from one activity to another we must change *our* mood; undergo an inner journey – otherwise, we're mentally 'in the wrong space'. Fortunately, moving from one room – and activity and mood – to another, always involves a *physical* journey. This can serve as an *inner* soul-preparatory journey, changing our inner state from one appropriate to where we *have* been, what we *have* been doing, to where we *will* be, what we *will* do. This soul-journey is a metamorphic progression, punctuated by a series of physical thresholds. Some movements and punctuation are abrupt, some fluid; some awakening, some barely conscious; some discordant, some harmonious. Some we experience kinaesthetically, others are visual gestures inducing eye-movement. All affect our *inner state*.

Strong mood transformations – such as arrival at a destination or coming indoors – require particularly strong markers. At such points, a complete change of materials to jolt our *senses* can mark these big inner steps. Sensory 'markers', such as a change in footstep feel and sound, movement in new directions or with new rhythm or effort, reinforce such mood transformations.

Traditional mood-shifting elements include dark porches, monastic cloisters, sweeping staircases. Contemporary everyday elements, such as doors, latches, steps, passage-constrictions, acoustics, colour and light, can do this. Whereas steps obstruct disabled accessibility, floor-material or pattern changes and threshold strips don't. Walking down a dark passage or going outdoors, perhaps through cold or rain require deliberate *intent*. So does opening solid, heavy doors. These make stepping from one mood-world to another more conscious, reinforcing a change of inner state. Wide or arched doorways – low over shoulders but, above heads, sufficiently high to avoid knockouts – lower proportion, so strengthening portal experience.

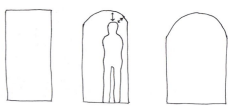

Low – but adult-safe – doorways enhance threshold experience

Archways, gates and bridges make clear arrival-threshold markers. *Dark* archways, *squeaking* gates and *hollow-sounding* bridges are even stronger. Entrance archways and 'gatepost' stones date from prehistory. Rivers, ferries and bridges have divided kingdoms, tribes and parishes for millennia. In much mythology, they divide life from death. The progression from constricted dark to expansive light often symbolized passing through death to new, revivified life. In addition to their sensory impact and change-of-state significance, this gives threshold-markers archetypal symbolic loading.

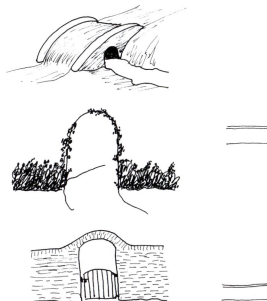

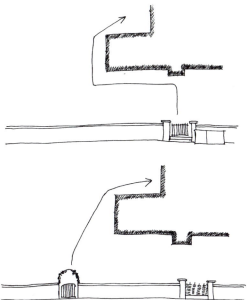

Threshold markers: archways, gates and bridges

Arrival entrance: before and after

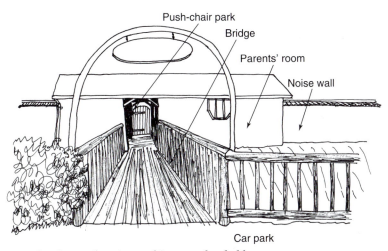

Push-chair park
Bridge
Parents' room
Noise wall
Car park

Bridge, gate and arch as welcoming, multisensory threshold

The arrival journey: pedagogical function

How do children get to school? This significantly influences the state in which they arrive, and continues reverberating long into the day. Many travel by car. Typically cars are filled with as many people as can fit in – making journeys overcrowded, hurried and fractious. This puts split-concentration stress on the driver – which feeds back to the

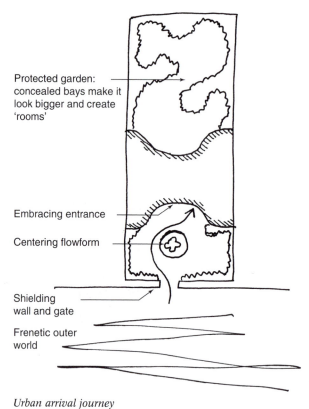

Protected garden: concealed bays make it look bigger and create 'rooms'

Embracing entrance

Centering flowform

Shielding wall and gate

Frenetic outer world

Urban arrival journey

children. Buses, with their squabble-potential and identical sensory-dysfunctional travel mode, are hardly better. After vehicle journeys, children aren't in a mood of quiet wonder, but more inclined to run, shout and push. Just as it's hard to eat slowly straight after a long fast drive, children driven to school need 'down time' to switch from highway-intensity to a more tranquil pace.[9] One effective way to leave behind car-journey-mood is by walking the last part. Events and sense-rich experiences orchestrated along this arrival journey focus attention in this new space, so car journey stresses cease to resound.

At one kindergarten (in Wales), we gave the children a 60-yard (50 m) woodland walk with several thresholds and sub-place moods to cross.[10] First a leaf archway, then a sun-dappled cliff edge (securely fenced) above the shining, singing river, then shady woodland. The path then goes uphill – so children gather themselves and quieten down. (Downsloping paths are too liberating; they encourage running.) Finally, it pivots past a firewood shed and through a gate, and opens into a sunlit brick-paved play-yard and sandpit. An invitingly gestured entrance faces this – slightly asymmetrically to avoid being too forceful. Next comes a passage, quiet, low, twisting, darker and blue(ish). These qualities further quieten children, bringing them more into themselves. The passage colour progresses from purple-blue – remembering the warm earthen red-brown exterior – to green-blue – anticipating the sun-flooded yellow cloakroom. This is another threshold: somewhere to *stop* and leave behind coats and boots – the accoutrements of the muddy, cold and wet outer-world. Classroom entrances are portal-thresholds. At this point, tiled flooring changes to wood. Doors have heavy wooden latches – tactile, auditory and requiring conscious effort. Entry requires a deliberate turn in direction. Although still on the ground floor, one room now *feels* upstairs as its windows look into treetops. These linear, sequential experiences now come to a final stop: the classroom, seasonally decorated, perhaps with a (safety screened) blazing fire in the grate.

Each of these changes marks a step in leaving one world behind and preparing oneself inwardly for a new one. Leaving chaotic, sensorially unbalanced overstimulation and lack of elbow-room, and stepping into socially harmonious, wonder-filled, quiet, stable security – a magical world.

Kindergarten arrival: path and internal sequence

For a Californian school – very different climate, place-mood and building (1950s ugly!) – children also had car-journey mood to shed.[11] We used a bougainvillea archway to make the disembarking area somewhere special, protected – its mood more for people than cars. The kindergarten path – formerly up sun-fried concrete stairs – now rises across a hillside in a tunnel of interlaced shrubs, light and shade splattered and aromatic with blossoms. Older children ascend a broader brick path. A water rill edges one side; craft-workshops, their activities in full and intriguing view, the other. Middle-school children swing into the courtyard formed between the building and rising hillside. High-school students climb this pine-treed slope beside the – now cascading – stream to its (wind-pumped) Flowform source in the high-school courtyard above.

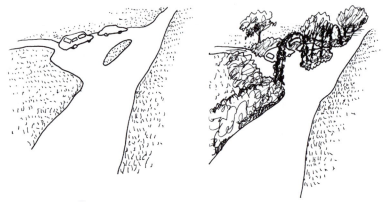

Bougainvillea archway to make disembarking area somewhere special

Approach journeys: kindergarten

Approach journeys: middle and high schools

A third school (in New England) was in forest, but accessed from an arterial road with its attendant noise, fumes and speed.[12] All the teachers wanted this totally screened.[13] I did too, but felt obliged to ask: what message would screening-walls give? How would anyone feel invited? Or even know the school existed? However aggressive the road, we needed to think of it as an asset. What benefits, therefore, could it bring?

Visibility from the road would be the school's best advertising. But rendering the road visible – hence audible – from the school, would destroy any oasis mood. We therefore reviewed the school's many activities. Which could be road-tolerant – able to say: 'Welcome. You can see me'? Which were fragile, easily compromised? These – saying: 'I'm magic, protected' – should only be *discovered* on progressing deeper into the site. What – as advertisement – *needed* visibility from the road?

To invite, the entrance would need to be clear and *welcoming*. Parking, being road-compatible, would be near the road to distance the school from this. It mustn't feel utilitarian, but should say: 'chat here' – so must be *beautiful*. Once they have arrived, small children would need to feel protected; older ones, safe but free; and high-school students should be able to look out into world. Non-noise-sensitive buildings tied to stone walls close the saddle between rock outcrops creating a noise-screen. Cresting the high ground, their line isn't straight, so, whilst preserving the mood-integrity of the 'school-world', don't look like 'keep out' walls. This zone houses school–public interface activities and buildings. Being fronted by human activity in full view – workshops, games, gardening and farming – it invites *interest*.

This established *where* things should be. But children arriving by car or bus would carry arterial speed-mood with them. How could we slow this down? Traffic-speed

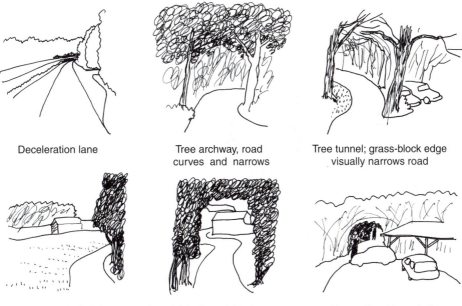

Deceleration lane	Tree archway, road curves and narrows	Tree tunnel; grass-block edge visually narrows road

Alternating dark–light; open–closed; left-view, right-view   Drop-off and bus-shelter, tree-tunnel footpath

Welcoming access

reduction would need to start with a slow-down lane alongside the main road. Turning in under a tree archway, this now becomes a country lane, intriguing and *inviting*. It then narrows and bends sharply, its surface changing from tarmac to gravel. After this contraction, dark under trees, a view opens expansively to the left showing pasture; then, to the right, tree-sheltered parking. Now comes another dark tree-vault and bend. Next, an opening reveals gardens, then physical education. This view is closed in the distance by a screen of 'education through the arts' workshops and a farmers' market shed (these also function as a noise-screen). The drop-off point – a roofed bus-shelter under another wall of trees – is the end of the vehicle journey. This breathing sequence of expansion–contraction, distance–closeness, darkness–light, left–right, and the punctuation of turns, portals and surface-change, progressively slow both traffic and children's state.

From the point where the lane swings back, a footpath tunnel of interwoven branches – lit, at night, by strings of sparkling 'fairy-lights' – leads to the school and kindergarten. Slightly curved, the destination doesn't immediately reveal itself. As arrival and departure are educational experiences, this path has a deliberate pedagogical function. But how long should it be? If too long, it would be hard for parents with infants in pushchairs. Furthermore, each end would require teacher supervision – a staffing burden. But how long is too long? This depends on culture. In Britain, 50 yards (45 m) seems good for kindergarten children. Many Americans think it's too long for *all* children. To help our decision, a Swiss teacher described a school where children walked for 20 minutes steeply uphill from the nearest bus-stop. All arrived glowing with health – sickness was rare, and inattention, rowdiness and disruptive-behaviour effectively non-existent. Despite general approval, we nonetheless felt that one mile (1.5 km) was a trifle excessive, especially for children carrying cellos through rain and blizzard. We therefore settled for 40 yards (36.5 m).

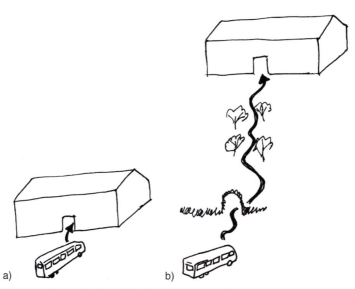

a)   b)

(a) Easily supervised, but institutional (b) Pedagogical, but hard to supervise

Arriving at kindergarten

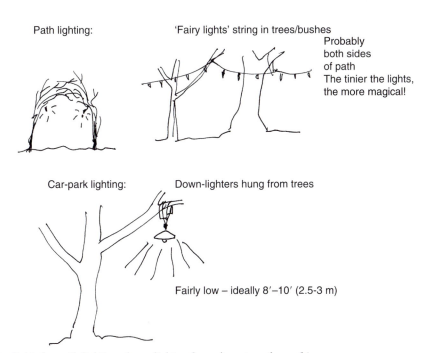

Fairy-lights for path lighting; down-lighters hung from trees for parking

Another school (also in California) was an island of magic – enchanting![14] But in a town, this insularity made outsiders feel unwelcome. How could it better enmesh with the surrounding community? Its approach journey needed a sequence of gestures: intriguing, inviting, welcoming, inviting, welcoming. (When planning this, we used wool to shape these: wool-colour for 'messages', line-shape for gestures.) These gestures started with the view from the two approach roads, continued to car-parking and drop-off points, then through the supervisory – and welcoming – 'gateways'. For the main school, this is the administration building for the kindergarten, the parents' room. From these rise paths, which then lead through the 'village' green and an unfolding progression of 'urban' courtyards.

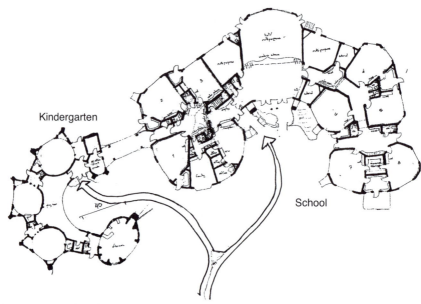

Welcoming gesture buildings

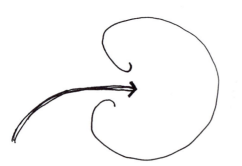

Archetypal welcome gesture

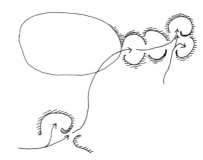

Welcome gesture on the ground, through existing courtyards and green areas

The periphery of the property was steep woodland, perfect for adventure play. The school's heart – the kindergarten garden – was reverential, tranquil. Ideal. But how could we reconcile such incompatible moods? We identified a range of activity-moods from open and rambunctious to protected, magical and sacred. This established a progressive sequence of mood-layers from the boundary slope with slides, swinging-ropes and equipment for adventure play, through 'village green' and social-courtyard spaces to the enchanted kindergarten garden.

At this school, the key to the arrival journey was the entry *sequence*: moods and activities, gestures and spaces.

In these examples, different circumstances required different aspects – physical, temporal and mood – to lead the design. The first was shaped by sensory 'quietening'. In the second, the atmosphere was transformed by sense-stimulating experiences. Breathing-rhythm deceleration shaped the third; and mood-layer sequence, the fourth. All serve the 'spirit-of-school'. In some, the vehicular arrival was critical; in others, the walking part. In all, however, both welcome and mood-induction were established by the arrival path – the state-of-soul transformative journey.

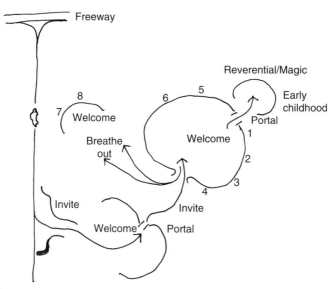

Path and building gestures

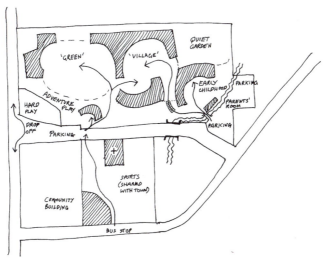

Entry from road

Administration building to greet visitors

Ascending path

Arrival at campus level

Magic heart: kindergarten building

Invitation and welcome gestures

Journeys of welcome

How children meet places affects their responses, expectations and behaviour. Self-esteem – fundamental to motivation – depends on feeling respected. Without this, why should children value themselves, others or the environment?[15] The arrival journey is, therefore, critical. What does it say? Does it convey child-valuing respect, or scornful disregard? This is both about how buildings welcome – or confront – children, and what children meet on the approach journey. Orchestrated sensory experiences, expansion–contraction sequences – both physical and soul-state – and progressively metamorphosing moods-of-place can transform obligatory journeys into delight. Unfolding scenes of interest, reinforced by invitation-gestures that intrigue, inspire and engage the will, are critical to this. Even arriving at school can make children feel deeply welcomed, raising spirits and motivating them for the whole day. Such welcomes potentially reverberate throughout their whole life.

Notes

1 Although the finding of a 1957 study of school closures and resulting bus journeys, this hasn't stopped small school closures! Lee, Terrence (1976) *Psychology and the Environment*. Methuen & Co.

2 Fenoughty, Susan *Outdoor Education: Authentic learning in the context of the landscape*.

3 Littlefield, D. (2005) Funds and games. *Learning Through Landscapes*, Building Design, March 2005.

4 Thörn, Kerstin *Att bygga en skola*. Västerbotton, Västerbottons Museum.

5 Rennnert, Klaus (1985) Evaluating the material collected from the kindergartens; an attempt to summarize. In Flinspach, Jürgen (1985) *Waldorfkindergärten Bauen*.

Unpulished translation by Luborsky, Peter (1988).

6 Olds, Anita Rui (2001) *Child Care Design Guide*. McGraw Hill.

7 Beck, Walter Thoughts of an architect on the building of a Waldorf Kindergarten. In Flinspach, Jürgen (1985) *ibid*.

8 Riscke, Elke-Maria (1985) Pedagogical aspects of kindergarten architecture. In Flinspach, Jürgen (1985) *op. cit.*

9 Olds, Anita Rui (2001) *ibid*.

10 Nant-y-Cwm Steiner School.

11 East Bay Waldorf School.

12 Meadowbrook Waldorf School, Rhode Island.

13 Consensus design with teachers and administrators.

14 Mendocino Waldorf School, California.

15 Thörn, Kerstin *ibid*.

Environment for children

CHAPTER 12

Outdoor places

Outdoor need

Humankind was born in a nature-formed world – the elementally balanced savannah. As Theodor Roszac observes, this has archetypal echoes: 'Every person's lifetime is anchored within a greater, universal lifetime. Each of us shares the whole of life's time on Earth'.[1] He considers this so central to the human unconscious, that '... repression of the ecological unconscious is the deepest root of collusive madness in industrial society'.[2] No wonder some deep part of us feels threatened by large buildings, abused by mechanical shapes and deadened by lifeless materials. No wonder green landscapes – from garden to wilderness – are so popular. No wonder children play more enthusiastically outdoors. Moreover, fresh air cleans the lungs. Its scents revive the soul. Consequently, 'children living an open-air active life ... seem to flourish in every way: their skin and hair change not only in colour, but in texture; their appetite often increases'.[3]

But not so many do. Many, as Fenoughty describes, 'live in an artificial "box"-like existence: the home is a box, the car to school is a box, the school is a box, children are increasingly attached to a box (computers) at school and, on return home, they attach themselves to another box'.[4] But where *can* they play outside? Are parks within impromptu walking range? Or must they be driven to them? Is the ground accessibly near, appealing and safe? Or are children confined to windy balconies? Asphalted or rooftop playgrounds allow letting off steam, but fresh air and running-around space isn't enough. The life of nature is a vital soul-nutrient.

But what about rain? Many children dress for fashion not weather, so don't enjoy wet or cold. Dressed appropriately, however, most love being out-doors. At school, canopied play-spaces let them play outside on rainy days. Waterproof clothing, however, allows them to do a wider variety of things. But wet ground means mud. Without somewhere for wet coats and

Outdoors in all weathers

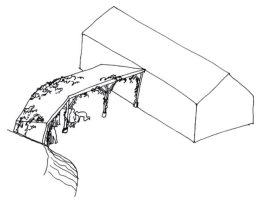

Shelter for all-weather play

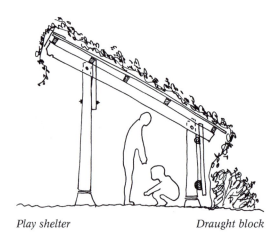

Play shelter   *Draught block*

muddy boots, adequately sized and conveniently close, *between* classrooms and gardens, mess easily deters staff from letting children out except in fine weather. In Scandinavia, despite sub-Arctic winters, children play outdoors all year round. For extreme weather, schools usually have an open-fronted hut facing a fire-pit. (Umeå Waldorf School – 3° below the arctic circle – has a fire-pit and log-circle for good weather, and a tipi with smaller fire, for bad.[5]) *Ur och Skur* all-weather activities for children of all ages – in forests for toddlers, on rivers, sea and mountains for teenagers – in and out of school, aim to change attitudes from user (exploiter) to appreciator (respecter and conservationist).[6]

In Britain, variations on this approach have been pioneered by Susan Isaacs' school, with 'jungle gym' trees and children responsible for bonfires, Margaret MacMillan's 'open air' schools as 'garden cities of children', and organizations such as Forest School Camps.[7] Most schools, however, are more cautious. Indeed, many have sold off much of their grounds. Nowadays, children have access to only one-ninth as much open-air play space as a mere generation ago.[8] Is it any surprise that environmental awareness is three decades – a generation – behind Scandinavia?

Gardens for the soul

Nature refreshes the soul. In hectic, hard-edged, traffic-dominated environments, eyes crave greenery and leaf shade for relief. To Olds, 'Trees, gardens, animals, water and views provide many physically and emotionally healing benefits, in addition to enhancing a child's knowledge of the natural world. Indeed, if we are to save this planet, exposing children to the wonders of nature at a very young age is essential'.[9] Meyerkort goes further. As, by collecting 'treasures' and making miniature 'places' such as mud-castles or beetle 'houses', children meet the universe through its microcosm; being in nature nurtures a 'feeling of belonging unreservedly to [their] surroundings'.[10]

But gardens aren't 'nature'. They're *pictures* of nature. These pictures reflect our attitudes. Paradise – from the Persian *Pairi-daeza* – means 'walled garden'.[11] Islamic gardens represented the four rivers of life with a cross inside a circle inside a square.[12] Typically, these gardens were centrally focused about a pool, fountain or tree. As small children go through a phase of drawing identical mandalas, these patterns have enduring archetypal significance. High-walled monastery gardens, German *Bauerngärten* – quartered into root, leaf, fruit and seed plots – and aristocrats' geometric gardens – their geometry

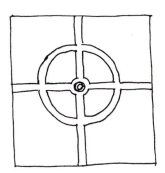

Seville garden[13]

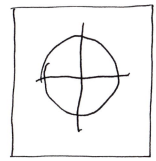

Children's mandala[14]

psychologically reinforcing their owners' secular power – continue this tradition. Their mood was calm, meditative and, in many cases, even holy.

Eighteenth-century English romantic gardens composed nature into *idealized* landscapes. Carefully orchestrated views integrated distant landscape but blocked anything unattractive. Such 'borrowed views', however, while valuable from windows, are compromised once we see or hear past obstructions. The opposite

Borrowed view, hiding middle-ground landscape

approach, 'Zen landscape', conceals views until revealing them with maximum impact. The irregular paving of Shinto gardens – precursor of 'crazy-paving' – encouraged *mindfulness* while walking. European labyrinths and Buddhist walking meditation, originally amongst trees, are about breathing meter in movement. Nineteenth-century industrialists, learning that meandering paths encourage soul-relaxing reflection, endowed naturalistic parks to refresh their workers.

In different proportions, these three, initially spiritual, themes – cosmology, composition and path – are present in *all* gardens – from formal palaces to sacred groves; exuberant, vertical, cottage-gardens to horizontal, suburban bungalow lawns and borders; geometrically arranged containers to barely modified wilderness. All, in some ways, are microcosms of, and reveal our attitudes to, nature. What attitude, what experience possibilities do lawns or tarmac reveal? As children feel their school's image reflects on them, what should school grounds say?[15]

For children, gardens are mood-places to *do* things in, not sit immobile looking at views. As 'good behaviour, budding sociability, respect and peacefulness are enhanced when children can play and move freely, be active and have the scope to recreate the world they experience', they need places that provide freedom, curiosity, interest, wonder, excitement and joy; places that encourage imaginative play and constructions.[16] Activity and creative opportunity are wholly contrasting moods to reverential state and magic. But children need both.

What do places mean? Even small interventions change their meaning. Man-made artefacts – from sculpture to mere painted stones – can jolt us to look with new eyes.[17] But what about 'wild' places? Primarily nature-formed, these are awe-inspiring. Even here, however, there's usually an imprint of human activity, but it's mostly indirect, such as grazing management. Cared-for places evidence human control in attentive, reverent, partnership with nature's vigour. In *neglected* places, this care is withdrawn. These speak of uncaring abandonment. Here, human impact carries no respect: paths are eroded, litter discarded. Nature 're-invades', usually with single species such as nettles, thistles or brambles: invariably a one-sided ecology.

Planned and manicured or wild and verdant, gardens are about *care*. Care to create 'heaven' on earth, or care to develop what's already there. Developing extant physical features, ecological progression, moods and spirit of place link places to their context. This is about *respect* – a crucial lesson for all ages.

Vegetable gardens

Gardening reconnects us with our archetypal roots. This gives it potent therapeutic potential. (For criminal rehabilitation, it's amongst the most effective.) To gardening therapist E. McDonald: 'Gardening is good therapy for young and old. The earth has great healing power ... Plants are indeed a source of great hope for our time and for the many people who are disturbed, frustrated, and concerned about the future. Knowing and understanding plants can give them hope and reassurance that with death there follows life, and the great cycles of the seasons are part of even greater rhythms of the universe that are not dependent on mortal man's manipulation'.[18]

But why grow vegetables? In supermarkets, all foods are available year round. This, however, is often at huge CO_2 cost. Moreover, it disconnects children from nature's rhythms. Gardening teaches that food is seasonal. As vegetables aren't saturation-advertised, they aren't 'cool'. Consequently, unhealthy diet is common. Food children have grown, however, they're proud to eat. This sparks interest in cooking and diet. Gardening's hard work also counters couch potato tendencies, bringing fitness benefits. Fenoughty reports that harvesting their own crops gives schoolchildren a sense of achievement, which increases their self-esteem. 'With increased motivation to learn, pupils were more prepared to settle down to other areas of the curriculum, with improved results.'[19] All this is generating a revival of school vegetable gardens.

Vegetable gardens may sound dull, but easily can be places of beauty. Many vegetables flower attractively and many flowers are useful companion plants. Instead of growing beans on islands of poles, they can form tunnels to walk inside, or tents or domes to sit in. Nor need rows be straight.[20] Gardening takes much care. Its slow results don't initially suit all children. But how magical when seeds suddenly become little plants! The sense of wonder that develops from caring for tiny plants and watching them grow can

Bean tunnel

make gardening a reverential experience. Consequently, whereas hard surface outside classrooms encourages frenetic play, garden plots exude a quietening influence.[21]

Through vegetable gardening, children experience tilling, sowing, weeding and harvest as a whole cycle, even if split by holidays.[22] But which produce matures within the school year? In Britain, these are autumn-planted vegetables and fast-growing spring ones such as nasturtiums, radishes and peas; also perennial plants such as herbs.[23] Autumn-ripening crops need to survive the summer holidays without weeding or watering. As, with these, school-leavers bequeath a harvest to starting classes, this shifts work from self-centred to other-centred. This introduces the idea of work as social gift – an important attitude to assimilate in childhood and carry into adult life.

What about other sorts of food, such as bread? Child-grown wheat, flailed, winnowed and ground, may only bake one bun each. But it's something *grown*, the product of *their* hands, not a slice-and-wrap factory. Similarly, Austin Green School grows pizza ingredients in a segmented pizza-shaped bed. When children bake pizzas in an oven they've built, they've been in control of the whole process. Knowing you don't need to be dependent hugely boosts self-esteem.

School vegetable gardens range from growing-tubs and window-boxes to class or individual 'allotment' plots. Some schools use community gardens or allotments.[24] But what if there's *no* land? The Pumpkin Shed organic market garden in Wales takes local primary school children. Through finding out what good or harm little bugs do, they learn how to deal with pests without poisons. Four- to seven-year-olds garden together in class plots. Seven- to eleven-year-olds have individual squares and choose what they grow.

> For little ones we work within the theme of food and the environment; where does food come from? Potatoes from Pembrokeshire – we visit a potato farm, oranges from Spain – we learn about why we can't grow them here. We grow, harvest and cook a meal. The bigger ones keep records in their gardening almanac, see how weather affects growing and study global warming and food miles: which is better, an organic lettuce from Spain or a local cabbage not registered as organic? They eat it and think about it. We do something on genetic manipulation with the bigger ones and we visit local farms.
> We start in March with a seeding project. From then I close the business every Tuesday to work with the children 'til winter. Harvest festival is in October, then we put the garden to sleep under a big mulch like a thick blanket. The children like to do that.[25]

Greenhouses and poly-tunnels extend the growing season, but in bad weather can feel too far away, a different compartment of life. Conservatories, however, bring winter-growing into daily view, lifting mood towards spring. As places to sit, chat and soak up light, warmth and peace, these encourage sociability. Opening off a café, a school conservatory's produce, flowers and greenery can feed both body and soul. Educationally, older pupils can grow, prepare and sell food, so learning how to manage a small business – including pre-planning (for planting dates and bed allocation), flexibility (for crop failures and customer preference), recycling (for compost) and closely attentive day-to-day management (for soil moisture, temperature, and weed and pest control). While 'farm shops', selling produce to parents, involve business-studies, cafés have additional social and artistic demands: quality customer service and appropriate seasonal ambiance.[26]

Conservatory café

Connection to source; living processes; the nutrient cycle; receiving fruit from, and sowing seed for, others; the hard-work side of an easy world; matching produce to consumer need – such lessons don't need to be taught or explained. They're *experienced* without the need for words and the prematurely hard-edged concepts that words easily bring. Moreover, things learnt through the ears last perhaps a week; through the hands, for life.

Kindergarten gardens

What about kindergarten gardens? Should they be reverent, educational or productive? Or can they be all three? For children of any age, gardens can connect to the life of nature and seasonal round. Vegetable cellars help complete experience of the whole food cycle. Children can, for instance, sow carrots, tend, pull, store in sand, then wash and eat them. Carefully wrapping apples in newspaper, weaving seed-corn 'dollies' to hang above mouse reach, makes storing a reverential experience.

Gardens teach the importance – and beauty of – multifunctionality. Roses are visually attractive, good songbird habitat and make intruder-proof hedges. Symbolically paralleling our autumn soul shift from dreamily expansive nature to mentally concentrated indoor life, rose-hips bring summer fruitfulness indoors for winter, both as decorations and tea rich in vitamin C. But roses have sharp thorns. Fortunately for winter bird-feed, they're not easy to collect. Snagged clothing and scratches teach that the world isn't 'sweet', but 'real'. However beautiful, intriguing and inspiring, it's never *completely* problem-free. Likewise, some plants are smelly, some prickly, but can be transformed into beautiful dye-colours through human *work*.[27]

Like buildings, gardens induce movement and posture, moods and aspirations. Upward-looking flowers are growing *up* towards the light. Just like small children, they're not yet weighed down. While older children can cope with the strong-willed, knotty-muscled gestures of oak trees, younger ones need species with lightness, such as birch and ash. Pine groves are too dark, brooding. Fruit trees bring 'sunniness'. They're also educational: blossoms are fragile – to become fruit, they need gentle treatment and respect. Moreover, pruned for branches within picking reach (6 to 7 inches: 2 m) fruit trees are safer to climb. 'Baby trees', however, aren't yet strong enough for that. Only 'grown-up' and 'grandfather' trees are. In such ways, infants connect with the natural world through empathy. They're open to its magic.

What makes places magic? Pantheistic presence is essential. Dark, secretive silent groves, gnarled old hollow tree-trunks, soft cushions of moss, tiny jewels of flowers and secret water, exhibit this. There's also something about feeling unexpected, separated from the 'ordinary' world. This feeds children's fantasy.

Are there fairies in the garden? Small children *know* there are – beautiful fairies, sad fairies, water, air and warmth beings, gnomes and monsters. What's important isn't what we, however vehemently anti-pantheist, 'know', but that we act *as though there were*. If there *are* fairies, we can't poison weeds, grub up trees, concrete gardens without feeling murderers. As Alan Marshall observes, 'Children learn to become the people they are, acting the way they do, by how the adults around them act, and how things happen in the environment'.[28] Reverential care, therefore, nourishes both garden *and* children.

Dark, secretive grove

Outdoor learning

What about schools? These are for 'real' serious education. Should they be 'places of instruction' or 'instructive *environments*'? Many teachers believe the latter.[29] Books aren't the only way to learn. 'Everyone knows that children would rather be out than in … There are more vivid, more practical, more inspiring ways of finding out about the world we live in.'[30]

Even the cheapest building is expensive. Even expensive gardens are cheap by comparison. Educationally, school grounds offer richer experience-potential than buildings – and at less cost. This makes them such vital learning resources,[31] that their loss has 'a detrimental effect on educational attainment'.[32] But to have educational value, grounds must be attractive. As Anders Szczepanski, director of Environmental Education, Linköping University, observes: 'Why care about an environment you feel no kinship with?'[33]

But, even with attractive school grounds, will outdoor learning automatically happen? What would facilitate it? Adequate whole-class seating space helps. As damp benches can be dried, they're less weather-dependent than grass. Shelter from noise, wind – and preferably also rain – is important. With increasing ultraviolet radiation, children burn more quickly in the sun, making shade trees or arbours essential. Willow bowers can also serve as outdoor classrooms.[34] (Willows grow easily from cuttings. But, as they dry out wet ground, shrinking clay soils, there's risk of structural damage if they're too near buildings.[35]) Layout-wise, amphitheatre arrangements suit listening; group work needs seats around tables. Different levels and scales of space suit re-enactments, role-plays and artwork display. Any activities need, of course, to be where they won't distract indoor lessons.[36]

Intertwine tops and temporarily tie

Weave in each year's shoots

Prune off remainder

How to make a willow bower

Whole class seating[37]

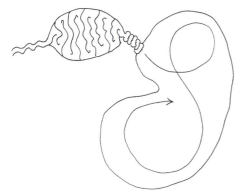

Streams and ponds as intestines, liver and kidneys

School grounds can be overtly educational. In playground nature reserves, for instance, rocks can show geology; ponds, butterfly meadows, trees, songbird bushes and nest-boxes teach biology. Landscaped grounds can also demonstrate how streams, marshes and ponds fulfil intestine, liver and kidney functions; how wind, dampness, drainage, shading and orientation affect plant growth and species. They can, as at Schule Sportplatzring, Hamburg, recreate biotopes: wildflower-meadow, hedgerow, heath-land, orchard, woodland, wetland and marsh.[38] This gives meaning to place names such as heath, wood or lea. For history, gardens typical of different periods can show how places used to be. Traditional cottage, monastery, Victorian and even – as at Ökowerk, Emden, Germany – Mediaeval 'witches' medicinal-herb gardens each have characteristic artistic moods.[39]

Recommended minimum range of habitats[40]

Vegetables and fruit
Woodland or coppice
Pond
Wet area
Short grass
Long grass meadow for butterflies
Hedgerow for songbirds
Old dry wall for insects
Roofed garden for wet days[41]

Diversity broadens habitat range and makes places more interesting and sensorially richer. 'Barefoot paths' add textural sensation to what we see, hear and smell. Plants vary immensely to the touch: smooth, velvety, rough, prickly; delicate, robust; dry, moist, feathery. Such sensory stimulus has therapeutic benefits for children with hearing, speech and special needs difficulties.[42] Additionally, colour and scent change with season. Wind-upturned leaves and rattling canes amplify weather. In most gardens and landscapes, sensory variety isn't contrived by design, but results from – and manifests – their ecology. This invites investigation. Authenticity appeals, intrigues and satisfies deeply; the arranged only shallowly.

As the Department for Education and Skills recognizes, first-hand experiences, getting their hands dirty, increases pupils' interest and understanding. Enthusiasm boosts commitment to learning. They allow all children – the more physical, more artistic and emotively led as well as the intellectual, academic ones – to experience a sense of achievement. With increased confidence and sense of worth, their behaviour also improves.[43]

No wonder – weather, clothing and attractive surroundings permitting – children prefer to be outdoors than in. No wonder that, to Summerfield Waldorf school: 'The ideal classroom is outdoors'.[44]

Educational benefits

It is widely recognized that outdoor experiences have more significance for children than indoor ones.[45] Outdoors, infants invent twice as many fantasy scenarios. All children play more, and more imaginatively.[46] Play is normally 'more free', more relaxedly expressive and socially harmonious in gardens than amongst hard, solely man-made, surroundings. Also bullying and aggressive games decrease.[47]

But what about education? Aren't classrooms the best places for learning? They're designed for teaching cerebral knowledge. But without hands-on experience, this is one-sided, partial – the least effective, least lasting, least meaningful way to learn. Limited space indoors limits experimentation. Moreover, it's hard to study much that is *alive* – only a few things can live indoors, and only when separated from their living context. Context gives meaning to things. Separation isolates them – from life, from relationships, from time continuum, and in our thinking. Not a good way to learn about the environment – which is all about life, relationships, time linkage and wholeness.

What about teenagers – whose education is more cerebral than sensory? Don't they need to be in classrooms? Many boys, however, find academic learning irrelevant, and classrooms prisons. Outdoor learning is widely recognized as a powerful method of engaging such pupils.[48] By switching from traditional didactic teaching to 'hands on' methods, Sportplatzring virtually eliminated adolescent behaviour problems. Here, 12- to 14-year-olds divide their time between theory indoors, 'garden classroom' and managing the school grounds' diverse habitats.[49] Similarly, as classroom education would completely turn-off the 'unredeemable' delinquents sent to Ruskin Mill, all activities there are nature-based. This is founded on Aenghus Gordon's view that 'nature is the best way to retune damaged senses'.[50]

Szczepanski also emphasizes that nature sharpens the senses and is the best medicine for nervous tension. Additionally, by understanding her cycles, children gain confidence that problems can be solved.[51] By hearing, smelling, tasting and feeling nature's variety and beauty, the German *Waldschulen* (Forest School) movement seeks not only to activate children's senses and understanding, but bring them to appreciate her irreplaceable value.[52] Planting trees in forests increases inner-city schoolchildren's confidence – even, for multi-ethnic children, in their unfamiliar host language.[53] With special-needs children, the motivation, responsibility and fulfilment benefits of such outdoor work are particularly pronounced. Szczepanski notes that physical activity outdoors stimulates comprehensive thinking, motivation and alert minds – increasingly necessary in our world of TV, computers and cars. Moreover, the real-life contexts encourage mutual responsibility for practical tasks and collaborative relationships.[54]

Outdoor learning develops visual and emotional literacy,[55] and can give every subject an *experiential* basis. By developing knowledge, practical skills and caring attitudes, it integrates head, heart and hands.[56] This lets children investigate things in a more concrete and sense-rich way, so understand and connect with them better.[57] From small children hunting, auditing and examining 'mini-beasts' (spiders, beetles, worms and larvae) to older ones integrating science, mathematics, language and art, it offers experience-based learning to all ages. As experience is essentially *trans-category*, this naturally implies cross-subject integration.[58] By relating soil-chemistry, vegetation and climate data to how places look, sound, smell and feel, children learn to understand places at a deeper level than any single subject permits. Diverse plants and insects over limestone, for instance, 'belong together'; they differ in ecology and mood – science and art – from those over granite. Likewise, those over clay differ from ones over sand. This introduces an artistic sense of unity underlying even exuberant variety – an essential step to recognizing the 'being' of a place or eco-system.

School grounds

Children shut indoors too long either go brain-dead or wild. Lunch and lesson breaks – 28 per cent of the school day[59] – allow children to relax from intellectual concentration, let off steam and socialize. Much time could be spent outdoors, were not playgrounds often, as Cherie Enns describes, 'leftover space fenced in ways that leave children peering out, similar to inmates'.[60] While robust areas are essential for all-weather play and gathering, hard surfaces suit 'hard' activities. Too much encourages 'hard' behaviour. 'Soft' playgrounds are more inviting, more educational and induce gentleness. Soft, however, doesn't mean just mown grass playing fields, too wet for heavy use in winter and featureless all year. Characterless places aren't inviting.

Entry through a garden can turn a school from institution to oasis. Fenoughty is emphatic about the importance of this: 'The school grounds, for many urban children starting formal education, could be the first outdoor landscape where they have the space to develop their physical and social skills ... and where they can experience the natural environment at first hand – their first stepping stone to understanding the wider environment beyond. The school grounds "experience" could make or mar a child's attitude to "being outdoors" in later life'.[61]

Landscaping is the easiest – and cheapest – way to transform place-mood

Greening playgrounds

Landscaped playgrounds are no mere luxury. Research confirms they 'can reduce bullying and crime; nurture teamwork and improve self-esteem; provide opportunities for kinesthetic learners and vocational learning and support all areas of the curriculum'.[62]

Landscaping isn't expensive. It's commonly 1 per cent of new-building budget. Doubling this brings great benefits for minute proportional expense. But this is still money. Although inconsequential in new projects, what about existing playgrounds? Can these be improved on minimal budgets? Many are just tarmac. Digging this up and planting grass sounds simple, but the most likely consequence is winter mud and summer dust. What then can we do?

Indigenous plants are cheap, sometimes free. Adapted to local conditions, they're more robust than 'strangers', better for local wildlife and more sustainable even if inadequately maintained. Native plants also respect local place-identity and show that the everyday can always be raised to the beautiful – two important lessons! Involving parents and grandparents – rare in British state schools, but central to the German *Grun macht Schule* movement – both saves labour costs and brings invaluable community involvement.[63]

What about design? Professionals know important things, but unless teachers – and preferably children – are involved, decisions won't be relevant to their needs. The ability to improve their surroundings confirms children's self-esteem,[64] and the ensuing transformations typically raise expectations and inspire further improvement projects.[65] With increasing responsibility for, proprietary pride in, and 'ownership' of, their environment, vandalism declines sharply.[66] Enns considers 'the critical importance of participation of children as they pass through adolescence cannot be overstated. Preparing children to participate more significantly as youth in the planning process can be a positive response to the problems of graffiti and the range of illegal activities'.[67] They learn a lot even from what doesn't work out right.

But *how* can children participate? Informal walkabout discussions and questionnaires produce information,[68] but more specifically, site-surveys and needs-analysis – by children – show what is, and what should be, there.[69] For site-analysis, they can draw and write about what they like and dislike.[70] To mark qualities such as: favourite, worst, sunniest, coldest, windiest and quietest, they can stick coloured dots on plans or run to actual places.[71] Children's survey-maps (who does what where?) can be backed up by observing their play: where do they run, hide, chat; what else do they do? Are the right things in the right places? Do they have the right microclimates? Are they easily maintained and supervised?[72]

How about design involvement? Everyone always has lots of ideas, but these can lead in many – often conflicting – directions. As doing your own thing rarely satisfies other people, the results aren't sustainable. Can priorities be agreed? Clear objectives focus thinking: 'we need to change the school grounds because ...'[73] Children soon find they have to learn *cooperation*. Fundamentally, co-designing is a *social* exercise.

Amongst many ways of co-designing, *brainstorming* is common. Lots of good, inspirational – and wacky, impractical – ideas come up, and somebody – or everybody – chooses the 'best' to put together. Unfortunately, if your idea isn't chosen, it's easy to feel rejected. At heart, this approach is competitive. It's therefore more productive – and much more affordable – to ask what children would like to *do* than what they want to *have*.[74]

Another method gathers ideas into common-theme groups, summarizes these, then synthesizes all these distillations. Everybody now feels included, but every idea has been moderated – usually compromised – by others. Like brainstormed proposals, these often assemble lots of things that don't innately belong together.

A fundamental problem with *ideas* is that what suits one may be an anathema to somebody else. Indeed, if two people have four points of dispute, ten will have a hundred; for a whole school, tens of thousands. Hence, to get anything done, what starts out as democracy easily slides into autocracy.

Instead of synthesizing *ideas*, I prefer instead to *condense* design. This has two phases: place-study and design – each with four layers. To get to know somewhere in meaningful depth, we look first at what *is* there, in exacting detail. (Had we done this before grassing everything, we would have known where heavy soil and water ponding would turn winter grass to mud.) We then look at transient factors: how it is used, when, in what weathers, what pathways and journey sequences do people take? (Had we done this, we would have known where foot traffic would kill grass.) We also review the place's biography from distant past to present. This gives us a sense of time as a *stream*. We can now imagine this time-stream into the future: how will the place – and its wider surroundings – be in five, ten, fifty years? (By doing this, our designs are unlikely to be compromised by changes outside our boundaries.) We next try to get a sense of the moods of the place's different parts. (Had we done this, we would have known where nobody would want to sit or play, and where they would.) And then we ask what the place *says*, what message it conveys.

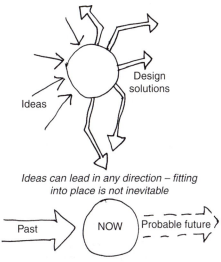

Ideas can lead in any direction – fitting into place is not inevitable

Design within time-steam inevitably fits

This is the crux. What *should* the place say? What message should it emanate? What are the core values it should express? What should be the 'spirit-of-place'? (Had we done this we would have known a sea of grass would be too boring, unimaginative – an abdication of our involvement, so not in the slightest sustainable.) Knowing what we want the place to say, how should we enhance, transform or redeem the moods of its parts to match the uses they suggest? Which parts, for instance, should be public, semi-private, boisterous or tranquil? How should these activity-mood-places link or barrier to create journeys and places? Knowing the soils, drainage and levels, doorways and access-points, shade, wind and microclimate, what land-moulding, ground-surfaces, planting, 'furnishings' and equipment should be where?

By condensing design like this, we start with what everybody *agrees* – what the place should say, how it should express the spirit of the school. Thereafter, every decision isn't a matter of competing individual preferences, but is servant of the previous layer of decisions. If we can't agree, instead of arguing (when the most persuasive-tongued, bombastic, stubborn or politically popular wins) we revisit the last decision. What would serve it best? This is consensus, not by abdicating or compromising individuality, but by rising above its narrow confines. It depends on *listening to the situation*. And listening is surely an invaluable life-skill – socially, ecologically and educationally.[75]

This kind of listening helps us see plants, animals and microclimate as related – a single, multilayered community. By recognizing the relationship between the scent and feel of air, qualities of leaf movements, bird and insect sounds, flower and foliage colours, the texture of view, we enter into the soul of a place. Our design interventions – whether modifying grounds or designing new buildings – will now *inevitably* be harmonious, ecological, not just the imposition of what *we* want.[76]

Only with such ecological integrity can places nourish us deeply and fulfil our unconscious archetypal needs, for, as Roszac writes, 'the needs of the planet are the needs of the person'.[77]

Notes

1 Roszak, Theodore (2002) *Ecopsychology: Eight Principles.* http://ecopsychology.athabascau.ca/Final/intro.htm.
2 Roszak, Theodore (2002) *op. cit.*
3 Ministry of Education (1952) *Moving and Growing.* HMSO – accompanied by strikingly different photographs of the same children in town and at the seaside.
4 Fenoughty, Susan, environmental education teacher consultant.
5 Actually, a Lapp *kåta.*
6 *I Ur och Skur*, Friluftsfrämjandet.
7 MacMillan, Margaret quoted in Dudek, Mark (1996) *Kindergarten Architecture.* Spon.
8 Letter by 110 childhood professionals to the *Daily Telegraph*, 12 September 2006, and subsequent interviews on BBC Radio 4 *Today* Programme.
9 Olds, Anita Rui (2001) *Child Care Design Guide.* McGraw Hill.
10 Meyerkort, Margaret *Kindergarten Architecture And Equipment.* Unpublished. Compiled By Elvira Rychlak.
11 Information from Zoarastrian, Zerbanoo Gifford. Or paradise can mean 'Beautiful (or well-watered) Garden' (Dunér, Sten and Katarina (2001) *Den Gyllene Trädgården.* Prisma). Literally, *Pairi-daeza* translates as 'wall around' (Baldwin, Cecelia (2004) The meaning of gardens. *New View*, Spring). Arabic, Armenian, Greek and Hebrew words are similar.
12 Dunér, Sten and Katarina (2001) *op. cit.*
13 After Dunér, *op. cit.*
14 After Kellogg, Rhoda.
15 Titman, Wendy (1999) *Special Places; Special People.* Quoted in Marshall, Alan (1999) *Greener School Grounds.* Learning through Landscapes.
16 Case study: Michael Hall Steiner Waldorf School, Sussex, in *School Grounds UK* 2 (2), 2002/2003.
17 Even just painting stones blue. Dunér, Sten and Katarina (2001) *ibid.*
18 McDonald, E. (1976) *Plants as Therapy.* Praeger Publishers, quoted in Venolia, Carol (1988) *Healing Environments.* Celestial Arts.
19 Such was the experience of the Rein Abrahamshool, Alkmaar, The Netherlands; Fenoughty, Susan (1997) *The garden classroom.* Unpublished Churchill Fellowship report.
20 These, however, need clear geometries so emerging seedlings are distinct from weeds.
21 When master-planning Mendocino Waldorf School, California, we were asked to do this.
22 Easy vegetables include: peas, beans, beetroots, cabbages, carrots, leeks, lettuces, nasturtiums, onions, potatoes, marrows and pumpkins.
23 Adapted from Ter Kleef Nature and Environment Centre, Haarlem, The Netherlands; as listed in Fenoughty, Susan (1997) *ibid.*
24 Department for Education and Skills (2003) *Growing Schools.* HMSO.
25 We dig school. *Vision in Action* 4 (1) (2001).
26 I'm particularly grateful to Dr Maria Castella for these observations.
27 Source: kindergarten teacher Elvira Rychlak.

28 Marshall, Alan (1999) *op. cit.*
29 My italics. This has been advocated for half a century. Ministry of Education (1952) *ibid.*
30 Edwards, A. (2002) quoted in An outside chance for learning, *Learning through Landscapes*, Building Design, March 2005.
31 House of Commons Education and Skills committee report, cited by Chillman, B. (2005) Ask the experts: *Learning through Landscapes*. Building Design, March 2005.
32 Sue Fenoughty, environmental education teacher consultant.
33 Szczepanski, Anders (director of Environmental and Outdoor Education at Linköping University) quoted in Fenoughty, Susan (1997) *ibid.*
34 West Devon Sustainable Schools Project. See, for instance a description of Lifton Primary School, http://www.westdev.co.uk/Pages/schools2.htm
35 Without root-barrier protected subsoil near foundations, buildings can crack, even collapse.
36 Chillman, B. (2005) *ibid.*
37 Hampshire County Council school.
38 Fenoughty, Susan (1997) *ibid.*
39 Fenoughty, Susan (1997) *op. cit.*
40 Fenoughty, Susan (1997) *op. cit.* Also Enns, Cherie C. (2005) *Places for Children*. University College of the Fraser Valley.
41 Dudek, Mark (2000) *Architecture of Schools*. Architectural Press.
42 Dudek, Mark (2000) *op. cit.*
43 Department for Education and Skills (2003) *ibid.*
44 Sandar, Ronnie, Summerfield Waldorf School, California (responding to a questionnaire about the ideal classroom).
45 Nordström, Maria (1995) in Lundahl, Gunilla, ed. (1995) *Hus och Rum för Små Barn*. Arkus.
46 Dongju Shin and Frost, Joe L. (1995) Preschool children's symbolic play indoors and outdoors. *International Play Journal* 3 (2).
47 Szczepanski, Anders quoted in Fenoughty, Susan (1997) *ibid.*
48 Frean, Patrick of Dean School, Plymouth, quoted in Chillman, B. (2005) *ibid.*
49 Fenoughty, Susan (1997) *ibid.*
50 Gordon, Aenghus (2003) Lecture at *On the Edge of Landscape* conference, Pishwanton.
51 Anders Szczepanski quoted in Fenoughty, Susan (1997) *ibid.*
52 Lohrmann, Iris (2003) Learning from nature in the urban landscape of Berlin. *Environmental Education* 73, Summer, published by National Association for Enviromental Education (UK).
53 Fenoughty, Susan (1997) *ibid.*
54 Szczepanski, Anders, quoted in Fenoughty, Susan (1997) *op. cit.*
55 Matin, D., Luca, W., Titman, W. and Hayward, G., eds (1990) *The Outdoor Classroom* and (1994) *Special Places, Special People*, Learning through Landscapes, quoted in Dudek Mark (2000) *Architecture of Schools*. Architectural Press.
56 Fenoughty, Susan (2001) *The Landscape of the School Grounds*. Comenius.
57 Nordström, Maria (1990) *Barns boendeförställningar i ett utvecklinspsykologiskt perspektiv*. Doctoral thesis, Statens Institut för byggnadsforskning, Lund University, cited in Farnestam, Sandra (2001) *Arkitektur i skolan*. Unpublished dissertation, Umeå University.
58 Anders, Szczepanski, quoted in Fenoughty, Susan (1997) *ibid.*
59 Marshall, Alan (1999) *ibid.*
60 Enns, Cherie C. (2005) *ibid.*
61 Fenoughty, Susan (2002) *Outdoor Education: Authentic Learning in the Context of the Landscape*. Comenius.
62 Littlefield, D. (2005) Funds and Games. In *Learning through Landscapes*, Building Design, March 2005.
63 This movement was founded in 1983: Lohrmann, Iris (2003) Learning from nature in the urban landscape of Berlin. *Environmental Education* 73, Summer, published by NAEE (UK).
64 Szczepanski, Anders, quoted in Fenoughty, Susan (1997) *ibid.*
65 Chillman, B. (2005) Secondary thoughts. In Learning through Landscapes, Building Design, March 2005.
66 Matin, D., Luca, W., Titman, W. and Hayward, G., eds (1990) *ibid.* and

(1994) *ibid*. Quoted in Dudek, Mark (2000) *ibid*. Also Chillman, B. (2005). Also the 1989 Elton report to the UK government specifically linked bad behaviour in schools to the quality of the outdoor environment. Dudek, Mark (2000) *ibid*.

67 Enns, Cherie C. (2005) *ibid*.

68 Chillman, B. (2005) *ibid*.

69 Fenoughty, Susan (2006): *7 Stages to Develop the School Site as an 'Outdoor Classroom' & Place for Play*. suefen@blueyonder.co.uk

70 Way, Emma (2005) Ask the experts. In *Learning through Landscapes*, Building Design, March 2005.

71 Chillman, B. (2005) Ask the experts. *Ibid*.

72 Advice from Fenoughty, Susan.

73 Fenoughty, Susan (2006) *ibid*.

74 For more details of this method and its application in varied circumstances, cultures and climate, proven over some fifty projects, see Day, Christopher (2002) *Consensus Design*. Architectural Press.

75 Bochemühl, Jochen (2003) Lecture at *On the Edge of Landscape* conference, Pishwanton.

76 Roszak, Theodore (2002) *ibid*.

CHAPTER 13

Environment for the developing child

Children and environment

So open and trusting are small children, they're easily influenced – often with lifelong effect. Long before psychiatric focus on childhood experiences, the Jesuits believed the first seven years shape character for life. To Steiner *everything* experienced in this period affects morality, character and even organ development.[1] What people do, say, and especially how they *are*, manifests their unspoken values, so has major effect. But what about 'lifeless' physical environment? This too manifests imprinted value-messages – with self-esteem, respect and behaviour implications. Its physical conditions offer experiential opportunities, and support, hinder or challenge everything we feel, do and even think.

Does, for instance, giving children plastic-surfaced chip-board desks that look like wood encourage honesty? For honesty-by-example, they need the genuine article. For the security born of trust, they need to recognize the tree source of wood, the earth source of stone or brick. Look-alikes or highly processed products provide neither.

Do rigid, compartmentalized surroundings help children develop beyond rigid, box-compartmentalized thinking? Might not form mobility and fluidity be more appropriate? Likewise, do harshly colliding shapes and forms foster social sensitivity? Elements that, instead of fighting when they meet, respond to each other, provide a better subliminal lesson. As harsh shapes frame harshly, what about windows – 'eyes' to the world? Curtains partially soften outline but gentle shapes do so even more.

Will children feel enthusiastic about school if its environment isn't inviting? But is it enough if rooms are nice? Just as kitchens, bedrooms and living-rooms have different spatial, organizational and microclimatic needs, so do kindergartens, classrooms, studios and common-rooms. Without functional practicality, needless stresses accrue. But, as different outer functions demand different *inner states*, rooms with different uses – even if initially identical – rapidly

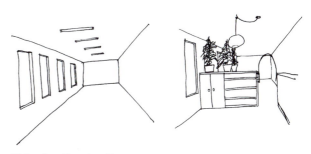

Using furniture to alter rooms

develop different atmospheres. But mood-range isn't infinite; it's limited by room character. Furnishings and paint can do much to change mood, but proportion, scale, room-shape and daylight quality are more difficult to alter. Furniture, fittings and finishes, however, are often half the cost of construction and are short-lived. In life-cycle cost terms, they're expensive. *Architectural* design that matches place-mood to use is more effective.

Age brings an additional aspect to place-mood. Children aren't small, uneducated adults, but *children*. Childhood is the journey of *growing up*. Much like flower-development, this journey is one of *opening to the world*. Small children need protection from the wider world; adults are only fully alive when engaged in it. Between these extremes lies an unfolding process. From childcare centre to university, we can characterize environmental *qualities* – though not actual *forms* – appropriate to each age as progressing from woodland glade, rich with dreamy elemental life; through garden, farm and fields, with animal-care opportunities; to the social challenges of village, town, then industrial city – where cultural riches contrast with squalor: places deeply in need of crusading idealism.

Children's activity-energy development is analogous to a stream; a pure spring, then a small but vigorously alive streamlet, growing increasingly powerful, occasionally destructively turbulent, eventually becoming a smoother river. Environmentally, young streams are deeply enclosed by landform and vegetation; then the landscape elements become more balanced, eventually becoming spacious and open, as do their rivers. We all, adults as well as children, need *both* life-enhancing and organizing qualities in our surroundings. We need both the stream's turbulent current and the sea's predictable tides. The relative proportions, however, vary with age and circumstance.

River as life-journey

Children's 'waking-up journey' progresses from just *feeling* to feelings associated with sounds. They imitate these, gradually recognizing them as words. Putting words together brings the feelings they evoke into relationship. This is the foundation of thinking.[2] As children grow, thought-generated forms become increasingly appropriate. Small children, however, live in evanescent moods, not neatly compartmentalized thoughts. They need fluidly life-filled surroundings.

How does life-energy affect form? *Every* living form, from leaves and tree-trunks to bones and hearts, is formed from water-flow deposits. Nonetheless, although fluid-formed, their archetypes – before distortion by local environmental forces (such as wind) are highly structured, even geometric. Ash-twigs bud symmetrically, but ash-trees never are symmetrical. Just as fluid, active, energy-generated forms are the forms of life, so, reciprocally, such spaces best suit, invigorate and nourish life. As in nature, however, without organizing principles these are ungrounded and meaningless. So, should buildings be symmetrical? Some feel the archetypal building is so much a picture of the human being, that it needs skeleton-like symmetry, letting freely placed furniture – like asymmetrical organs – enliven rooms.³ Symmetry, however, is lifeless; but *balance* is alive.

Structured lines are about order. Straight lines (their power deriving from their tension) arranged at right-angles make a very clear, organized geometry, but if unrelieved (as, in classical architecture, by texture and moderating 'transition elements'), its emphasis on *order* easily makes buildings feel they're ordering *us*.⁴ This makes them feel *institutional* – unresponsive and uncaring. Likewise, straight-line *principles* exist throughout nature, but no shapes are 'dead-straight'. All have the slight irregularities of life, not the tension and precision of machine-produced ones.

Archetypal child's drawing of house as 'face'

Symmetry and asymmetry, straight and curved, geometric and fluid, conscious and dreamy: how can these polarities be interwoven into a multinutritious balanced whole? Appropriate balance is never just a centre-point between extremes, but varies according to circumstance: context, culture and, especially, *age*. For small children it lies more towards the life-filled, curved, dreamy; for teenagers, more towards order, straightness, wakefulness. Children's developing needs – increasing light, unfolding enclosure-gestures, growing firmness and more upright-inducing space – parallel their own bodily growth and soul journey.

As children grow, they move differently and play different games. Their imaginative thinking evolves into intuitive and lateral thinking. As their relationship with each other and the outside world changes, their rooms and buildings need to similarly metamorphose. Like children themselves, these need to grow from low, small-scale, soft and fluidly formed to taller, bone-structured and upward-gesturing; from protectively enclosed to outward-looking and socially engaged; from nurturing to inspiring. Enfolding earth-mother softness protects infants. But to support the dignity in growing up, adolescents need higher ceilings and windows, upright-proportioned spaces, firmer, clearer and graceful.

Any design for children must take account, not only of their smaller stature and lower eye level, but also of the stage they have reached on their developmental journey.

Unfolding gestures for each age

Small children

At birth, children enter with independent bodies into the physical world. Babies need a protective environment – physically sheltering, and with a mood of womb-like loving security. This means warmth, quiet and gentle surroundings, quiet filtered purple light and soothing rhythmic motion – womb-like qualities. Spatially, this protectiveness – like womb, or nest – has a spherical, enclosing gesture. Until they're seven years of age, children are still 'coming to earth': forming their bodies, and developing separate individualities. Though no longer babies, echoes of these womb-qualities still nourish them. These, however, evolve. Purple-filtered light, for instance, may metamorphose from translucent cradle-veils, blue over crimson, for babies, into rose-lazured rooms with darker, bluish or violet 'nest'-corners for infants.

As infants become more consciously aware of their surroundings there is a wondrous newness to everything they see, hear and feel. By contrast, we adults are blasé and unobservant. Small children avidly and without discrimination drink in every sensory experience. These penetrate their whole beings so thoroughly that they colour behaviour, and can influence psychological, sensory and even physical development.

So open, undefended, are they, and so unconsciously and unselectively do they imitate, that surroundings affect their play. Fast-moving, loud and overstimulating or dreamy, gentle, magical environments induce matching responses. Children play differently with inflexibly formed, simply experienced solids such as building blocks, or with fluid materials such as water, sand, clay or dough. Elusively formed things – such as tree roots and cloth – support their vivid powers of imagination. 'Living' forms, spaces, textures, colours, light and materials encourage imagination-mobility. As kindergarten children don't connect to their environment through thinking but through sensory experience, particularly touch, balance, movement and a sense of well-being, they need touch-inviting textures, expanding–contracting and balanced posture-inductive spaces. Harmonious and gentle environments nurture their sense of reverence.

Their natural sense of devotion leads small children to unconsciously assume the world is moral – the way things should be, an example to follow. Consequently, they can't help imitating everything around them, good or bad – even our most casual or unconsidered actions. This makes it important that everything they meet – people, things, places and buildings – is infused with moral values worthy of their unselective imitation.[5] Their natural, unquestioning trust is confirmed when everything around them – toys, furniture, buildings – manifests loving, care-rich craftsmanship. This brings the experience that 'the world is good' – vital for positive values in later life.[6]

Young children need *security*, so play more confidently in close orbit around an adult. When ill, they want to be treated like babies: lying snugly and quietly, but close to the centre of things. Hence cosy, darkish alcoves off main rooms make good kindergarten sickbays. Here, 'big' children (six year olds) love to take care of the sick 'patient'.[7] A special 'sick-time' hot-water bottle, mattress and blanket, makes the invalid feel securely 'held' with loving care.

Until they're six years of age, consistency, warmth and long-lasting relationships are children's primary needs.[8] It may be 'natural' for small children to be at home, but nowadays many spend more waking hours in school than at home. One-third of American under-five year olds attend childcare centres 10 hours a day, 5 days a week, 50 weeks a year[9] – almost twice European adult work-hours! In childcare centres, 'home-groups' of six to eight children in 'domestic' space can provide compensating homeliness.[10] 'Family' atmosphere is essential, but which is more suitable: a 'house' sort of building rich in 'home' associations, or one shaped by therapeutic and pedagogical considerations – a more 'magical' space? Or domestic mood for smaller children, magic for kindergarten age?

Houses, however, are mostly shaped for adult needs; rarely are children considered. Matching space quality to age isn't easy as children grow so quickly. Altering buildings is rarely practical but cross-corner furnishings, curtains, cloth tents, room dividers, nests and nooks can inexpensively soften rooms.

In every home, kitchens are centres of 'homeliness'. With baking smells, grown-up things going on around you, and human-warmth aura, what better place for a child to be? Here, even playpen-confined children are at the heart of home life. Just as loving food-making makes houses into *homes*, and acquaintances into friends, it gives a kindergarten or school a heart. In kitchens, infants make early connections between smell, taste and appearance,[11] learn about dangers such as fire and hot, sharp or fragile things; then how to *use* utensils, brooms, oven-gloves and suchlike – how to live safely in a not-quite safe world.

Labour-saving machines, although freeing adults from drudgery, impoverish small children, who want to participate in and imitate everything. As Elke-Maria Riscke points out: 'To see jobs being done by hand with care and joy and suitable seriousness, in some cases with exertion, to see the adult do his or her work with love, not being continually in a rush and holding to the right sequence of steps in a job: for the child, these are irreplaceable formative impressions and experiences'.[12] Watching, however, isn't enough. Small children want to do whatever adults do. As *real* cooking is an important part of grown-ups' life, kindergarten classrooms need child-accessible kitchenettes. In Germany, these – including child-scaled stoves and equipment – are obligatory. In many US states, however, they're illegal.[13] Here, interior windows and fire-dampered vents can at least allow view and smell.

Should kitchens have counters or tables? Tables are social. Many can work, or sit, around them. Round or squarish ones focus everyone towards the centre. (Oblong ones with over three seats per side don't.) For disturbed children, however, working side-by-side is easier. Just as walking *beside* people eases getting to know them, they talk about problems more easily when *not* looking into someone's eyes.[14] Conventional kitchen counters face antisocially outwards, towards walls or windows. For supervision – and children sharing adult sinks – they need to face *into* classrooms. Hot-plates and kettles must, of course, always be beyond child-reach.

Should kindergarten kitchens be child-sized? This suits children – but not adult backs! Sinking kitchen floors or raising platforms makes one counter-side right for adults, the other for children. Another simple device is pull-out boxes (like inverted drawers) to stand on. Such solutions appeal to architects, but offer no stimulus to initiative. At home, children fetch stools to stand on – why not at school? (For safety, these should be broad-based boxes.) Educationally, this

Child-accessible kitchen

Sunken kitchen for two-level counters

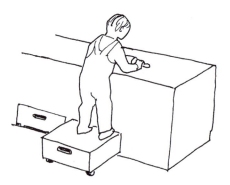

Pull-out boxes

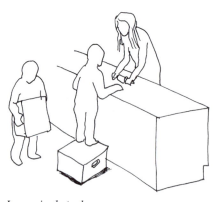

Improvised stools

involves deliberation, balance, inventiveness and will-commitment to overcome obstacles. Children feel a sense of achievement – even more so when, around age six years, they're big enough not to need steps. As in most things, simpler, freer, less designed, is usually better – and invariably cheaper!

Likewise, child-height sinks leave nothing to grow up to, no challenge to surmount. One school with three sink heights found all ages *only* used the highest one – the adult sink.[15] Not everything, however, should be adult-sized. 'Large' toilets can frighten small children – especially vacuum toilets with their monster-like roar and powerful suck-down-a-hole to the unknown. Although Margaret Meyerkort insists on adult height wash-basins, door-handles and fixtures – as at home – she does use child-sized furniture. For teachers' backs it's better if children's tables are adult height, with their chairs adjusted to fit this. (Norwegian 'Trip-trap' chairs can 'grow', so children can keep the same chairs throughout school.)

Should children have child-sized chairs? More pertinently, how long should they have to sit in them? Though individualized chairs acknowledge children as special, they – unlike the floor – create bad posture.[16] Actually, *all* chairs are bad for backs – adults' too – if you sit still. Children don't get backaches because they *fidget*. Before their backs are strong, the freer they are to move, the better for muscle and skeletal health and flexibility. Children *need* to move: squat, kneel, sit, lie or squirm on the floor.[17] Warm, comfortable floors – wood, cork or linoleum, with cushions, mattresses or rugs – encourage this. Chairs, however, as inanimate laps, have an important inner developmental role.[18] With their backs supported, small children are less conscious of their bodies, so more able to relax into a dreamy state, and fully enter into the world of imagination.[19]

What environmental qualities do infants need? Just as outdoor spaces 'held' by enclosing hedges, walls or not-too-permeable fences help them feel secure, they need 'indoor-feeling' buildings – not unprotectedly overlit. Importantly, these must feel *stable*: well-rooted in time and place, of durable materials and with protective enclosing spatial gestures.

Large buildings bewilder, even frighten small children. They need ones small enough to comprehend, of non-dominating scale.[20] Likewise, though low-ceilinged large rooms feel oppressive, even only ten-foot (3 m) ceilings can be too high for them. Some kindergarten teachers think seven-foot (2.15 m) ceilings – uncomfortably low for adults – optimum.[21] But children also need upright-inductive space. Shaped ceilings – rising in the centre but low where meeting walls, especially at corners – resolve this conflict.

Beyond this, infants need surroundings that 'love' them. How can *buildings* do that? Cosy, warm, soft colours comfort both body and soul. Warmly embracing pinks do that, but need great care, as sentimental sweetness is stifling. Peaceful spaces are secure. Circular or similarly embracing nest-gestured shapes, both in plan and three-dimensions, are sheltering; they 'hug' their occupants. Nests are womb-homes: round, warm and protected, never square, hard or window-walled.[22] To be 'alive', however, circular plans need enlivening by organic evolutions, metamorphoses and dynamic energy. Geometrical rigidity can make anything dead. Also, flat ceilings are distinctly un-nestlike; they collide uncompromisingly with walls, negating any planned softness and leaving it feeling contrived and meaningless.

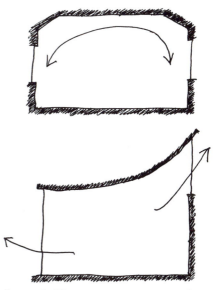

Secure, holding, attention-focusing gesture; insecure, out-flying, attention-dispersing gesture

In terms of wakefulness, spherical-quality spaces suit small children's dreaminess; harder, more axially organized and facetted ones suit teenagers. (Rotating a sphere in our hands feels dreamy, but a cube's angles jolt awareness of its hardness, making rotation more deliberate.)[23] Not surprisingly, spheres symbolize the cosmos – the great dream around us; and rectangles – boxes we store things in – symbolize matter.

Rectangles are good for organizing material things, for clarity of intellect. But small children aren't *things*, nor yet materialist thing-collectors; and their relationship to the world isn't intellectually awake – like adults – but dreamy. In fact, rectangular spaces have nothing to offer infants. They can actually be *harmful*. Just as eviction from their world-representing tipi circles and enforced settlement in 'square gray houses' severed the Lakota-Sioux from their anchoring cosmology,[24] rectangles deny the soft, enfoldingly protective, spherical, prenatal memory that is children's soul-anchor.[25]

Between circle and rectangle are circular-gesture shapes with planar facets, such as pentagons and hexagons. Pentagons, however, have 108° angles and apparent, but changing, axiality. Even adults need a developed spatial consciousness to orientate themselves in these. For children, pentangular rooms, even sand-boxes, can be disorientating.[26]

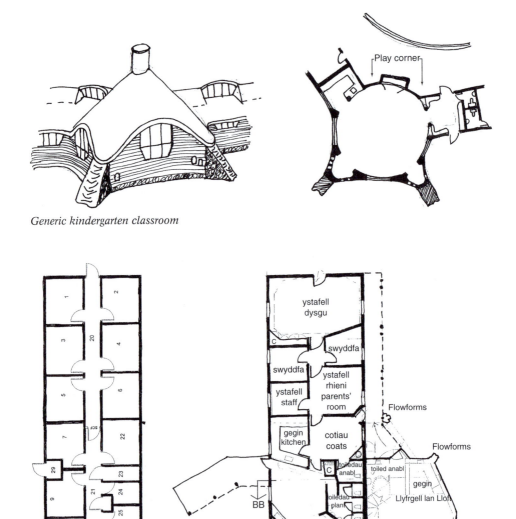

Generic kindergarten classroom

Pre-fabricated shed converted to kindergarten

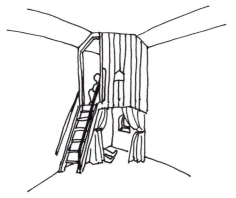

Hidey-hole corner in rectangular room

To Architect, Walter Beck, 'next to the family's dwelling, the kindergarten is the first spatial surroundings belonging to the child. The child is still malleable and takes in forms more intensely than the adult, who is already misformed. Structures form the germinating soul of the child and its feeling of life much more strongly than is generally imagined'.[27] This gives early-childhood architecture – especially its embracing, protective, circular gestures – a therapeutically compensating role.

How does all this translate into architecture?

I have tried to build these qualities into a Steiner kindergarten. For many children, kindergarten is their first consistent social experience outside home. A regular part of every school-day, therefore, includes society-building games. As circles encourage sociability, many are 'ring-games'. To further support socializing, the classrooms are circular, centrally focused by conical ceilings and flooring pattern. As circles are unambiguous, hence lifeless, shapes, however, they're more hinted at than completely *defined*. Circles have no corners; but corners, like behind-the-sofa and under-the-table spaces, are the places children are drawn to for individual and small-group imaginative play. The plan of each room, therefore, is a sort of circle-with-corners. These 'corners' are in the form of soft-cornered play alcoves, some below floor level, as 'under-the-tables'.

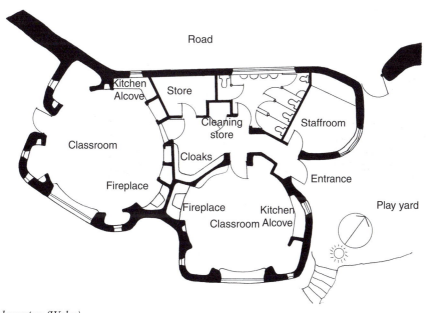

Kindergarten (Wales)

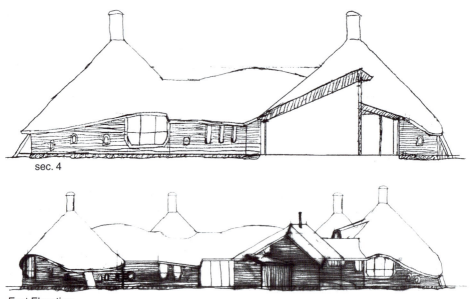

sec. 4

East Elevation

Kindergarten (USA)

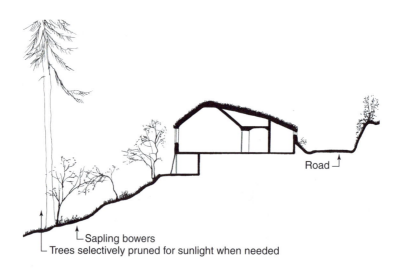

Road

Sapling bowers
Trees selectively pruned for sunlight when needed

Kindergarten building shields child-realm

Tiny windows – each a different coloured glass – give each alcove its own distinct mood. Some alcoves have several differently coloured windows. The resulting colour interplay changes throughout the day with sun direction and strength. Major windows are clear, but as walls and ceilings are lazured, the mood is set by coloured *light*. The colour is pink, making classrooms feel secure, calm and warm – activity-inducing in a gentle, dreamy way.

Amongst excessively free curves, children might never 'come to earth'. To stabilize this, therefore, all curves have an underlying firmness. Some are geometric – classroom-circle arcs; some – constructed from straight lines (literally, with concrete blocks or plasterboard sheet) – embody straightness within curvilinearity; and some, 'sculpted' in wall-plaster, are generated by invisible form-giving forces – gravity, thrust and latent movement. Similar pressures are forming children's bodies and souls. As straight lines would be dead, many are faintly curved; others are enlivened by texture. All, therefore, contain hints of the life-enhancing qualities of curves.

Externally, the building is rooted durably into the ground, walls flaring at their base and ground surfaces sweeping up to it. To anchor it into place, the building grows seamlessly out of the boundary hedge-bank at the point it turns a corner. Both literally and metaphorically, this raises nature into the human sphere. Building and hedge-bank also shield the 'child-world' magic grove from occasional traffic disruptions.

Being turf-roofed, the building risked appearing camouflaged, self-effacing. Exterior walls are, therefore, earthen-red lime-render, not overly concealed by climbing plants. Nor is 'gnomey-ness' an appropriate lesson. Children shouldn't be *ashamed* of being human, but enjoy *harmony* with nature. Interiors, therefore, are well – but enchantingly – daylit, with ceiling uplift to counter any subterranean-feeling. Both inside and out, building and garden seek to feel as magical and as full of reverent wonder as an ancient fairy tale.

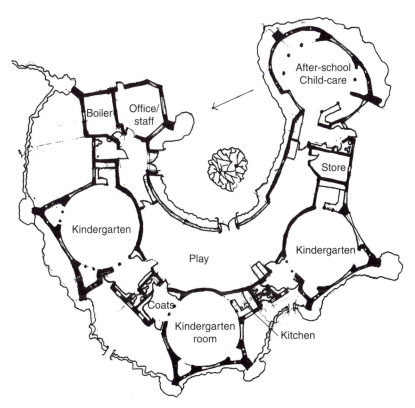

Mid-childhood

Around their seventh year, children start to change their teeth. With every cell in the body by now renewed, building up the body requires much less life-energy; there's enough to spare for the demands of education. Becoming aware of opposites – such as fair and unfair, and us and them – children instinctively begin to develop balance and rhythmical abilities – commonly manifest as skipping, singing, rhymes and rhythm games. Harmony between extremes and balance in architectural surroundings support this striving towards inner balance. So does bringing contrasting experiences – such as outside–inside, dark–light or constricted–spacious – and 'events' – such as windows, doors and cupboards – into unifying relationship by rhythmical (but not repetitive) relationships.

Again, like flowers, children grow into the light. They increasingly need sunlight until, as teenagers, they start to sunbathe. For increased daylight and more open classroom mood, they need bigger windows. To avoid distraction, however, views still need to stay above human-activity level.

As the need for security declines, children increasingly enjoy *challenging* play. By eleven years, climbing frames mean: 'Look what I'm *going* to do!' Then, sitting atop them: 'Look what I *have* done!' Their curiosity horizons also opening, they want to see how things work, how they stand up. This means clearer, firmer spaces with upwardly posture-inductive gestures, ceilings rising with age. Rooms need progressively firmer, clearer, spatial organization and greater distinction (albeit subtle) between walls and ceiling – their conversation less melting, more 'audible'. Likewise, facets are more awakening, 'decisive', than curves.

Upward-inductive building gesture

Like kindergartens, primary schools also need to feel homely. Some 1960s village schools even had – along with study alcoves, workshops, kitchens and library – 'living-rooms' with rocking chair, window-seat and fireplace, and curtained-off bedroom alcoves – with beds, bedside-drawers, mirrors and shelves.[28]

But aren't schools for work? Shouldn't they perhaps look like offices? Many offices are grid-planned, glass-walled rectangles – good for thought- and product-organizing. All are well lit. But 'illumined', organized, thought – the opposite of what kindergartens need – needs only gradual introduction. Children are still growing *towards* it.

Unlike younger children – whose needs, behaviour and dreamy relationship to the world are still coloured by prenatal experience – children between change of teeth and puberty live very much in the present. For this present to be nourishing, it must *every-where* be so infused with artistic quality, that they experience: 'the world is beautiful'.[29]

What does this mean architecturally?

The world certainly *wasn't* beautiful in a 100-year-old school needing renovation. Our first priority was to make it child-welcoming. Built in the days when children were sub-dued by discipline, there wasn't one window to see out of. To make classrooms less claus-trophobic, we lowered them all. For child-scale, we reduced wall height by interceding sloping planes between walls and ceilings. Sloping lower at the corners, this made rooms more protectively gestured, intimately scaled, while allowing ceilings to rise in the centre for upright stature-induction. This shaping also allowed windows, wall, ceiling and shape-of-space to gently 'converse' with each other – wholly transforming the formerly institutional atmosphere.

Minor extensions left blocked-in windows – good opportunities for niches and alcoves. We re-ren-dered gloss-smooth, hard-plas-tered walls in softer hand-finished textures, and lazure-painted them for levity, light and age-appropri-ate mood. With dormers and roof-windows, we contrived to bring sunlight even into north-facing rooms. 'Journey-spaces' – entry, passages and stairs – now meta-morphose along their length, and everywhere shapes, forms and spaces 'speak to each other' in life-filled, but peaceful, harmony.

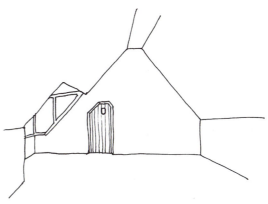

Dormers bringing sunlight into north-facing rooms

A new wing offered the opportunity for *new* forms. A subtle metamorphosis flows rhythmically along this linear extension, distinguishing each classroom's identity. Though twisting with life, spaces are simpler; small and large ones contrasting in breath-ing rhythm. Being for older children, this wing aims for maximum legibility: what rooms are for, how they're constructed and structured, and how the environmental systems work.

Sustainability issues were central to its design. For solar (pre-)heating, a conserva-tory/social-space runs along its southeast face. This is separated from classrooms by a heat-store wall, glazed above door-level, for maximum light. To be fully visible, solar water-heating panels are *below* windowsills. Grey-water processing reed-beds (largely flag iris) are also in prominent view.[30] Both for deference to landscape and warmth retention, the building is dug into the hillside. Though its back grows out of nature, its glazed front is erect, forming a weather-protected courtyard. Its *form*, therefore, speaks of 'harmony with nature' but the *space* it creates is social.

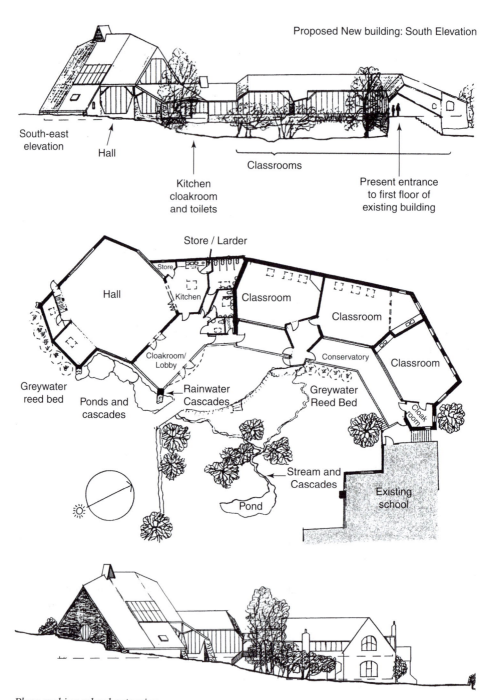

Proposed New building: South Elevation

South-east elevation

Hall

Kitchen cloakroom and toilets

Classrooms

Present entrance to first floor of existing building

Store / Larder

Store

Hall

Kitchen

Classroom

Classroom

Conservatory

Classroom

Cloakroom/ Lobby

Cloak room

Greywater reed bed

Ponds and cascades

Rainwater Cascades

Greywater Reed Bed

Stream and Cascades

Pond

Existing school

Place-making school extension

Teenagers

The ability to direct memory and anticipation to deliberate ends distinguishes humans from animals. Even two-year-olds, by balancing chairs on refuse bins to access forbidden poison cupboards, think logically. But young children can't think *abstractly*, can't use thinking as a means to understand the world. Teenagers can. No longer living in a dream world, but one clearly illumined by thought – they need big windows. Seeking strong – often excessive – experiences to enmesh them in the excitements, imperfections and challenges of life, their interests, criticisms and crusading ideals are now focused *outward* into the world – the world they want to explore, experience, and transform for the better.

Teenagers of 12- to 13-years so enjoy socializing, gossiping indoors, that they often need pushing out. They want privacy behind closed doors; teachers are less keen! At 13 to 15 years, they enjoy sitting in niches. Though feeling private, these need to be visible, allowing staff to informally visit.[31] Despite *wanting* secretive spaces for illicit activities, adolescents *need* outward-looking rooms. Sunlight-flooded social spaces, window-seats with expansive views and study-corner window alcoves serve both awake thought and expanding interests. At this self-critical age, however, window-walls, or even excessively large windows, leave them too vulnerable.

Teenagers want to exercise their intellect, whether in understanding (other people's) car engines, reading whodunits, out-smarting video-games or finding rational reasons to criticize their parents. This criticism, however, is driven by a search for truth; they're trying – like scientists – to find out what the world *is*. Not surprisingly, they find it's less than perfect, not up to their ideals. Though inexperienced enough to easily deceive, any dishonesty they meet breeds cynicism – deeply destructive and often precursor to nihilism. It's vital, therefore, that teenagers experience 'the world is true'.[32]

Honest building materials and construction are part of this. Structural honesty, visible systems (such as pipes and ducts), space clearly matched to function, and well-lit airy spaciousness also help counter ungroundedness. Another aspect is *legibility* – the extent to which teenagers can understand the reasons for things; how and why buildings are constructed as they are. To match their growing consciousness, architectural elements need clearer distinction (though planes still shouldn't collide: this is, after all, a violent age – emotionally and, sometimes, physically). Truth, however, isn't limited to what we can see. It's also about how the invisible systems of buildings enmesh with the wider environment. These *ecological* relationships bring up *moral* issues such as environmentally damaging building design and materials.

Teenagers are inspired by a future yet to come – a world built of hopes and ideals. Solely *physical* functionalism does nothing for these. Uninspiring buildings devalue them; inspiring ones respect and motivate them. Inspiration depends on both design *and* motivating values: aesthetics and ethics. Striking design not underpinned by values feels somehow empty, false. Inartistic design, shaped only by ethics, feels dry, empty of feeling, even moralistic.

Soon teenagers will reach the stage when their feelings, intellect and physical abilities can be brought into a more or less harmonious balance. An environment where the goodness of the crafts, beauty of the arts and truth of the sciences interweave, can nurture this integration. They are now ready to embark on the journey of adulthood, a journey shaped by experience from without, whereas childhood is one shaped by unfolding within.

How can all this work architecturally?

For a Californian high-school, respect was a primary concern. This meant making a place that the students would feel 'theirs': socially focused but with clear class-group identity and expansive views out. Being in a hot climate, building *forms* were shaped by cooling; but *layout* by social cohesion and outlook into the wider world. Like a hill-top village, the classrooms crest a steep slope. Sitting-bay windows give extensive views over both town and countryside. Low-roofed cloakrooms, toilets and storage rooms link these upright spaces into a three-quarter circle. At one end is the café-like, student-administered common-room; at the other, the eurhythmy-room, shared with the lower school. The circle is closed by a tree and shrub windbreak on a mounded bank.

Classrooms are paired into individual buildings, their roofs rising to a high apex to maximize ventilation air-lift. Deeply overhanging eaves ensure summer shade, whilst allowing solar-heating by low-angle winter sun. A snaking shade-roof unifies everything around a 'village green' with a pool in its centre. Recycled rainwater feeds a Flowform here. Its overflow becomes a stream, rippling, cascading and gliding beside the stepped path from the main entrance. Pumped by the constant wind, and sometimes also rain-fed, this water varies in flow according to weather and season.

The building shapes teach about solar winter-heating, summer shading and natural cooling. The wind soughing above, but screened at person level, emphasizes wind-sheltering design. Building construction is clearly legible. Lime-plastered straw-bale walls and round-wood pole structure demonstrate environmentally friendly building.

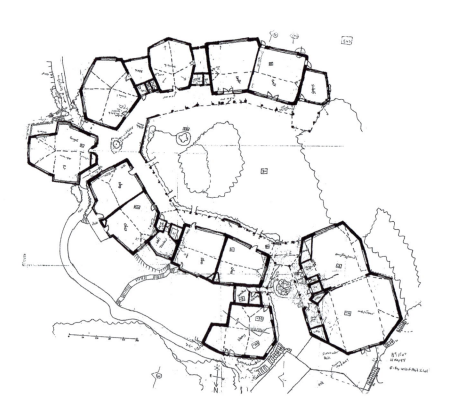

Shape-induced cooling, solar water-heating, rainwater harvesting and recycling are constantly on view – daily environmental lessons. Socially, the layout is about community, student-respect and responsibility. All this encourages task-in-outer-world motivation.

Nourishing children's developmental journey

Such observations of how children progress from birth to adulthood can shape *physical environments* – buildings and outdoor spaces – to support their developmental needs at each stage. Approaching design by listening to developmental needs and unfolding situations treats children as human beings on a journey through life. Quite opposite to the institutional picture: an unruly herd, for which there's an obligation to provide, and which it is necessary to control.

By growing places out of the meeting of *children's needs, place* and the specific *circumstances*, we can create places of soul-harmony that support children's unfolding development and both nourish and inspire them at every stage.

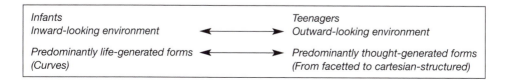

Notes

1 Steiner, Rudolf (1919) *The Foundations of Human Experience*. 1919 Lectures. Anthroposophic Press.
2 Steiner, Rudolf () *Faith, Love and Hope*.
3 Riscke, Elke-Maria (1985) Pedagogical aspects of kindergarten architecture. In Flinspach, Jürgen (1985) *Waldorfkindergärten Bauen*. Unpublished translation by Luborsky, Peter (1988).
4 For more about how geometry and shape-qualities affect us see Day, Christopher (2002) *Spirit & Place*. Architectural Press.
5 Steiner, Rudolf (1919) *The Foundations of Human Experience*. *Ibid*.
6 Davy, John (1975) On coming to our senses. In Davy and Bittleston, eds (1975) *The Golden Blade*. Rudolf Steiner Press.
7 From kindergarten teacher Elvira Rychlak.
8 Lifeways North America.
9 1995 figures, cited by Olds, Anita Rui (2001) *Child Care Design Guide*. McGraw Hill.
10 Male, D. dot@dmale.fsnet.co.uk.[AQ]
11 Venolia, Carol (1988) *Healing Environments*. Celestial Arts.
12 Riscke, Elke-Maria (1985) *ibid*.
13 Olds, Anita Rui (2001) *ibid*.
14 Maria Castella, teacher.
15 Dudek, Mark (2000) *Architecture of Schools*. Architectural Press.
16 Huult, Marie. In Lundahl, Gunilla, ed. (1995) *Hus och rum för små Barn*. Arkus.
17 BBC Radio 4 *Today* Programme, 6 May 2004.
18 Meyerkort, Margaret *Kindergarten architecture and equipment*. Unpublished. Compiled By Elvira Rychlak.
19 Meyerkort, Margaret () *op. cit.*
20 Ministry Of Education (1952) *Moving and Growing*. HMSO.
21 Olds, Anita Rui (2001) *ibid*.
22 Beck,Walter (1985) Thoughts of an architect on the building of a Waldorf kindergarten. In Flinspach, Jürgen (1985) *ibid*.
23 Riscke, Elke-Maria (1985) *ibid*.
24 Neihardt, John *Black Elk Speaks*.
25 Riedel, Martin (1985) Some notes on the effects of architectural forms. In Flinspach, Jürgen (1985) *ibid*.
26 Riscke, Elke-Maria (1985) *ibid*.
27 Beck,Walter (1985) *ibid*.
28 Ministry of Education (1961) *Village Schools*. Ministry of Education Building Bulletin No. 3, June. Cited in Dudek, Mark (2000) *ibid*.
29 Steiner, Rudolf (1996) *The Foundations of Human Experience, ibid.*, and Davy, John (1975) *ibid*.
30 The building form resulted from a consensual design process involving teachers and myself. (This is more fully described in Day, Christopher (2002) *Consensus Design*. Architectural Press; and Day, Christopher (1998) *A Haven For Childhood*. Starborn Books.)
31 Meadowbrook Waldorf School teachers.
32 Davy, John (1975) *ibid*.

PART VI

Sustainability lessons from surroundings

14

Learning to care for the environment

From reverence to conscious care

Is care for the environment natural to humans? Or is it something wholly new to be learnt? Are there foundations to build on? Or must it be 'taught' as a 'foreign language'?

For newborn children, the world is new: everything fascinating and wondrous. To Roszak, 'The ecological unconscious is regenerated, as if it were a gift, in the newborn's enchanted sense of the world'.[1] Is this ingrained by countless generations of living amidst 'nature'? Or is it just romantic sentimentality? Or is it both archetype and *necessary*? Widespread conscious *understanding* of ecological relationships and nature's fragility is only recent. Aesthetic appreciation, and awe of nature, however, are found in *all* cultures in *all* (recorded) times.[2] Jane Jacobs calls these 'habitat-preserving traits', essential to human survival. Had we, over millennia, just taken what we wanted, we wouldn't now be here.[3]

All children seem to be born with a nature-reverential attitude. If this is so essential to being human, no wonder that, as Enns relates, even 'modern' city children view 'nature as a significant part of what they value in their neighbourhood'.[4] Though under daily assault, if this reverential attitude is nurtured, it can mature into a caring-for-environment attitude. If destroyed, cynicism – and in adolescence, nihilism – follow.

Unfortunately, as children grow, they often meet disenchantment. Exaggerated 'virtual' stimulation makes the real world seem dull. How many children ever see sunset, moon or stars? Or regularly hear birdsong? Ugliness and sensory boredom foster environmental alienation. Does this matter? To Hannes Weigert, 'Alienation from nature ... is inevitably linked to an alienation from ourselves. This estrangement from our own humanity is certainly one of the main reasons for the numerous social and political problems besetting our society'.[5] If true, this places major responsibilities on environmental design.

---

reverential wonder → *explorable* → *alterable* → *usable* → *conscious responsibility*

reverential wonder → *disenchantment* → *cynicism* → *nihilism* → *exploitationism*

Which route will we encourage?

Absorbing values

Children learn attitudes and behaviour, not in class but through *everyday* life. Places made, decorated, lit or maintained, with *reverence* emanate these values, conferring beauty. Not *applied* beauty, where artistic ideas originating *elsewhere* are imposed; but *reverent* beauty: appreciation of everything we have been given – by nature, human effort and maturation processes.

Care is partly attitude, partly habit. To establish habits, it's best to start young. Children love to *do* things. They involve their whole being, every ounce of concentration, in adult-modelled activities such as baking, washing-up and making things. They work with *care*, even reverence. As Meyerkort notes, from kneading dough and cutting carrots, to cleaning windows and raking leaves, many domestic, maintenance and garden activities, besides balancing fine and gross motor movements 'carry a social as well as moral component in that *work is love in action'.* Small children experiencing this acquire a foundation for *care* in work and *respect* for environment.[6] These values, though often dormant throughout rebellious adolescence, fertilize ideals that, when their adult identities emerge, they can then *consciously* embrace.

Like kittens, children are eternally curious; 'must' see *everything* going on. Adult's work isn't aimless but clearly 'important' – as absorbing as play is for children. This makes it especially appealing to participate in and imitate. Conventional architectural 'good' practice and children's needs, however, often diverge. Hiding away service areas is to children's loss. Indeed, to urban designers, Lennard and Lennard, 'the isolation of children and youth from the common adult world, their exclusion from the natural learning environments of social life, work and cultural activities, has serious consequences for their emotional and social development'.[7] Once we sanitize activities that *we* don't enjoy, life is no longer whole, colourful – or even true. Cleaning, laundry, maintenance, repair, cooking and much we think utilitarian, unsightly or everyday fascinate small children – to watch and, especially, *do*. Only later do these become chores. Some activities need special equipment, such as small brooms and barrows or anti-scald temperature-controls.[8] Even those too dangerous for children's involvement are better in full view – but out of reach – than hidden away.

Work – or water delight?

Approaching cleaning as *care* demonstrates that places are *valued*, hence welcoming and morale-boosting. But what about teenagers who don't want to do anything? Schools that involve pupils in cleaning, maintenance and repair, experience reduced vandalism and 'accidental' damage. Partly, this is because vandalism means more work for vandals, but more importantly, such involvement breeds a more responsible *attitude*.[9]

Small children don't learn by being told, but by copying. Even by just watching others work, they subconsciously *absorb* both *values* and *how to do* things. This is the basis of all

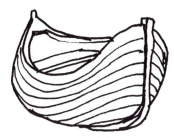

Useful and beautiful

traditional in-family apprenticeships; generation after generation following the same crafts. Absorptive learning develops, in later life, *respect* for work and craftsmanship. Some schools therefore build workshops to

Craft workshops along entry route to school, so children pass them daily

rent out to craftspeople. Children can watch unprepossessing raw materials transformed into things simultaneously useful and beautiful. Interfacing between school and 'real' world, extensive glazing can keep work in daily view without disruptive visits. Watching care and commitment can enthuse, motivate and awaken a sense of mission – vital to counter teenage cynical disillusion, and essential if children are to bring appreciation and responsibility to the world they will soon be shaping.

Notes

1 Roszak, Theodore (2002) *Ecospsychology: Eight Principles.* http://ecopsychology.athabascau.ca/Final/intro.htm

2 In the West, until the end of the Middle Ages, wilderness was terrifyingly *awe*-full.

3 Jacobs, Jane (2000) *The Nature of Economies.* Random House.

4 Enns, Cherie C. (2005) *Places for Children.* University College of the Fraser Valley.

5 Weigert, Hannes (2004) Transforming our Relationship to Nature. (Translated by John Barnes.) Anthroposophy Worldwide No. 8 October 2004.

6 Meyerkort, Margaret Kindergarten architecture and equipment. Unpublished. Compiled by Elvira Rychlak.

7 Lennard, H. and Lennard, S. (2000) *The Forgotten Child.* Gondolier Press. Quoted in Enns, Cherie C. (2005) *ibid.*

8 Anti-scald temperature controls should be routine, but in older buildings, often aren't.

9 So successful was this initiative, pioneered by security guard Martin Giles, that it has been exported from Britain to Sweden, with equal success. *Dagens Nyheter*, 1 September 2001.

CHAPTER 15

Making nature's cycles visible

Cycles and nature

Nature's systems are cyclic: in a finite world, the *only* sustainable systems possible. But that's not how we, and especially children, *experience* the world. We don't live in 'systems' – but in houses. Moreover, our environment has no visible boundaries, so doesn't *feel* finite. Nonetheless, awareness of sustainable cycles is central to understanding environmental cause and effect, and the *whole*-ness of our world. How can children learn this in ways that have meaning for them?

Books can quantify every flow of energy or matter. But numbers are dead abstractions; not something we experience, emotionally engage with, nor easily relate to actions and choices in everyday life. If books can't do this, can *daily life experiences* develop awareness? How? What potential lessons are there in our everyday environment, waiting to be demonstrated?

Solar cycles

The most obvious of all cycles are the sun's: seasons and days.

Parts of buildings – such as columns or corners – acting as sundials, can cast shade onto clock-faces and calendars in paving. The shadows tell the time, but they don't visibly move unless very long – as those cast by the 100-foot (30 m) sundial in the Team Disney Building. Just before sunset, shadows on open ground are also long enough to show movement. Placing sundials so that shadows run downhill can achieve the same effect.

Windows facing different directions show the sun's rotation, orientating us in time and space. Sun-cast traverses the floor with hour and season. Similarly, pools outside south windows move reflected sunlight around walls and ceiling, though as a general rippling glow without hard edges. As schools run to timetables, sun position is predictable for every timetabled activity.

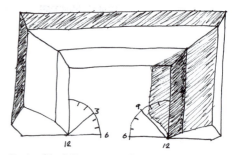

Parts of buildings as sundials

Careful orientation can arrange sun in play-yards, classrooms, entries, arrival-paths and after-school play corners *at the required times*. For this, it's rarely necessary to fell trees; carefully targeted pruning often suffices.

Porch as sundial

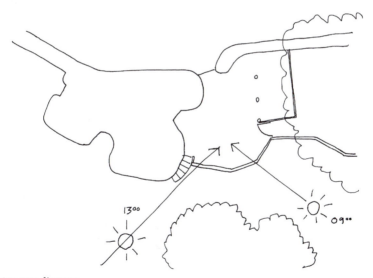

Kindergarten sun diagram

Seasonal cycles

Living principally indoors, seasonal extremes are obvious, but not their cyclic continuum. Evergreen trees and mown grass change little with the seasons. Naked deciduous trees, on the other hand, mark the onset of winter; snowdrops, the year's upturning. Spring unfolds with flower-colour progression.[1] Deciduous vegetation outside windows enhances seasonal colour-mood changes. Young leaves, luminous yellow-green, amplify the joy of spring; heavy green ones cool harsh summer glare; crisp gold, they redeem autumn's darkening days; then finally, thin twigs let open sky maximize winter's scant light. Indoors, seasonal decoration and weekly changing nature-corners parallel these mood transitions, anchoring children into the cycles of life, death and rebirth, outer activity and inner thought. As teacher Carol Petrash notes, 'Young children thrive on rhythm – not the rigid holding to a timetable, but the rhythmic flow of one thing into another. It gives them a sense of security and well-being to know that as it was, it shall be again. For many children today, a connection to nature and the passing of the seasons is one of the few constants in their lives'.[2] To Green, experiencing the routines of day and week and cycles of the year develops a sense of process wholeness. This he regards as crucial to counter attention deficit. Otherwise, 'malnutrition of this sense leads to a sort of nervous activity ... lots of information about bits and pieces, but no sense for the whole process'.[3]

The seasons flow between warm, cosy, socially focal indoors and light, airy, spacious and restful outdoors

Nature's seasonal cycles teach us there's always something to *look forward to*. They show how life hides in the winter earth, then emerges into the visible; how it metamorphoses, moving up trees and flowers then descending – as seeds – for burial in the earth, before bursting forth again. Gathering seeds, even from (uncooked) food left-overs, and planting them, lets us participate in this cycle. The cyclic progression of the seasons reminds us that life follows death as surely as death does life.

The nutrient cycle

Where does food come from? Where does it go to? Why isn't the world buried in sewage?

Food isn't static. Nutrients *flow*; they continually cycle through living and lifeless things. But abstract knowledge – food-cycles on the blackboard – has nothing to do with the world as *experienced*. Children learn one thing in school: another – at supermarket or burger-bar – in life.

Half the nutrient *cycle* is about how the earth feeds us – and what our food costs it. Typically, every calorie eaten takes ten to produce and deliver.[4] This is mostly transport: in Britain, it accounts for 40 per cent of all truck traffic,[5] costing £8 billion (shoppers driving to supermarkets adds another £1 billion[6]). This raises issues such as food-miles, local food and local shops.[7] Science forecasts that soon anything can be grown anywhere, but genetic modification brings serious corporate control, cross-pollination and health worries.

The other half-cycle is about how we feed the earth. Chemical fertilizers are polluting and energy-expensive to manufacture, and weaken plants and soil-life. They're neither sustainable nor healthy. By contrast, composting turns garden, food and animal waste into rich, dark, crumbly soil. Composting isn't hard to do. The micro-organisms who do all the work just need the right food and conditions. Moisture is essential. Composting is an aerobic process. Without air, damp organic waste putrefies – a slow, smelly and pathogenic breakdown. Fibrous matter ensures aeration. Paper, straw, wood-chips and plant-stems are too carbon-rich on their own, so need nitrogenous matter, such as coffee-grounds, leguminous plants or urine to optimize the carbon:nitrogen ratio.[8] Sewage contains both urine (sterile and useful) and faeces (pathogen-rich – a serious health hazard). Separation at source makes both easier to process – good for compost, and also for consciousness. Separating toilets, besides saving water and recycling nutrient, have, therefore, an important educational role. Are these acceptable in schools? In Sweden they've been used in schools and apartment blocks since the early 1990s.[9]

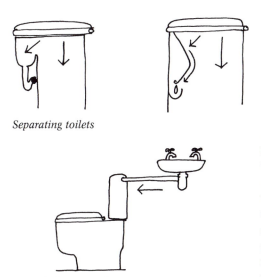

Separating toilets

Re-cycled water toilet

Indoor composting means special compost chambers or – much more simply, worms. Vermiculture (worm composting) is straightforward: just add (perforated) trays of vegetable waste on top of those the worms are already working on, and keep warm and moist. Being the fastest compost method – and in constant view – this technique gives the clearest lesson. But it needs thermal and moisture care – also during holidays. Though easy, this is rarely guaranteed at home, so it's less of a 'take-home technology' than conventional composting.

Outdoor composting is both simple and robust. Just add layers of garden and food waste (and manure *or* lime, if available – but not *mixed*[10]) until the heap is large enough or bin full, then leave – usually for a year. This means two – or preferably three – heaps: one growing as more is added to it, one shrinking as it decomposes; and one matured from which compost can be taken.

Something mysterious happens deep inside compost heaps. But this needn't be permanently out of sight. A 'compost window' – with insulating shutters to maintain middle-heap temperature – can show worms and other creatures at work.[11] (This is simple in theory: a

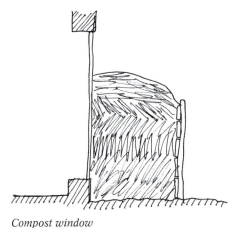

Compost window

window. But as decomposition makes an aggressive environment, it needs careful choice of materials and design.) Decomposition also produces heat. Piles of cut grass sometimes catch fire – dramatic but wasteful and unsafe! The ratio of heat-generating volume (x^3 for a cubic heap) to heat-dissipating surface area ($5x^2$) means the larger the heap, the hotter it gets. Compost piles can even be heat radiators – free heat and a free lesson on bio-energy.[12] Turning compost moves the cool outside to warm inside – both stifling weeds growing on outside faces and ensuring even decomposition.

For hygiene, tidiness, low attention requirements and speed of decomposition, compost boxes, cages and bins are best for moderate volumes. Wire-mesh cages allow hens to scratch for worms and pickings, mixing and manuring in the process. Unlike weeds and raw vegetables, cooked food and meat attracts rats when composted, so rodent-proof

Compost-heated radiator

bins or a distant location are needed. But, whether in heaps, cages or bins, piles of rotting food are a health, smell and visual disaster, so someone must keep them tidy, also arrange teams for turning and carting to the garden. Devon Steiner School rotates these responsibilities amongst 14-year-olds. At Summerfield, students compost on the farm, under the groundkeeper's supervision.

Not all food waste need be composted. Chickens like leaves, peelings and fruit. No bird, however, should ever eat dough – as they can't pass wind, flatulence can kill them. Poultry like – but, because of disease risk, *mustn't* get – meat or cooked food. The more things that eat waste on its decomposition journey, the more nutrition is locally extracted and the more cycles within cycles. This means a longer – so more stable and complete – total cycle.

Sewage

Concentrated and in the wrong place, excrement is pollution, but recycling it is essential to the life of nature. Conventional sewage works do this but are ugly and smelly, so best out of sight. This means they're usually out of mind. *Visible* treatment systems, such as reed-beds, can make attractive – and odour-free – water gardens. One (for a college) was even featured in a TV garden programme![13] Fish in downstream ponds make the nutritional cycle clear – although it's not a good idea to eat them! Even in

Sweden – where cold winters stifle biological action – a number of schools use reed-bed and lagoon sewage treatment.[14]

Grey-water has only one-tenth the pollution content of *treated* sewage effluent as released to rivers.[15] This makes it much easier to deal with. Even improvised plumbing alterations can separate this. Wash-basin water can go directly to irrigation. Kitchen-sink water needs de-greasing by filter – as does run-off from roads and parking. It can then flow through a progression of plant root zones to remove phosphates and nitrates. This bio-engineering sequence needn't be mechanistically laid out but can be contoured, with roots compartmented to prevent dominant species taking over, but plants visually interwoven above ground. (Many, like flag iris, are attractive flowers.) The treated efflu-ent (if necessary, ultraviolet-sterilized) is clean enough for toilet flushing. Unlike rain, which varies with season, grey-water volume is more or less constant. Since volume reflects occupancy, there's no risk of toilet cisterns running dry. As water is already a significant (and constantly rising) cost for schools – and, with climate-change, increas-ingly limited – there are economic and convenience benefits besides the obvious ecolog-ical and educational ones.[16]

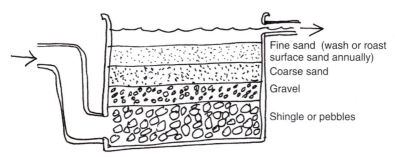

Fine sand (wash or roast surface sand annually)

Coarse sand

Gravel

Shingle or pebbles

Filter to clean microbiological pollution[17]

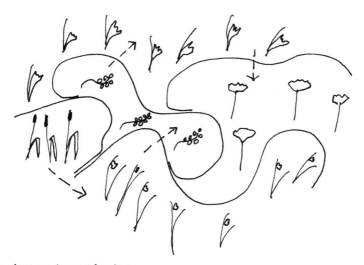

Interwoven plant species root-barriers

The water cycle

All life depends on water. Like nutrients, water constantly flows through every living thing. It also cycles through sky, earth, rivers and oceans. Though gravity, capilliarity, osmosis and biochemistry play their part, this hydrological cycle is primarily driven by the sun. In nature, evaporation lifts water from the seas, to condense as clouds. Rain falls on earth, collects as streams, which then replenish the sea. To simulate this cycle, we can use pumps instead of evaporation, header tanks to represent clouds and ponds (or cisterns) for the sea.

What's the best way to pump water? Electric pumps are easiest and don't use much energy. But why use any? And what educational value do they have? Children better understand where water comes from, if *they* are the ones who pump it – especially if it's fun. (There are also less conscious fun-pumps such as the South African carousels, which pump as children push them round.[18]) As in nature's hydrological cycle, the sun can power pumps, but photovoltaic panels reveal no *visible* reason why water should move. Wind pumps, however, show how wind energy (itself largely sun-powered) lifts it. Unlike electric pumps, wind pumps are low speed, simple mechanical devices – no motors, electricity or batteries to go wrong. For pumping water, wind *generators* are technological (and cost) overkill. Why use expensive, high-speed, high-maintenance, electro-mechanical devices to do a low-speed, low-maintenance, mechanical job? Wind-pumps, however, have one disadvantage. Water collects at the bottom of things, making the lowest land best for pools, and therefore pumps. Unfortunately, this is usually the most wind-sheltered.

Wind pumps don't stop when header tanks are full, but pump whenever there's wind. Overflow, therefore, is inevitable – but this can return to source ponds as a tiny stream. When it rains, this same stream-bed can also collect run-off.[19] Not only are open channels cheaper than underground pipes, but they're more educational, fun and easily maintained. Shallowly dished paving is even cheaper. This lets water pencil, trickle, sheet or gush according to weather.

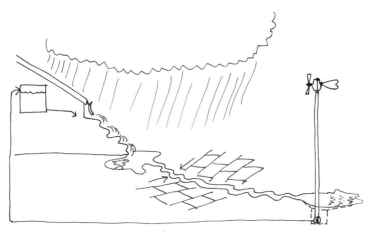

Rainwater to shallow rill, stream and cascades, then to pool. Wind pump to header tank, to Flowform, to the same stream. Rain gives lots of water down the stream, wind gives some. In fine weather, there's still a trickle

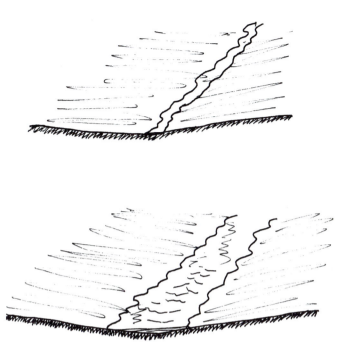

Shallow paving: variable water widths

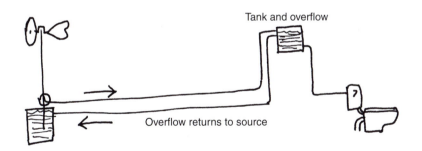

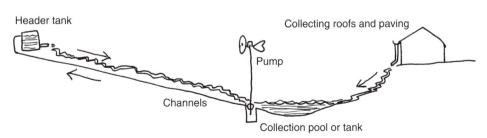

Wind pump systems

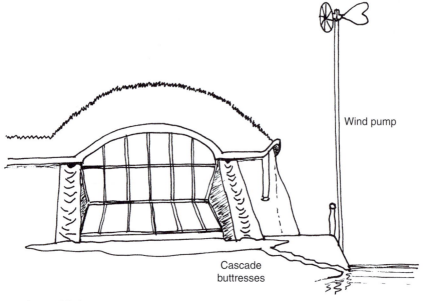

Water cycle at a kindergarten

Cycles and life

These are cyclic systems. They're simple to set up and maintain. Some are fun to play in; others, attractive. None are out of sight. They're all systems children can *experience*.

Air and warmth-energy also cycle through the whole world, shaping weather and climate – but invisibly. These, therefore, are more easily experienced as *elements*. The most elusive of all cycles is life. Life feeds off life. Also each individual life is cyclic: from 'somewhere' pre-birth to 'somewhere' post-death. Children aren't ready to deal with this intellectually. Unable to relate verbal description to their limited life-experience, how could they understand? Nature's cycles, however, provide rich analogies. By involving their interest in cycle-streams, profound universal meanings can resonate in their being.

Notes

1 Where I live, the sequence is white, yellow, blue, pink, white.
2 Petrash, Carol (2005) Creating a Seasonal Garden: Bringing Nature Inside. *Messenger, the Waldorf School of Mendocino County*, 16 November.
3 Green, Jeff (2006) Sensing the world and ourselves. *New View*, Autumn.
4 Lecture at Eco-fair, Wales, July 2005.
5 BBC Radio 4, *Today* Programme; 15 July (2005).
6 BBC Radio 4, *Farming Today*, 4 March (2005).
7 In Europe, even in 1995, these averaged 2200 miles. (Guépin, Mathias (1995) Community supported agriculture. *News from the Goetheanum* 16 (3), May/June.)
8 But it's wise to keep human urine off vegetables!

9 As pioneered by Luleå University, which has a chair of recycling. Urine is stored underground (at 4°C) for sale to farmers. It's diluted ten times before spraying on fields.

10 But caution: even ground limestone is bad for lungs and eyes! Hydrated lime is aggressively alkaline; quicklime downright dangerous.

11 As composting is a digestion process – this window must be rot- and corrosion-proof.

12 Mollison, Bill *Permaculture: a Designer's Manual.*

13 The six-lagoon wetland sewage system at Rudolf Steinerseminariet in Järna, Sweden.

14 As at Björko Friskolan, Linköping, Sweden, described in Fenoughty, Susan (1997) *The garden classroom.* Unpublished Churchill Fellowship report.

15 As at Summerfield Waldorf School, it's even done in California – notorious for rigid public health officials.

16 *Good Stewardship: National Audit Office Examination of Value for Money at Grant Maintained Schools 1995–96.* Report by the Controller and Auditor General, HMSO (HC 697).

17 Mollison, Bill *Permaculture: a Designer's Manual.*

18 BBC World Service, *Making a Change.* 23 January (2005).

19 As did landscape architect Gareth Lewis at Svenhogskolan, Sweden, described in Fenoughty, Susan (1997) *ibid.*

CHAPTER 16

Living with the elements

The elements and us

Are the four elements just convenient labels? Or do they mean something to children? What children aren't irresistibly drawn to sand, water and fire? Or don't enjoy balloons, streamers and kites? The classic children's holiday is elementally rich: sun, sea, sand and open air. The 1930s social reformer Alva Myrdal considered experience of the elements a primary need for children. She advocated that all schools provide access to wind, water, earth and fire.[1] But is this any more than a 'nice' idea?

Elemental *states* – solid, liquid and gaseous, and their quickening by energy – describe every *physical* thing. (Add *life* – a Vedic element – and they describe *everything* in the world.) They also describe the human being. Physically, we have solid bodies, but are about two-thirds water;[2] we have lungs full of air, and are warm-blooded. Temperamentally, we can be grave, persistent, flighty or dynamic; different balances profiling each unique person. These parallel nature's elements: gravity-bound, ever-flowing, freely mobile and flaming. The elements are, therefore, fundamental constituents of our world – and of us ourselves. Experiencing them reconnects us with our archetypal roots, nourishing us. Their absence starves the soul.

The elements, one by one

What *are* the elements? How can we get to know them? At how many levels can we connect with them?

How different are their characters: earth – its forms condensed, crystallized, fragmented or moulded – is about stability. Water – directionally flowing, uniting – is about fluid movement. Air expands, blows, audibly vibrates. Warmth energizes, transforms, radiates outwards but socially focuses. We also meet them differently: earth – solid matter – obstructs our free movement; it confronts us. Water – fluid – is shaped by its surroundings. Air, we are always surrounded by, impossible to separate ourselves from.[3] Fire exists only in transformative activity; it's a *process*, though we experience it as a (substance-less) 'thing' – almost a living being.

But earth is more than just solid lumps. It's also hardness and texture; sand heaps and clay, their forms established by gravity and adhesion. Water isn't just something to splash in; we can lose our whole being in its many songs, movements and moods. Air, fresh or stale to breathe, also bears scent and sound messages impossible to escape from. Warmth brings sociability and cosiness.

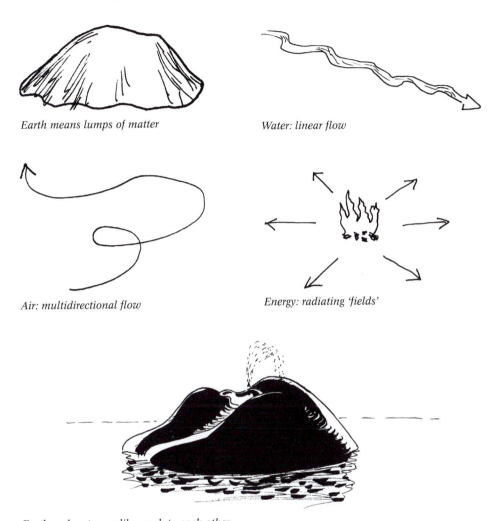

Earth means lumps of matter

Water: linear flow

Air: multidirectional flow

Energy: radiating 'fields'

Earth and water readily speak to each other

What is the distinct *essence* of each element? How can we meet, become aware of, enjoy and work with these?

Earth

Earth is solid, heavy and fixed. 'Made' a long time ago, it feels old. In its visual texture and crystalline structure is imprinted its creation-biography. Crystals fascinate children. Rocks of all sizes attract them. They're drawn to climb on boulders and cliffs; small stones inspire them to build; pebbles, they collect. But are they interested in geological

Gnome-world tree-roots

education? For this, Hamburg Botanical Gardens has a 'stone garden': different rock types arranged like a Japanese meditation garden.[4] For children, the earth-bound layer of rocks, roots and tree-trunks is a fitting world for gnomes, trolls and earth-beings. Quite different from leafy tree-tops where semi-etherealized matter brushes air – the place for fairies.

Earth is the realm of *form*. Anything children need to know about form and substance depends on experiencing solid materials. They love to make things: castles, caves, pies, cakes, animals, people, etc. Malleable materials, such as sand, mud, clay, wax, even snow, soap and bread, readily lend themselves to this. Through

mud-slump, sand-collapse, dry-cracking, wet-dissolving and erosion, they encounter physical properties such as durability, malleability, self-mobility and water-solubility. Making things is an enthusiasm-generating vehicle for many kinds of learning.[5]

Sand encourages exploratory play

Of all form-making materials, sand is the most accessible for children. Beyond being irresistible fun, sand-play brings multiple educational benefits. It has been found to help language, mathematical, creative and social skills, as well as encouraging scientific experimentation.[6] What does it need? What sand and where? Sand characteristics and price tend to vary from quarry to quarry. Many sands stain

hands and clothes. (Children don't mind, but some parents do.) Silver sand doesn't, but is expensive. Paving grade is normally cheapest. Indoors, as children tend to sit in sand-boxes, filling their clothes, sand-tables keep everything cleaner. Outdoors, lorry-load *mounds* are cheapest, but sand-*pits* in paved yards enable overflow to be swept back in, so are less messy.[7] Mats and buckets by doors to sand-heaps encourage emptying out

Cat-proof fence

of shoes before coming in.[8] Where should outdoor sandpits be located? Although sand drains well, it does so slowly, so stays drier on well-drained ground. Sand play is so engrossing that children easily get chilled. Cold-climate sandpits therefore need to be in sunny, wind-sheltered, places.[9] Also the sunlight effectively sterilizes the sand.[10] Cats, however, regard it as ideal for toilet use, so – unless distant from homes – cat-proof fencing or covers are necessary for hygiene. (Fences above 5 foot (1.5 m) high, topped with floppy wire-netting overhanging the cat-side, keep them out.[11] These also keep cats from birds-nests; and even deter burglars – not that many steal sand.)

What about mud? For making things, this even surpasses sand. As a sculpture medium, clay is more form-responsive than play dough. Hand-dug clay doesn't make only pottery. With cob, wattle-and-daub, adobe or other techniques, children can build.[12] At Nibble School, Järna, Sweden, pupils actually built clay school buildings.[13]

Children are natural builders. From babyhood on, they balance piles of things (espe-

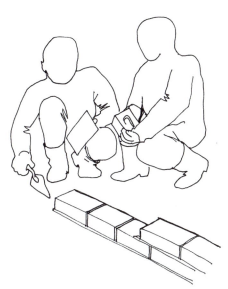

Nant-y-Cwm School: children helping build the kindergarten

cially fragile ones), then make towers, caves and 'houses'. In the kitchen, they love to make bread animals or ginger-biscuit houses (glued with dangerously hot melted sugar). Outdoors, left to their own devices, children use all manner of materials to build with. 'Creative playgrounds' utilize urban detritus such as tyres, cable-spools, poles and piping.[14] But they can also build in school. In Denmark, state primary classes design and build buildings.[15] All Steiner schools give five-week building lessons for 10-year-olds. (When 16 years of age they revisit building; but now as architecture.) Building lessons on 'real' projects mean free, super-keen labour. Helping build a kindergarten, Nant-y-Cwm Steiner School children laid bricks with such enthusiasm I could barely keep their wall vertical![16] For children, even humble projects such as sandpit walls or outdoor bread-ovens, are unforgettable fun. Through building, children directly experience form and space. They learn about structure, materials, tools, construction principles and techniques – and, without realizing it, social cooperation, time-sequence organization and how to use their bodies. Building isn't just for builders – it's fun for all children.

Children build all sorts of buildings – different imaginations, materials, construction techniques and jointing give widely differing forms. But what sort of buildings should surround them? Culture, climate, context and, of course, age suggest the elemental bias: should buildings be earthy, fluid, airy or energetically dynamic? Or what combination and balance of these qualities?

One aspect of earth is that it's rooting, anchoring. It doesn't easily move, like water and air; nor finish, like fire. You know were you are with 'solid earth'. Earth is about stability, durability. Stone endures. Stone buildings more easily feel ageless than brick, stucco or wooden ones. Rocky landscapes speak of this time-resistant strength. Earth-sourced building materials, from stone and brick to rammed earth, make earth-based demands on construction and form. Masonry arches are held together by gravity. Heavy, flared bases root buildings into ground. Archetypally, gravity-bonded structure, solidity and reliability are characteristics of earth-element buildings. These qualities are all about *security.* This is a major need for small children. Teenagers need the opposite: airy, spacious, confinement-free buildings – ones that don't pin their utopian idealism down, but give it wings.

Water

While earth is about changelessness, water is about movement – life. But, like life, water's movement isn't simple. It exhibits flows, counter-flows, rhythms, energy transfers, inversions and evolutions. Educationally, as life is constantly mobile, sensitivity to fluid movement helps us understand it. Water-play is the first step. Children love this – moving water, or things or themselves, in it. (Is it true we evolved from fish?) Because the constantly reshaping form of water mirrors their fluid, ever-alive thought processes, it's important for children's healthy development.

Sociable paddling

Small children can spend hours scrubbing, then hosing outdoor steps in cascades of bubbly water, selling soap-foam ice-cream (a by-product from washing clothes – also fun), damming streams and throwing in stones, drawing ripples with fingers, or even just stamping in puddles. Simple equipment, such as large, shallow, low sinks, indoor water-trays, outdoor taps and hoses, and ground sufficiently uneven to hold puddles, bring great pleasure.

The *quality* of water is important to whether or not we appreciate it. Dirty water is foul. Clean, hygienic, water has

Manipulating nature

Making dams

high amenity value. But this depends on a healthy eco-system. For ponds, natural swimming pools provide a good model. (In Austria, Germany, and Switzerland, there are more than 1000.[17]) These use shallow 'regeneration zones': 12 inches (300 mm) of shingle,[18] planted with indigenous bog, marsh, waterside, submerged and floating plants in root-separated 'plant pockets'. Water is drawn down through this, then pumped back to the pool.[19] As there's no topsoil, the plants draw nourishment solely from decomposing matter, bacteria and pollution. They convert this to biomass which, cropped each autumn, can be composted for use on land.[20]

Algae are a common problem. Most are just unsightly, but some blue-green species are toxic to vertebrates. Warmth accelerates algal growth, so they can grow fast, take over – then die. The ensuing mass decomposition robs water of oxygen, killing aquatic animals. Mostly, algae get nitrogen from farm fertilizer and manure run-off, but possibly also from air.[21] Algaecides – usually copper compounds – both poison aquatic eco-systems and risk sudden additional toxin release when the algae die. Fortunately, zooplankton, enzymes, carp and other fish eat algae. (In swimming pools, however, fish aren't welcome. They attract water-fowl, whose droppings pollute and nitrogenate the water – and, worse, herons, whose stabbing beaks can damage liners.[22]) Barley straw reduces algae; reasons are unknown, but possibly its cellulose balances nitrogen. The more self-correcting are biological systems, the more likely are they to *work*, the less effort to maintain – and the more true they ring.

You can move *things* in ponds, but moving *water* allows you to dam, put in water-wheels and race boats. Cascades, rills, mini-waterfalls, fountains and sprays, give multi-farious play opportunities. Even improvised sluices change how water moves. 'Flowform' water's endlessly inverting gentle spirals and lemniscates can mesmerize children (and adults) for long periods. Indoors or out, just watching and absorbing water movements, textures and songs can be calming and healing.

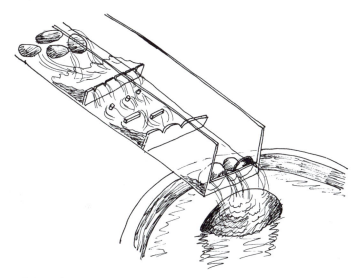

Water texture slides indoors

For older pupils, water offers lots to study. The sounds, colour, movement, viscosity, transport characteristics and droplet size of flowing water change with temperature.[23] From how it responds to obstructions, children learn about standing-waves, laminar-flow, differential speed, back-eddies and water-flow patterns. Straight-line flow isn't natural to water. Curvilinear movements are. Water trickled down a smooth inclined surface starts straight, but within seconds, starts to develop meanders. As water exhibits molecular memory, its movement and vibrational (electrochemical) biographies become imprinted.[24] (Homeopathy is based on this.) These affect its influences on life. As well as pollution, geometric confines reduce its life-supporting attributes. Fewer fish, for instance, live in canalized rivers and pollution self-cleans more slowly than in naturally shaped ones. So strong is this propensity for living movement that fluids even spiral along tubes. The spirally inverting currents of natural streams undercut alternate banks and transport and deposit stones and silt, creating many diverse habitats for flora and fauna. Beyond practical applications such as non-destructive gravel mining, river maintenance and game fishing, understanding water flow also aids fluid thinking.

Few schools, however, have their own streams – but they're easy to make, using rainwater or treated grey-water. Amenity streams are simple, but at Royston High School, pupils built one specifically to demonstrate water flow characteristics.[25] Shape, streambed and flow-speed affect water's song. Judiciously placed stones and cascade lip notches can 'tune' water features, even streams. Artificial streams, however, tend to disappear into artificially hollow-sounding chambers. Synthetic (hence everlasting!) rags here can dampen this sound.

Water-flow is governed by three basic rules: it always flows downhill; anything that can block, probably will; (almost) anything meant to hold water, will leak. This means levels are critical to where and whether water flows, shallow gradient streams are sure to clog, and ground downhill from ponds is usually damp. Circumventing these rules is technically easy, but invariably brings problems. Also, the water will look 'out-of-place'. These rules, together with sensitivity to water flow patterns, establish the levels, location and design of watercourses and ponds.

Most children, however, see more rain than ponds and streams. Rain is normally depressing. But if we're warm and dry, there's something very secure-feeling about *hearing* it drumming on awnings, skylights or roofs – especially corrugated-iron! Likewise, coloured lights reflected off wet paving induce an inner glow to redeem dark-evening gloom. In such ways, rain ceases to be miserable, but becomes heart-warming. It can also be exciting. Sheeting off unguttered roofs or shooting from gargoyles, it's dramatic. It can run down chains, twirl inside transparent rainwater pipes (ensure access to clean out slime!), course down buttress-cascades or riven slate slabs, then flow in streamlets,

Coloured lights reflected off wet paving

Rainwater buttresses

textured or ribbed for ripples, swirls, standing wavelets and musical sounds. Carefully located, these can also reflect lighted windows for dull-weather benefit.

By their example, rigid forms set a context for rigid thinking. Mobile, living forms induce mobile, living thinking. But this isn't only about water to play in. Watery *qualities* in children's daily environment also do so. As, from root to leaf-tip, all plants are conduits of water, their forms are concretizations of water flow. Vegetation, therefore, brings watery qualities to otherwise dry, hard, mineral buildings – even box-conceived, box-thought-inducing

Riven slab

ones. Buildings also – through mobile forms, rhythmic undulations, accelerating-decelerating curves and shapes that invert from concave to convex – can exhibit water-like fluidity and life: simultaneously active and gentle.

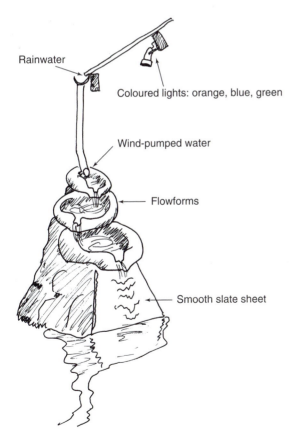

Rainwater

Coloured lights: orange, blue, green

Wind-pumped water

Flowforms

Smooth slate sheet

Rain-boosted flowforms

Water's moods resonate with our own. It responds to everything we do to it. Our playing with water liberates its many movements, forms and sounds. From water-sculptures to rainwater-streams, buildings and landscaping give manifold opportunities for *it* to play around us. Water is also often tranquil – but rivers, even lakes, depend on renewal-water constantly flowing through them – both horizontally and vertically. This fills their tranquillity with life. Whether in water-design, soft landscape or architectural form, this non-assertive balance between dynamic mobility and restful tranquillity, the life-filled active and the quietly eternal, can only be found by entering into the *spirit* of wateriness.

Air

Air is so much around us, we rarely notice it. We can smell it, feel its movement, but air itself is wholly invisible. We do, however, see its *effects*, and hear its *interactions* with solid material.

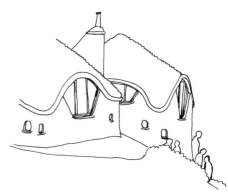

Rainy day entrance   *Fluid building forms*

Wind-shriek through ventilation grills, melodically fluting tubular steel gates, banging doors and humming wires are rarely intended, but the notes, loudness, rhythms, harmonies or discordances of wind-chimes and Aeolian harps describe weather *mood* as clearly as do cowbells the state of a herd; lulling or jangling tones communicate contentment or ill-ease. Insect-buzz, birdsong, leaf rustle, wind sough, murmur, hiss, roar or shriek lets us 'read' weather with eyes shut. Its mood enters our unconscious. Visually, streamers and flags deliberately celebrate air-movement. (Traditionally, these were extended sense-organs for sailors.) Similarly, curtains, awnings and trees 'converse' with air. Their movements, sounds and lapping shadows make breeze visible and audible, adding psychological respite to physical cooling.

Through sound and scent, air is *the* medium of communication – particularly of mood. We breathe air's *qualities* into our souls: long before recognizing any chemical effect, polluted air *feels* depressing and 'fresh' air invigorating. Open windows invite in a spirit of *freshness*. They connect us to the world outside, to *life*. Outdoor sounds, including those of human activity, vary throughout day and year, locating us in time. The scents of flowers, earth, mown grass, damp leaves, frost and snow emphasize season. The first balmy smell of spring, reinforced by spring birdsong is irresistibly intoxicating. Windows let all this in. Ducted air can't; it has no interest in *delight*.

Despite invisibility, air can be powerful. Increasingly extreme weather puts new emphasis on wind-shedding building form and wind-breaking landscaping. As symbols of appropriate technology, wind generators are almost *de rigeur* for eco-projects. Safety, however, limits schools to small ones. (Kinetic energy is proportional to the square of propeller-tip speed, making big ones dangerous, should anything break.) As badly built wind generators can shake themselves to pieces, can school children make them? Cardinal Hinsley High School pupils did. They made two to power their 'green classroom'. (Like hamster-powered electricity, they also boil kettles by boy-powered bicycle.[26])

As turbulence reduces efficiency, wind generators need height – optimally, 33 feet (10 m) above any obstacle within 330 feet (100 m). Buildings may seem obvious places to mount them, but risks to structure need careful attention. Also, vibration can cause headaches, stress and can even (literally) drive people crazy. As this is a huge potential market, there is much development of low-vibration microgenerators and vibration-insulating mountings.

Nonetheless, great care is needed to avoid transmitting vibration to noise-sensitive areas. Theoretically, roofs can accelerate wind into the propeller zone but most roof-forms make turbulence more likely. How much turbulence? Tethered balloons can show this.[27] Are wind generators too noisy to be near? No. This is a fiction. Roads are many times louder.

Would a wind generator on every school measurably slow global warming? No. But even inefficient wind generators have inspiring demonstration value. Their effect on attitudes should not be underestimated. Attitudes have far greater impact than gadgets.

Flying

As with most things, awareness progresses from play to using, then understanding. Small children enjoy twirling paper 'windmills' and watching bubbles.[28] Older ones fly darts, kites, even Chinese lantern-kites or, spreading their coats wide in gales, 'fly' themselves. Next comes experimenting: how do different-shaped 'air-sculptures' move? Then making instruments such as Aeolian flutes. Controlling sails – on model boats, real ones or sail-powered go-carts – is all about experientially *understanding* air. As we no longer live in a sail-powered age, this may seem outdated knowledge, but it's central to natural cooling – essential to energy conservation. Also, more technically, the future of pollution-affordable aviation depends on utilizing stratified air-currents – just as balloonists do. But beyond any such practical applications, air teaches a vitally important lesson – especially relevant in our material-cause-demanding culture. It unequivocally demonstrates that the world isn't limited to what we see.

Fire

Children love to play with fire; they're natural pyromaniacs. But fire is dangerous. Its drama can be overpoweringly seductive. Are children and fires safe together? Aren't fires needless risks? Children deprived of them, however, are soul-deprived, so increasingly likely to light their own. This magnifies risk many-fold. For safety, therefore, they need to learn to *respect* and *control* fire. But this they can only do through experience.[29]

Apart from annual bonfires and the barrel-fires of adventure playgrounds, however, few children experience open flame. Many cities are smokeless zones. Many buildings are fireplace-less; they're heated by boilers. Industrial boilers are soul-less boxes with bolted-on bits and lots of

Children are natural pyromaniacs

pipes. Even wood-pellet boilers are unattractive and have noisy augers and unsightly lorry-load sized hoppers. These, therefore are usually hidden in cellars or sheds. Out-of-sight, however, means out-of-mind. Boiler-rooms with windows let children look in and perhaps hear their power. Sometimes they can even cart bio-fuel, such as straw, logs or site-produced wood-chips to boiler, and ash to compost heap. Such ways of connecting children to the bio-energy cycle ensure heating is never out-of-thought.

Fireplaces are grossly inefficient heaters, but there's something magically transfixing about open fires; whole stories unfold in flame pictures – children can watch them for hours. Scandinavian and German kindergartens, therefore, commonly seat children around outdoor fire-pits. Some Waldorf kindergartens gather children round stoves for stories. Glass doors, essential for safety, don't deny the sights, sounds and smells of fire. The cosiness of flame-heat is unmatched; similarly, fire-cooked food-appeal, even if

Bread – or pizza – ovens of brick or clay

burnt! Brick or clay outdoor ovens (clay needs rain-protection) are easy to build and safe to operate. (For doors, planks draped in wet sacking usually suffice.) At Summerfield – after growing, mowing, threshing, drying and grinding wheat – children gather and split wood, tend fires, cook and bake bread. This makes the whole process of food preparation comprehensible and accessible. Central to this is the transformation of substance wrought by fire. Fire also transforms things through burning, melting and smelting. At Solgården School, kindergarten children watch older ones firing pottery, blacksmithing, charcoal-making and cooking over open fires. Whether working with, or even just watching this, children learn much.

Transformation is another key life lesson. It teaches that nothing is permanently bound by its composition and form. Moreover, so central to life are combustion–transformation processes, that to not understand them is intellectual – not to mention soul – impoverishment. As architect, Kerstin Thörn points out, 'Learning about oxidization and fire without experiencing fire is like learning about craftwork without making anything'.[30] Even more importantly, fire has deep archetypal roots – involving food, warmth, society and safety. Until recently, you couldn't live without it. Hence its magnetism – especially for children. This makes fire a *soul-necessity*.

The elements and everyday life

Why do we consider some landscapes, cities and buildings beautiful? Is it something to do with elemental power and how elemental qualities converse and interweave?

Why do we feel at home in – or near – some buildings? Is this something to do with archetypal elemental resonances? Is it that materials of, or grown from, the earth help root us into time and place? Is it that mobile forms induce similar eye movements, the fluidity of which enlivens us? Is it that space and light make us feel free as air? Is it that by their feel, texture and colour, materials that warm us in cold climates – or cool us in hot ones – help psycho-thermal balance? Does this mean earth-sourced materials (and perhaps timber)? Organic curvey-wurvy forms? Extensive glazing? Red or blue paint? Not necessarily. Indeed, such formulaic responses would be both dead and context-disregarding. But it does mean we must think very hard when we choose materials, forms, fenestration and colour. Are these elementally nourishing? Or do they counter the mood, temperament-support, associations and messages appropriate to age and circumstance?

The life of nature is woven of solid, liquid, vapour and warmth: the durable, cyclic, ever-moving and energized. Our technology, power and products utilize these elements. Whether natural landscape or built forms, places that respond to, celebrate and *symbiotically* work with the forces of nature, are inevitably ecologically harmonious. These help children feel embedded in, and sustained by, the *processes* of nature.[31]

To live in harmony with nature requires understanding – both scientifically and empathetically – in a whole, multifaceted way, how these work and interweave. Holistic understanding requires 'knowing through feeling'. Cerebral knowledge without feeling-related experience is useless. For small children, this means exploratory and sense-stimulating play; for older ones, background awareness, only semi-conscious; for teenagers, rational understanding. At all stages, from living *in* to knowing *about*, delight always sharpens awareness. Multilevel awareness develops different ways of seeing, feeling, thinking, relating to and doing – of making and using things. Without this, we can only exploit.

This is a primary reason why elemental experience, investigation, play and delight should be part of every child's life.

Age	State	Need
Small children, still in the world of spirit	Building their bodies	Anchoring earth
Mid-childhood	Bursting with barely controllable life-energy	Watery rhythm
Pre- and early teens	Moody and led by feelings	Airy levity
Teenagers	Self-centred unless enthused	Enfiring inspiration

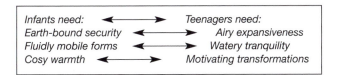

Infants need:		Teenagers need:
Earth-bound security	⟷	Airy expansiveness
Fluidly mobile forms	⟷	Watery tranquility
Cosy warmth	⟷	Motivating transformations

Notes

1 Alva Myrdal, the Swedish social reformer, cited in Lundahl, Gunilla, ed. (1995) *Hus och Rum för Små Barn*. Arkus.

2 Water constitutes 70 per cent of a newborn baby's body, 62 per cent of an adults body; 84 per cent of blood. Vilma, Luule *A Teaching for Survival*.

3 Bockemühl, Jochen (2005) reported in Rohde, D. (2005) Chemists conference at the Goetheanum: bridges of understanding. In *Anthoposophy Worldwide* 10/05.

4 In Barnsley, England. Described in Fenoughty, Susan (1997) *The garden classroom*. Unpublished Churchill Fellowship report.

5 Sandven, Jostein (2003) *Kroppslig erfaringsdanning – uteskole arbeid med rom*. Paper to Freskerutdanningskurs, Vasa, Finland, 23–25 May 2003.

6 Fenoughty, Susan (1997) *ibid*.

7 1 ton of sand is around 1 m³ in bulk.

8 Meyerkort, Margaret *Kindergarten architecture and equipment*. Unpublished. Compiled by Elvira Rychlak.

9 Olds, Anita Rui (2001) *Child Care Design Guide*. McGraw Hill.

10 Olds, Anita Rui (2001) *op. cit.*

11 Barrington, Rupert (1971) *The Bird Gardener's Book*. Wolfe Publishing.

12 For example, the Zentrum für Schulbiologie und Umwelterziehung, Hamburg – as descibed in Fenoughty, Susan (1997) *ibid*.

13 Lundahl, Gunilla, ed. (1995) *ibid*.

14 Olds, Anita Rui (2001) *ibid*.

15 These are taken down at the end of the year and the materials re-used. Fenoughty, Susan (1997) *ibid*.

16 Nant-y-Cwm Steiner kindergarten.

17 Their popularity is fuelled by recognition that chlorine is a poison and skin irritant, associated with asthma and eczema; and trihalomethanes are suspected carcinogens. Littlewood, Michael (2004) Natural swimming pools. *Building for a Future* 14 (1), Summer. AECB

18 This is important to limit nutrients.

19 This can vary from 2 inches (50 mm) to 18 inches (450 mm) in depth. Littlewood, Michael (2004) *ibid*.

20 Littlewood, Michael (2004) *op. cit.*

21 King, Shawn (1996) Managing the blooming algae. *The IPM Practioner* XVIII (7) July.

22 Littlewood, Michael (2004) *ibid*.

23 Viktor Schauberger used this to practical effect. See Andersson, Olaf *Living Water*.

24 Hall, Alan (1997) *Water, Electricity and Health*. Hawthorn Press.

25 Marshall, Alan (1999) *Greener School Grounds*. Learning through Landscapes.

26 To Cardinal Hinsley High School, London 'technology education must at the same time be ecological education'. Marshall, Alan (1999) *op. cit.*

27 Vertical-axis machines don't yaw and buffet, but aren't widely available. Martin, Nick (2005) Can we harvest useful wind energy from the roofs of our buildings? *Building for a Future* 15 (3), Winter. AECB

28 Three parts washing-up liquid to one part glycerine in distilled water makes good bubbles. *Families, Festivals and Food*. Hawthorn Press.

29 This, at least, is the experience of the Mulleborg nature school – part of the 'Ur och Skur' preschool movement. As described in Lundahl, Gunilla, ed. (1995) *ibid*.

30 Thörn, Kerstin *Att bygga en skola*. Västerbotton, Västerbottons Museum.

31 Meyerkort, Margaret *ibid*.

CHAPTER 17

Levels of life

Children and animals

Children feel a natural affinity with animals. But do animals belong in modern urban childhood? Pets certainly give pleasure. But more than this, they help 'domesticate' children – teaching them how to relate better socially, avoid unintentionally mistreating other beings and communicate without words. Through pets, children encounter life, death and reproduction, directly experience biology, and learn ownership and sickness-care responsibilities and the foundations of respect for nature.[1]

Children have a natural affinity with animals

Petting isn't just one-way. Care and appreciation is reciprocal. Pets emanate trusting, non-judgemental love. They offer constancy, stability and opportunities to be unashamedly intimate, even in public. Their 'praise' confirms *our* importance; they also facilitate contact with strangers;[2] and, for adults, reduce the risk of heart attack. They give children the chance to *be* loving and responsible. Stroking animals and absorbing their appreciation, even rough boys become gentle.

Animals (normally) aren't expensive, but demand *time*: regular attention, food, companionship and care. You can't abandon responsibility for them. But they give back so much.

Animals teach compassion and responsibility

Through handling – especially *touching* – them, children get to know animals in ways impossible by just seeing them.

Animals and school

What about animals in schools and institutions? As team games – requiring even numbers – often leave one child out, Forest School Camps arrange a dog to play with. Both lone child and dog love it! School pets, even next-door cats, have an important 'petting role'. So significant are they that children – describing their ideal school – requested a heart-shaped front-door with a heart-shaped cat-door.[3] Allergy to pet-hair, however, may require pets to live outside or in a cat-lovers' hut (contents: sofas, cats and cat-lovers).[4]

Children's ideal school – and cat – door

In our touch-deprived society, children easily develop inhibitions about contact with others. This can lead to social withdrawal.[5] For disturbed children, contact with goats and rabbits, in particular, has been found to help overcome this.[6] To heal social or behavioural disconnection, therefore, Steiner curative-education usually includes farms. Mariagården, Sweden, for instance, uses sheep to reconnect special-needs children with the cycles and responsibilities of life.[7] Sheep aren't 'pets', but 'molly-lambs' (bottle-fed orphans) follow their surrogate 'mothers' around, hence 'Mary had a little lamb … it followed her to school …' (a friend even kept one in boarding-school; like the rhyme, it kept inviting itself into lessons). Despite mowing grass – and, unfortunately, flowers – for free, sheep aren't common in school. So beneficial are they to healthy social development, however, that Martin Riedel recommends sheep-milking huts in kindergarten playgrounds.[8]

Small animal corner

For Olds, animals – as well as teaching about the living world – are delight-magnets, which infants so look forward to meeting that they don't mind parting from parents. In her child-care centres, animals in the vestibule 'greet' arriving children; more robust ones, such as tortoises and rabbits sometimes roaming freely.[9] With small-animal display areas in semi-private child-cosy niches, low-level fish tanks – for children playing on the floor – mid-room cages (open-topped for hamsters) and wire-netting gerbil runs hung from ceilings, animals aren't compartmented off into science areas but are part of everyday life. Olds advocates a wide range of animals: ducks, birds, rabbits, pigs, cows, ponies, horses, bees, chickens, geese, cats, dogs, goats and lambs (but, because of the risk of meningitis, no parrots).[10] Geese, however, frighten children; large pigs are dangerous[11] and bees not

Mood-setting vestibule with indoor plants, animals, fish and lots of light

always nice. Horses, though popular with teenage girls, are expensive to own, look after and pasture. Smaller animals are safer and easier.

But should pets be in school? The Royal Society for the Prevention of Cruelty to Animals considers the risk of inadequate pet-care is too high. And how do animals cope with a constant turnover of carers? There are also questions about what message cages give. Should the animals not be free?

These aren't easy questions to answer, as much depends on individual circumstances. Is the responsibility structure robust enough? Is it based on legal obligation or commitment, love? At heart, this is a matter of attitudes and values. Are animals just there for *our* exploitive fun? This is simpler with 'agriculturally productive' animals. We – at least – are used to seeing these fenced – although this doesn't guarantee that *they* enjoy this. San Francisco Waldorf School's tight urban courtyard has hens, chickens and rabbits. The children love them. Chickens, however, are often banned within

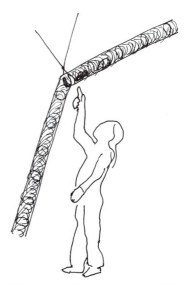

Wire-netting hamster tube in child-care centre[12]

cities for 'non-agricultural zoning' reasons, or – although few cockerels are louder than trucks – noise. Ducks are safely 'ornamental'. But they're less hygienic – sometimes making water unhealthily bacteria-rich. Also duck eggs are laid in wet, squidgy, pathogen-friendly conditions, so less safe to eat.

But what about health risks? At one extreme, 'farm schools' give children full exposure to manure – and sometimes blood. At the other, some schools so fear intestinal parasites

Entry courtyard with animals and birds

and bacteria – and associated litigation – that they forbid animal contact, and sometimes even farm visits. But children, in fact, catch more illnesses from other children. Logic would suggest closing down schools – but this rarely happens! (Similar hygiene arguments also prohibit dogs in hospitals, despite statistically proven benefits – and more illnesses caught from other patients.[13]) Fortunately, basic hygiene – washing hands before eating – almost eliminates risk. A wise additional precaution is to inoculate school animals against human-transmittable diseases.[14] As the socially developmental benefits of keeping animals far outweigh any health risks, animal contact is perhaps better weighed against fights and stabbings than tummy-bugs. Health-wise, children's immune systems don't properly develop without exposure to dirt and bugs – which animals provide at low infection risk. Moreover, as social tensions often manifest as illness, childhood *without* animal contact may well cause *unhealthier* subsequent adulthood. The benefits of learning care for the living world may prove, in a few decades, to be even more significant – for all of us.

Farm animals, food and the foundations of life

Where does food come from? Does it matter whether children know? Is this irrelevant knowledge or something that, by connecting them with the foundations of life, helps counter alienation?

A recent survey found that one-third of city children didn't connect eggs to chickens. Some thought cows 'made' them! (Through which part of their anatomy?) Two-thirds thought cotton came from sheep.[15] Ethnic minority children, lacking rural roots and role models, are particularly disconnected from agriculture. Farm visits help. For children, they're goldmines of fascination and fun. But farms are dangerous: big machinery, heavy animals, high stacks, deep pits and ponds. Moreover, not every farmer finds wild city children easy. Animals are easily panicked, and crops – often unrecognized – frail.

There is a project that brings deprived inner-city school classes to stay on organic farms, and introduces them to farm-work. Initially, with early rising, mud, manure and all-weather work, the children don't know what has hit them! By the end of a week, however, cocky ones have found that cockiness can't get you through everything; quiet, shy, children have found that they can contribute as importantly as louder ones; academic under-achievers have found that their physical strength means their work is valued. Also, as farm-work keeps them outdoors all day, they experience the day's cycle differently. To one girl: 'Being able to watch the sunset made me feel so special'. For many, just touching an animal is a daunting experience – a fear to overcome. Day-old chicks are so fragile, it brings out reverent care to handle them. Even tough, street-wise boys, awed by the wonder of baby lambs, treat them gently. The farmer thought these children learnt more in one week than in the rest of the school year – and experienced it so deeply that, unlike classroom lessons, it will influence their whole lives.[16]

Can farm experience be *in* school? German *Gartenarbeitschulen* include animal-care, typically with sheep, goats, geese and bees. Even in Berlin, there are twelve such schools.[17] Ohio Montessori Farm School gives 12- to 15-year-olds responsibility for almost all farm tasks.[18] All Summerfield classes – kindergarten to 18-year-olds – do farm work, integrated with the curriculum, every week.[19] For such children, the nutrient cycle is no abstraction, but daily experience.

Is this to train children to be farmers? No. Its purpose is to prepare them for *life*.

Songbirds

What about wildlife? All living things – from bacteria to people – can only live within specific environmental parameters. Understanding habitat needs isn't only essential for their survival, but also key to understanding them.

Songbirds bring delight; watching them is a free nature lesson. But their presence isn't automatic. Birds are opportunists – if conditions are suitable, they'll come. If they aren't, they either won't come or won't survive. To optimize their habitat, local wildlife trust advice is indispensable. It's more educational, however, to visit typical habitats and note their vegetation species, density and height, and elemental characteristics: soil, moistness, shelter and orientation. Such observation develops an 'inner picture' of place-*quality*, enabling similar physical conditions, security, microclimate, food supply and ecology to be created in wholly different contexts, even city playgrounds.[20]

Birds have four essential habitat requirements:[21]

1. suitable nesting sites
2. suitable roosting places
3. a regular supply of food and water
4. safety.

Woodland-edge provides a broad range of environmental conditions and forage – ideal for songbirds. Joined-up greenery with maximum 'edge' (and impenetrably thorny woodland-edge shrubs such as blackberry and hawthorn), multilevel canopy with nut, seed and winter-berry shrubs (such as Cotoneaster, Pyracantha), and dead wood for insects and grubs, recreate these conditions. Safety is crucial – particularly from cats and grey squirrels, but also from larger nest-robbing birds.

Few small birds nest in larger trees. Most choose between nesting sites between 3 and 10 feet (1–3 m) above the ground. Hedges or brush – dense or thorny against predators, and with leaf-cover against weather – 10 feet (3 m) high, make the most popular nesting sites.[22] Traditionally constructed buildings also offer many nesting and insect-forage opportunities. (Modern materials such as glass, concrete and steel are too smooth for bird claws to grip.) Creeper-clad or dry-stone (or fissured brick) walls and 'green' (vege-tated) or 'brown' (rubble covered) roofs increase forage opportunities.

Buildings make good homes for bird nests

Easy adaptations can encourage nesting. As nests against walls are potentially the safest of all locations, these appeal to small birds. Amongst 'house-nesting' birds, swallows appreciate 2 inch × 2 inch (50 mm × 50 mm) battens 3 inches (or 70 mm) below shed roofs (they also need a 2 inch × 3 inch (50 mm × 75 mm) hole – usually above the door – to get in). Swifts need 1 1/4 inch (30 mm) holes under eaves, usually behind fascias. House-martins build mud nests on anchoring textures under eaves. Weighted strings hung from the fascia in front deter nest-destroying sparrows. Other birds like ivy-cloaked walls, gaps between stones and artificial nests, such as sacking pouches and bundles of twigs (all weather-protected by eaves or 'roof' boards). Doves willingly inhabit dovecotes. Riedel suggests these outside every kindergarten.[23] Nest-boxes for small songbirds should have 1 1/8 inch (28 mm) entry holes – larger gives access to robbers. As birds normally consider old nests too unhygienic to use, lids need to be removable for cleaning out.[24] It's vital, of course, that all nest-box entrances and nest-starter-aids are above cat-jump level, and protected from both rain and ambush by roof, or similar, overhang. Optimally, nests should be around 6 1/2 feet (2 m) up and, for shelter from hot sun and cold winds, west or northwest facing.[25]

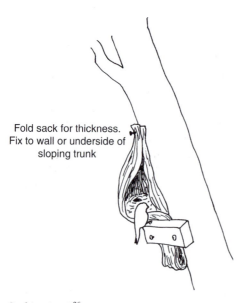

Fold sack for thickness. Fix to wall or underside of sloping trunk

Sacking 'nest'[26]

But birds nests are private. Disturbed birds can abandon nests. Even unaccustomed noises and bright lights can frighten them away – leaving eggs to cool and die.[28] How then can children see nest-building, egg-hatching and chick-feeding? One way is from a *human-sized* bird-house. Can children make these? Hamburg Centre for School Biology and Environmental Education pupils built one with windows only into nesting boxes. Being very dark, children can watch without disturbing birds at all.[29]

Most birds have several favourite perching places. From these they both sing and check safety before flying down to drink or feed. Good view for birds means good view *of* birds – so artificial perches – wooden tee-bars, some 6 1/2 feet (2 m) high – can be located where children can best see them.

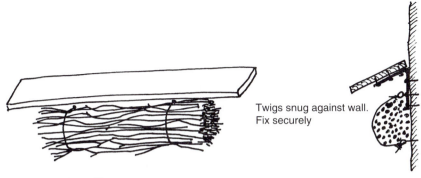

Twigs snug against wall.
Fix securely

Twig-bundle 'nest'[27]

Roosting has different environmental demands. In winter, birds roost most of the time. Minimizing body-heat loss is essential to survival. This means wind-shelter – especially from north and east. Thick evergreen foliage (such as ivy or dense holly) keeps off rain and snow. Preferably, this is so thick that birds only need to shift position a little when the wind changes. Like perching and nesting, 6 1/2–10 feet (2–3 m) is the preferred roost height of songbirds.[30]

What about bird-feeders? Outside windows, they're in constant view. It's nice, however, if the dropping-rich 'white lane' between feeder and nearby perches avoids entrance doors. Safety from cat ambush is paramount. To conceal nest location, birds don't like to feed near them, so feeders shouldn't be too near nest-boxes.[31] Birds become dependent on feeders, so starve if food isn't replenished, especially in hard weather. This makes a winter-holiday responsibility for someone.

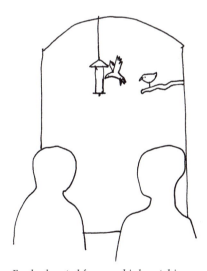

Feeder located for easy bird-watching

Birds also need to drink. As they only require 0.5–1.5 inch (10 to 30 mm) depth, ponds should have shallow gradients but must hold enough water not to dry out. For winter drinking, an unshaded bank at the north ends of pools accelerates ice thawing. Most songbirds also bathe. They therefore appreciate a sunny location to speed feather drying. As foliage can conceal cats, low branches or mid-pond logs are safer than bushes to drink and bathe from.[32] In such ways, songbird habitat needs can shape both building and landscaping design; also planting, pruning and maintenance.

Insects

If biology is about birds and bees, what about bees? The lazy drone of bumblebees and the self-important pollinating of honeybees are part of the mood of summer. Bees also need habitat to attract them. Traditional cottage gardens, vertical, so packed with flowers, have high bee-appeal. Monocultured lawns don't. Honeybees, though hardly pets, do all sorts of interesting things: pollinate flowers, 'dance', make wax, create geometric cells – and honey. Although bee colonies can rob and fight, separate hives aren't essential. Multicolony bee-houses, common in Europe, can even be indoor cabinets – though each colony must have its own bee-route direct to open-air. If – like ant-colony 'windows' – the indoor side(s) are glazed, everything they do is easily visible. As bees fly towards light and crawl uphill, high opening windows (curtained to prevent attracting the inhabitants when opening hives) are useful to clear escaped (or lost) ones from rooms. Unfortunately, bees sometimes sting.[33] Fortunately however, when commuting to flowers, they fly in 'bee-lines', namely straight. Hives on roofs, upper floors, above sloping ground or with 'rising-tube' exits keep flight safely above head level. Similarly, 'bee-fences' (hedges, or even just wire-netting) in front of hives make bees rise to a safe level before their honey-flow flight missions.[34] Are bees possible in school? In cities? In Hamburg, Gymnasium Blankenese students manage theirs – and even earn honey as reward.[35]

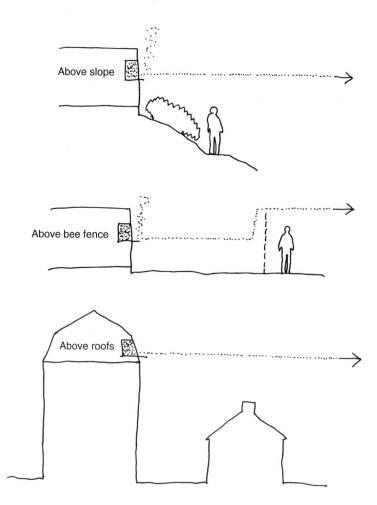

Bee flight

Ground insects, even spiders and creepy-crawlies, can also be fascinating. If adults handle them confidently and respectfully, even replacing stones they hide under in the same way, children learn to do the same.[36] At Klostergarten Environmental Study Centre, Oldenburg, a wall of multihole bricks makes an 'insect village'.[37] For many insects, however, visibility means danger. How can children observe their 'private lives'? The Hamburg environmental centre uses a wall-mounted, multicompartment box. Opening its door exposes insects 'at home'.

However interesting, not every insect is nice. Not everyone likes midges and mosquitoes. Fortunately, bats do. Even the tiny Pipistrelle eats 3000 midges a night – a boon on summer evenings. Old buildings suited bats well. New ones don't have cracks and ways-in to warm spaces. Bat-boxes, 'bat-bricks' or deliberate gaps between tiles or boarding to access cavities can substitute for these. As heat takes about four hours to pass through bricks, bat-roost cavities need to face south or east for sun-warmed day-time sleep.[38]

Butterflies can access nectar in deep-trumpet flowers, such as jasmine, which bees can't.[39] Some plants, particularly buddleia and nettle, attract them. They like sunny, wind-protected meadows with varying length grass and wild flowers. Woodland-clearings or rides are ideal. As subtly different habitats favour different species, close observation of the *quality* of their appearance and flight gives insight into the ecologies of places.[40] Butterflies do something wonderful: caterpillars become hard ugly chrysalises – to all appearance, dead.[41] Yet from each, a beautiful butterfly emerges, opens its wings and flies! Just as plants sprout from dry, shrivelled seeds, butterflies are a gentle analogy of life rising out of death.

Aquatic life

Slimy, wriggly pond inhabitants fascinate children. Much biology can be learned – and inspired – at the poolside. Lots of invertebrates live in ponds. Fun ones such as pond-skaters and water-beetles, beautiful ones such as dragonflies and damselflies, interesting ones such as pond-snails and freshwater mussels and intriguing ones – some so tiny, they're only visible through magnifying glasses or micro-scopes. Gymnasium Blankenese has an under-water window. Like glass-bottomed buckets, this shows a whole world hitherto unimagined – a magically inspiring lesson about the invisible wonders of life.[42]

Pond-making gives a double lesson: nature-study and plant-care. Ponds are best planted in winter, using starter plants, microlife-rich soil – or even just a bucket of water – from a local *natural* pond. (Native flora by supporting native fauna, have natural biological controls. Foreign species, however, are common in garden-ponds. As these can take over and become uneradicable,

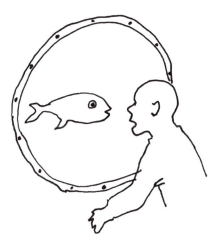

Underwater window

garden pond water should *never* be used.) Immature ponds are often covered in blanket-weed. Though unsightly, fauna come to depend on this. It's safe, however, to remove one-third each autumn (after tadpoles but before amphibian hibernation); but anything more drastic threatens many species' survival.[43]

Mosquitoes can't lay eggs in fast water, but love ponds. Fortunately, many fish eat mosquito-larvae. As warmth accelerates biological activity, depleting oxygen, fish generally need cool water. Running water re-oxygenates and – through increased evaporation – cools it. For protection and shade, fish like deep water and plants or stones to hide under. But should fish be in small ponds? Ones larger than minnows eat too many tadpoles. Unless there is adjacent wetland, this makes pond ecology one-sided. Simple ecologies have little resilience to unpredictable external events, such as droughts, floods and extreme temperatures – all likely with global warming. If ponds ever dry out, fish die, but most amphibians survive. These live long enough to miss an occasional breeding season. Amphibians like damp, sun-warmed, fertile margins, at least 2 feet (600 mm) wide. Unable to climb vertical walls, they need shallowly sloping sides and, to safely move between forage habitats, corridors of cover: dense vegetation, logs or stones.[44]

But how small can ponds be? Frogs and smooth newts only need 10 square feet (1 m²). For some dragonflies 43 square feet (4 m²) of water suffices, though most need 540 square feet (50 m²) of damp-margin habitat – achievable around smallish ponds by 'pleating' edges. Frogs spawn among submerged plants in shallow water; newts, a little deeper.[45] Deep water increases habitat diversity for more species to exploit. In cold climates, depth is essential to avoid frozen fish. But insects, important food, need shallow areas. Ponds therefore need deep(ish) water, shallow ledges, water-weed, damp edges and shade. Unfortunately, this combination makes the perfect recipe for a child-trap. Any deep water *must*, therefore, be inaccessible to children. For child safety, everything must also be in full view.

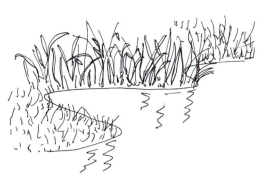

Pleating pond edges to enlarge damp-margin habitat

As small means ecologically fragile, larger ponds are more resilient. If circumstances don't change too abruptly, flora and fauna can adapt; with summer water-temperature, for instance, new species colonize ponds. In all living systems, habitat diversity broadens species range, conferring stability from both ends: more species able to survive new conditions, and more places retaining previous conditions. Even garden ponds can support complex ecologies and food webs. This makes them rich educational resources.

Lessons from the living world

We only need to think about dead objects once. They store easily on shelves. Live ones crawl, slither, fly or grow, off them. We must actively involve ourselves with them. All living organisms change with time. We can't understand them without knowing their temporal and contextual aspects: biography and rhythms; and cause-and-effect contexts – such as habitat, food-chains and pathology. A *living* world is a world of *connections*: fluid, not rigidly boxed. For living thinking, children need contact with living things.

   Living with other living beings is what life is about. What better way to learn how to do this harmoniously than by caring for living things? But care also means care for habitat and ecology – care for living *relationships*. What better way to learn *this* than by seeing, hearing, handling, playing with, smelling, 'breathing' these in daily life from early childhood on?

Notes

1 *Talking Pets: Pets are Good for People* (1986) Pedigree Pet foods.
2 Hunter, Linda Mason (1990) in *The Healthy Home*, Pocket Books, cites separate studies in confirmation of all these assertions.
3 A request relayed to me by a *Blue Peter* (children's TV programme) presenter during the design of a multicultural centre in 2000.
4 As at Emerson College, England.
5 Green, Jeff (2006) Sensing the world and ourselves. *New View*, Autumn.
6 Olds, Anita Rui (2001) *Child Care Design Guide*. McGraw Hill.
7 An anthroposophical home and school for special needs children.
8 Riedel, Martin (1985) Some notes on the effects of architectural forms. In Flinspach, Jürgen (1985) *Waldorfkindergärten Bauen*. *Unpublished* translation by Luborsky, Peter (1988).
9 Olds, Anita Rui (2001) *ibid.*
10 Olds, Anita Rui (2001) *op. cit.*
11 Exceptionally amongst animals, pigs have no fear of humans. Farm folklore claims stories of pigs eating babies.
12 After Olds, Anita Rui (2001) *ibid.*
13 *The Independent* newspaper.
14 Olds, Anita Rui (2001) *ibid.*
15 A survey in a Scottish city, reported on the *Today* Programme, BBC Radio 4, 2 May 2002.
16 BBC Radio 4, 23 June 2003.
17 Literally: Garden Work Schools. They're for 3- to 20-year-olds. Lohrmann, Iris (2003) Learning from nature in the urban landscape of Berlin. *Environmental Education* 73, Summer.
18 Newberry, Beatrice (2002) Natural born learners. *The Times Magazine*.
19 They work under the farmer's direction. This farm comprises three cows, nine sheep, chickens, ducks, rabbits and bees.
20 For more on how to use observation to build an 'inner picture' of a place's essence, see Day, Christopher (2002) *Consensus Design*. Architectural Press.
21 Barrington, Rupert (1971) *The Bird Gardener's Book*. Wolfe Publishing.
22 Barrington, Rupert (1971) *op. cit.*
23 Riedel, Martin (1985) *ibid.*
24 Barrington, Rupert (1971) *ibid.*
25 Specific details here are for British birds and conditions.
26 Barrington, Rupert (1971) *ibid.*
27 Barrington, Rupert (1971) *op. cit.*
28 Barrington, Rupert (1971) *op. cit.*
29 (Zentrum für Schulbiologie und Umwelterziehung, Hamburg) Fenoughty, Susan (1997) *The garden classroom*. Unpublished Churchill Fellowship report.
30 Barrington, Rupert (1971) *ibid.*
31 Barrington, Rupert (1971) *op. cit.*
32 Barrington, Rupert (1971) *op. cit.*
33 Thundery weather, horse- and fear-scent increases the likelihood.
34 I am indebted to beekeepers, John Drakes and Col. Francis Day, for this information.
35 Fenoughty, Susan (1997) *ibid.*
36 Marshall, Alan (1999) *Greener School Grounds*. Learning through Landscapes.
37 Fenoughty, Susan (1997) *ibid.*
38 East-facing allows time for heat to travel through bricks. Johnston, Jacklyn and Newton, John *Building Green*. London Ecology Unit.

39 Olds, Anita Rui (2001) *ibid.*

40 Heaf, David (2006) Summary of articles. *Archetype* 11, September.

41 Indeed, inside them is liquid mush – neither caterpillar nor butterfly form at all!

42 Fenoughty, Susan (1997) *ibid.*

43 This information, from Royal Society for the Protection of Birds (RSPB) (2002) *Ponds for Wildlife*, is particularly for a British climate. Nonetheless, these principles, if not exact detail, apply to all ponds.

44 RSPB (2002) *op. cit.*

45 RSPB (2002) *op. cit.*

CHAPTER 18

Learning sustainability through daily experience

Towards a sustainable lifestyle

Everyone agrees sustainability is a 'good thing'. But how should this affect what we *do* in everyday life? Without an experiential bridge, our brains (and words) can think one thing, but our habit-based behaviour does another. Similarly, school-based cerebral learning teaches one thing but life-based absorptive learning teaches another.

Absorbed lessons start in early childhood. Most children love dolls – they treasure and imagine life into them. But what happens when these break? For soft dolls, a few stitches in doll hospital (out of child-sight, for dolls are 'alive', not 'things' to sew up!) and loving nursing cures even serious injury. Indeed, many toys accumulate character with wear and tear. But plastic dolls, once broken, are irreparable. All that loving care poured into them – and suddenly, they're rubbish. This is a first lesson in disposability. Unless we're careful, life teaches many such anti-sustainability lessons.

Facing the future: developing sustainability consciousness

For children, before they were born was 'a long time ago'. Fifty years hence is unimaginably far ahead – full of optimistic possibilities beyond imagination. For adults, anticipating global warming, rising sea level and mass migration, it's tomorrow. Human damage to the environment is appalling. Most has happened within one generation – our generation. This is indisputable. But this isn't something to teach children. Thinking people are bad is no way to grow up! However accurate our predictions of catastrophe, it's nonetheless vital that our gloom – and often cynicism – doesn't infect children's hope. For them, it's essential we re-cast our doom-laden predictions as *challenges*. More helpful is to demonstrate how to live sustainably by example. Fear paralyses – but challenge inspires.

Time	50 years ago	Now	50 years in the future
Children	Unbelievably old-fashioned. They fought with swords	Now is just now	Exciting, wonderful, full of hope
Adults	The golden age	The world is going to the dogs	Doom! Apocalypse!

What does living sustainably mean? Solar panels on the roof, a windmill in the garden and bottles collected for driving to the bottle-bank? Or is it more about attitude? Something about respecting, valuing and loving our environment; recognizing and minimizing environmental costs; ensuring our impacts remain within cyclic systems? Is it about living *with*, rather than *in spite of*, the forces of nature?

What about urban surroundings? How can *built* environment help children *absorb* sustainability values, habits and experience-based skills? What does this mean for buildings and furnishings, playgrounds and gardens? As 'environment', these are background ambience – not chosen focus of attention – but are they acceptable of wear-and-tear, maintainable, repairable and lovable? If not, what do they say to us?

This casts new light on material choice. Should furniture be wood, particle-board, metal, concrete or plastic? Besides price, cleanability, toxicity and 'abuse'-resistance, we need to consider maturability and reparability; also how something smells and feels to touch. This about how things feel as neighbours, how we can trust them, feel anchored by them – and most of all, what values they teach us.

This raises issues of where things come *from* and where they go *to*. Traditionally, earth, stone and trees made buildings; cruck-frames, like ship-ribs, were cut from curved boughs. Everything came from, and all waste returned to, the local soil. Nowadays timber comes from further away, but it still was once trees. Many things, however, are made of industrial materials. Where do these come from? How did they get like they are?

Whether through industrial processing, complex technology or geographical distance, the more remote are their materials' sources, such buildings – however practical – alienate us

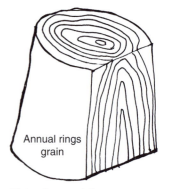

from the *process by which they have become.* By contrast, making things such as coat-hooks from small branches, or paper from wood-shavings, links product to source. When children see sheep sheared, then card fleeces, spin wool and knit clothing, they experience making as a *process*. By using waste wool for toy nests, pet bedding or compost, it's complete, waste-free and rooted in life. This closes the cycle – from soil-fed grass to soil-feeding compost. At one level, this process is about enrichment by human work riding harmoniously on nature's cycles. At another, it links producers to consumers symbiotically, not competitively. Goods flow one way along the link; money, the other. This shows how human work and re-imbursement can parallel nature's systems. Both ecologically and economically, the relationships

Annual rings
grain

Natural materials connect to source

 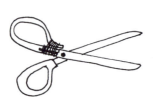 

Connection with source: coat hook, scissor-handle and whisk cut from hedgerows

are established by symbiosis. Such visible connection to source, comprehensible processes and relationships of mutual benefit help us 'know – and trust – where we are', even in unfamiliar surroundings. Environmentally, the better we connect to the materials, processes and skills of which a building is made, the easier to imagine how *we* could build it; the easier it becomes 'home' not 'alien institution'.

Material choice also raises issues of extraction, processing, transport-energy, pollution and bio-degradability. The environmental costs of *chemically* processed materials, such as plastics, usually greatly exceed those of *thermally* processed ones, such as brick. Does user-benefit match environmental costs? For how many minutes is a plastic bag used? How many millennia will it last? If making plastic typically requires 15 synthesis operations, each only 50 per cent efficient, how much of the original material becomes final product? 0.02 per cent![1] And the rest? Some is recycled; some makes other products; most is waste, some – such as vinyl-chloride from PVC manufacture – is highly toxic. The average classroom and its contents – including children's clothes – is a sobering lesson in cradle-to-grave environmental costs. But it's also a lesson in how easily things could have been done differently.

One aspect of 'waste' is that it isn't a material fact, but an *attitude of mind*. Nature – as we constantly hear – doesn't produce waste. Only humans do. But we only do so because our product focus is narrow. Much waste we don't even notice. We routinely dump dirty water – including spilt oil – down drains. Once washed out of sight, the ground looks clean again. But is it? The Austin Green School uses a cross-section geological model to show what happens. 'Oil' (dye) spilt on the ground and 'rained' in with a watering-can, can be seen percolating into the underlying aquifer. True – bacteria decompose oil, but only slowly, and mostly only in shallow, humus-rich, topsoil. Most liquids rapidly sink deeper, often contaminating drinking water. Some biocides, antibiotics and hormone mimics (from plastic by-products) resist bacterial breakdown so recycle into tap water.

Cross-section geological model to demonstrate pollutant percolation into aquifers

Should pollution-awareness start with global warming or dog-shit? The devastating consequences of climate-change can't be overstated. This makes CO_2 the most serious of all pollutants – but it's inoffensively invisible, odourless and (effectively) non-toxic.[2] Rubbish, by contrast, is highly visible; it directly touches our emotions. We *feel* sickened by a littered beauty spot, but only *think* concern about greenhouse gasses. Is litter, therefore, the best starting point to change awareness?[3] Many schools think so. Most playground rubbish is packaging, dropped by children. To minimize this – and also for children's health – some schools only allow fruit for snacks. An unanticipated consequence is that children's behaviour markedly improves.

Packaging can easily be dismissed as someone else's 'fault' (but wasn't it *we* who bought it?). But litter is largely a problem of *attitude*: 'Dropping litter is a bit like proving you are hard and not a goody goody.' 'If I used a bin, my mates would take the mickey out of me.'[4] How can non-littering become an issue that *inspires*, not just one of compulsion? Amongst schools that address this, Eastchurch Primary children survey their village rubbish-densities.[5] At New Milton, pupils bury waste, then dig it up a month later. What has happened to it? What decomposed? What didn't?[6] Civic refuse sites, however, bury waste too deep for air, so even lettuces remain recognizable – although hardly appetizing – after 40 years. Anaerobic decomposition produces methane: an inflammable and explosive greenhouse gas. Some refuse sites are 'mined' for methane or minerals, some dramatically explode or burn, but most aren't thought about at all. They just silently waste land, waste resources, breed rats and flies, pollute nearby water and contribute to global warming. This makes a strong argument for composting and recycling.

Recycling is a *process*. Tracing the route of objects through this, it's obvious that dissimilar materials must be kept separate; once mixed, recycling is uneconomical, if not impossible. Cluster waste-bins enable easy sorting – thereby raising *consciousness*. While glass recycling banks are often surrounded by broken shards, so unsafe at school, those for clothing, textiles, newspaper and printer cartridges become community resources. The sorted waste is even saleable – perhaps to sponsor charities. Where should recycling banks be located? They need to be parent-accessible – both to maximize use and to encourage parents dropping off children to chat and get to know one another. Though easily screened by hedges, they're unsightly and can be noisy, so shouldn't front classrooms. Message-wise, located by the entrance gate they announce environmental responsibility. Hidden at the back, they're ashamed of it.

Cluster-bin recycling

Re-use *always* saves more energy, resources and pollution than recycling. *Local* re-use saves yet more. Moreover, it connects children with the local economy. Some municipalities and charities have organized this. Reggio Emilia's refuse service collect, sort and display sub-standard factory products, normally waste, for schools' use. British 'Scrap Stores' offer scrap card, paper, plastic containers, foil and suchlike.[7] In poorer countries, much that we (in the West) consider waste is too valuable to discard, and is made into all manner of beautiful, useful things. By imparting value to others' waste, we can link narrow, blinkered, linear systems into closed-cycle communities of production.

Re-use also has consciousness-raising value. Tree-conservation campaigner Julia Butterfly Hill suggested schoolchildren quantify its potential. If half a class discards all

Namibian houses made of bottles, built by children at a music school

waste paper and the other half re-uses whatever practical, how do their waste volumes compare after a month? For the annual total, double, then multiply by the number of classes in the school, and months in the school year.[8] As paper is about twice the density of softwood,[9] what volume of wood, how many trees would re-use save?

Two generations ago (wartime), virtually everything was mended – or adapted for another use. Today, little is. What does our throw-away attitude teach children about valuing our environment, caring for our irreplaceable planet? Repair extends the lives of objects – for zero environmental cost – by adding *human care*. Mending things shows we value them. Besides saving money, doing this in children's view – or, better, with their participation – gets them used to care, repair, frugality and resourcefulness. Toy and furniture 'hospitals' help establish these values. Instead of forced lessons, repair can build on children's natural interests in taking-apart, re-building, adapting and mending things.

Mending develops care and attitudes of responsibility. It also strengthens understanding of connections to things: how they're made, where their materials come from and how to improvise replacement parts from what's around you. Knowing they can mend, or make, anything needed with whatever materials are to hand helps build children's confidence. Natural materials make this much easier.

Energy use

Heating and cooling buildings is a major cause of climate change. This accounts for nearly half of all global pollution, nearly half of all the greenhouse effect. Most of this is wasted energy – needless waste, because *conserving* energy is invariably cheaper, easier and more effective than producing it. But although draughts chill us, most energy loss leaves no sensory signal, so energy-conservation easily remains an unexciting, abstract concept. How to raise awareness? Visitor accommodation at the Centre for Alternative Technology, Wales, addresses this by providing 'rations' of firewood (also water). Once used up, visitors have the effort of getting more!

Largely, we're unaware of either heating or cooling happening – warmth or coolness are just 'how things are'. Even energy-conservation measures are rarely noticeable. Temperature readings in different places, such as either side of curtains, or sun and shade, help children relate thermal *experience* to *understanding*. Spatially *non*-uniform heat raises awareness. Focal, radiant heat – as from stoves – declines with distance. Air heat is stratified – as changing a ceiling light teaches. Different heat *zones* contrast. For thermal comfort, what sort of places do children need? Weather range – and even temperature preferences, which vary up to 8°C (14°F)[10] – necessitates considerable variety: from sunny alcoves for cold weather and shady, leafy, breeze-washed, water-refreshed places for hot.

We naturally adjust how we do things to thermal conditions – in heat, we walk slower and seek shade; in cold, we avoid wind. We boost heating, open windows and add or remove clothing as required. But this isn't automatic behaviour. It's *learnt*. Children easily overheat or chill before they realize something is wrong – even worse once they're fashion conscious.

In most schools, someone (or some*thing*) regulates heat (or cooling), and electric lighting is usually on all day. Life goes on without children having to think about climate control. But this changes if they deliberately compare how different rooms perform thermally in different weather and seasons. How can they be improved? Should under-window radiators be topped by shelves to avoid heating windows *behind* curtains? What shutters, blinds, light-shelves, reflectors or other devices – many within the skill-range of older children to make – do rooms need? Whereas automatic systems never need thought, such daily involvement develops both conscious awareness and an automatic climate-responsive, energy-conservative attitude. This prepares children to take responsibility for classroom energy use: in winter, closing curtains and shutters at night; in summer, opening night-vents, closing them by day, and adjusting shades and reflectors. Classroom meters can connect energy-use to what children do – or don't do. The costs saved can even fund prizes for energy-conserving classes.

Too complicated for children? At simplest, Eastchurch Primary schoolchildren switch off unneeded lights, and report classroom temperature variations, so controls can be adjusted. In cold weather, they're responsible for closing doors and windows.[11] More demandingly, in Haute Vallee School, Jersey, classroom energy monitors operate wind-tower dampers, windows and thermal blinds, themselves.[12] Energy consumption has such major planetary consequences that responsibility can't be learnt too young. It needs to become an unshakable habit.

Recognizing the sun's energy

Sunlight, our planet's energy source, is just 'there'. We enjoy sunbathing, and feel good on sunny days. But sunlight doesn't *feel* like free energy. Likewise, houses heated by large south windows are just 'houses', but even basic solar water-heaters are clearly 'inventions' – something to wonder at.

As glacial melt-water trickling over black rock can become bath-warm, pumping water over dark, sun-orientated roofs is the cheapest way to warm swimming-pools.[13] (Black-bottomed pools are even cheaper, but give the illusion of frightening depth.) Some solar water-heaters are technically sophisticated, but most combine the dual principles of black cars (dark – or thermally selective – surfaces absorb radiant heat) and greenhouses. (Long wavelength light comes in through glass – or CO_2. Short wavelength heat doesn't easily go out through it.) Solar collectors are less shaded, less damage-prone when sited high on roofs, but they're more *educational* at *low*-level, in full view. Judiciously placed, collectors can reflect

Water running over dark-surfaced, sun-orientated roofs

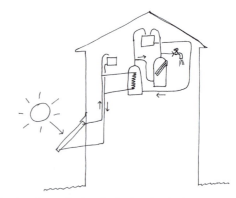

Basic solar collector for hot water system – can be part of a shed-roof, or a shade over south windows

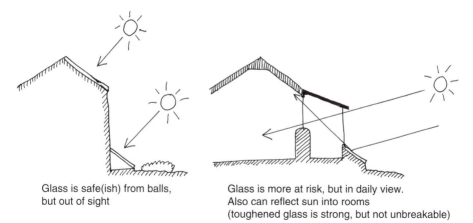

Glass is safe(ish) from balls,
but out of sight

Glass is more at risk, but in daily view.
Also can reflect sun into rooms
(toughened glass is strong, but not unbreakable)

Visible solar collectors

shallow-angle winter sun onto ceilings to maximize daylight. (Care, however, is needed to avoid glare.) Low-level placing also maximizes collector-to-tank height so the heat-exchange fluid can thermo-siphon. Thermo-sensor controlled, pumped systems are more efficient, but thermo-siphon ones have less to go wrong. Also, they demonstrate physical laws: heated water rises, cool descends, and hot water stratifies. Technically undemanding to make, solar hot-water systems only require basic plumbing and carpentry skills.

The easy comprehensibility of solar hot-water systems makes them accessible, but they don't symbolize the future – indeed they've been around for over a century. Children often regard the past as 'old-fashioned' – suitable only for oldies. But they have a natural optimism about the future. For them, new means good, future means better. Photovoltaic panels represent this future. These, however, are the most expensive, least efficient way of harnessing nature's 'free' power – currently costing 38 times more per Kilowatt than solar space-heating.[14] Energy-wise, some experts calculate that they *never* recoup the energy invested in their manufacture – although this is contested. Nonetheless, their high symbolic value inspires. If they power something visible such as a fountain, cascade or, as at Summerfield, farm electric-fencing, this inspiration is grounded, not abstract. Their cost may be difficult to justify on homes but, for schools, they have an important attitude-motivating role.

Thinking green

To have any effect, sustainable consciousness mustn't be a compartmentalized subject, but must permeate, indeed shape, everything we do. As the National Primary Trust recognizes, 'There is little point in reforming the … curriculum unless the aims professed and lessons taught are reflected in the day-to-day life of the school and its relations to the wider community'.[15] But how can this happen?

One model is Kullerbyttan Day Nursery, Linköping, Sweden.[16] This aims to develop environmental awareness through 'caring responsibility for people, society and nature'. Besides growing much of its own food, it has an environmental purchasing policy for everything bought. Avoiding disposable items, it uses cloth towels, re-uses paper for drawing; sorts paper, milk cartons, glass, batteries, metal and plastic for recycling; and composts all waste food – some, for teaching purposes, by worms. To encourage energy awareness, children are responsible for switching off lights (all low-energy) in empty rooms. They – with teachers – do all the cleaning, using only bio-friendly cleaning materials. By helping children understand that they're part of the natural cycle, they learn to work in harmony with their environment and actively improve it.

Organizationally, one teacher is responsible for environmental education: giving ideas, keeping staff informed, annually evaluating the environmental programme and, with the site-supervisor, kitchen and cleaning staff, monitoring performance. All staff attend environmental-education training days every term. As everyone shares commitment to this approach, many cross-linkages appear, and the 'impossible' suddenly becomes accessibly achievable. 'Thinking green' becomes *being* green.

Environmental audit

Today's schoolchildren will have to cope with *our* generation's myopia. Fortunately, young people are generally more enthused by sustainability than their elders. They may not know *how* to do it but, doubly fortunately, teenagers know *everything*. They particularly excel at finding what's wrong with what adults do. Why not ask *them* what's wrong with their school?

School audit

Once completed, the children can be asked – *without forewarning* – how to remedy the faults. And later again, to actually *do so*. This way they learn the inseparability of criticism and responsibility.

Element	Questions	Examples
Substance		
What comes in to the school?	Past: Where is it from? (Trace the whole journey backwards, including transport distance, high energy inputs, pollution costs)	Food to canteen, pupils' food to cookery class; materials to workshop and art room; new furniture; paper, stationery and computer supplies; etc.
	Present: How economically or wastefully is it used?	
What goes out?	Future: Where does it go to? (Whole journey to decomposition; including transport distance, high energy inputs and pollution costs)	

(continued)

Element	Questions	Examples
Water What (mains) water does the school use	Where is it from?	
What is it used for?	How much for each use? Where does grey water and sewage go? And then where?	Drinking, cooking, washing up, cleaning, hand washing, taps left running, toilet flushing, irrigation, etc.
How much water falls on the school grounds? (area × rainfall)		
How much rain falls on hard surfaces? (area × rainfall)	Is any used? Could it be? If so, for what?	
Air How is the classroom, corridor, canteen air?	Is it too stuffy, smelly, draughty, hot, cool, etc.? Where do smells come from?	Flooring, furniture, computers, cleaning materials, chalk dust, marker solvents, kitchen, art room, traffic and boiler exhaust, refuse, tarmac, trees, flowers, grass, etc.
How is the playground/ playing field air?	Where is it windy, sheltered, noisy, quiet? Are these places in the right locations?	
Energy How much energy does the school use?	Where is sunny? Where could be solar warmed? Where is too hot? Where could be naturally cooled?	Coal, heating oil, gas, methane, wood chips, geo-thermal, electricity, etc.
How much heat is lost from the building? Where does most of this escape?	How much is due to construction faults, how much to use patterns and human behaviour?	Poor insulation, draughts, doors left open, uncurtained windows, etc.
How much electricity does the school use?	How much electricity is wasted? How can this be reduced?	Electricity used for non-electrical uses; lights, computers, equipment left on, etc.
	How is the electricity generated?	Nuclear, coal, oil, gas, wind, hydro, tidal, wave, etc.
	Are alternatives practical?	Wind, PV, microhydro, Combined-Heat-and-Power (CHP), etc.
Traffic	How many cars come to school? What extra trips do school demands cause? (number × average round-trip mileage ÷ miles/gallon)	Late classes, parental deliveries, etc.
	How much carbon dioxide does the school generate?	

Sustainability in daily view

Why are neighbourhoods as they are? Where did their constituent elements come from and go to? And at what environmental cost? The towns, roads and landscape around us didn't appear overnight. They grew and changed. Their history shows which materials, techniques and systems proved sustainable, and which obsolete. However 'old-fashioned' tradition may feel, we can learn much from what did and didn't work, and from the processes by which places evolved. What lessons are valid for modern circumstances?

Neighbourhood environmental audit

- *Buildings*: What are they made of? Where do these materials come from? Are they recyclable? How? How old are they? How much longer might they last? How do they perform energy-wise?
- *Food*: From how far away does it come? How long are farmer-to-table chains? What are the cost mark-ups?
- *Goods*: What comes in, goes out? From how far away do they come? How long are producer-to-user chains? And cost mark-ups?
- *Waste*: What happens to it? How much is recycled?
- *Economy*: Where do people work? What money comes into the area, what goes out?
- *Traffic*: What type of vehicles are common? How many single-occupant cars? How much public-transport? How many bicycles? Where do people walk; where don't they?
- *Water*: How much does the town use? (population × gallons/day (UK: 31; USA: 122)).
- *Rainwater*: What happens to it? How much falls on the town area? What ground surfaces – permeable and impermeable – are there? How much of each?
- *Flooding*: Has there been flooding of local areas since records have been kept? How often?
- *Sewage*: What happens to it? Where? Does any return to the land?
- *Air*: Where is the air clean, where not? What pollutes it? Where does clean air come from? What refreshes it?
- *Energy*: What major energy sources are used? Where do they come from?
- *Trees*: What species? Where? In what soil, climate and human-use conditions? Do they connect to woodland, hedgerow or rough land 'reserves'?
- *Wildlife*: What birds, animals and insects? Where are there more; where less? What habitat types are there?
- *Microclimate*: Where is it sunny, shady? Where windy, sheltered, stuffy? Where damp, dry, dusty? Where is most and least comfortable?
- *Noise*: Where is it noisiest; where quiet? Where does the noise come from? When?

How do these factors relate to each other? What improvements would you like? How can we:

- Improve building longevity and recyclability?
- Improve buildings' energy performance: reduce heat-loss and overheating?

- Reduce 'carbon cost'?
- Encourage local food? Shorten farmer-to-table chains?
- Encourage local goods, work and money-flow?
- Encourage recycling?
- Compost sewage, recycling it back to the land?
- Reduce traffic? Make walking, cycling and bus-travel easier?
- Conserve and use rainwater?
- Prevent flooding?
- Improve microclimate?
- Clean air?
- Maximize living ground-surface?
- Find appropriate places for trees?
- Encourage wildlife?
- Control, screen or mask noise?

And finally:

- How could this be self-financing?
- What can students themselves do – *now*?

Notes

1 König, Holger (1989) *Wege zum Gesunden Bauen*. Ökobuch Verlag.
2 At a mere 5.4 per cent, CO_2 is fatal. Fortunately, the CO_2 content of air is only 0.034 per cent. König, Holger (1989) *op. cit.*
3 This is the view advocated by Environmental Campaigns (ENCAMS) in their Keep Britain Tidy campaign.
4 Kids Confess to Causing a Mess! In *Review*, 2002–2002, ENCAMS.
5 Marshall, Alan (1999) *Greener School Grounds*. Learning through Landscapes.
6 Marshall, Alan (1999) *op. cit.*
7 Marshall, Alan (1999) *op. cit.*
8 Hill, Julia Butterfly (2002) *The Legacy of Luna*. Harper.
9 Fairweather, L. and Sliwa, J.A. (1970) *AJ Metric Handbook*. Architectural Press.
10 Wyon, David (1992) User control of the local environment. *Building Services Journal* June. Others, however, have found a much narrower band – down to 0.6°C. My own experience is nearer to Wyon's findings.
11 Marshall, Alan (1999) *ibid*.
12 School designed by Architecture PLB, described in Dudek, Mark (2000) *Architecture of Schools*. Architectural Press.
13 These don't need the high-temperature water provided by solar panels. All they need is *lots* of warm water. Large area tile, slate, corrugated-sheet or asphalt roofs are ideal for this. As roof-perching birds aren't house-trained, however, water may need cleaning by fine sand filters and ultraviolet sterilizers. Anti-perch ridges help.
14 As of 2005. Their price, however, reduces every year.
15 Huckle, John *Burning Issues in Primary Education: EDUCATION FOR SUSTAINABILITY*. National Primary Trust.
16 Paraphrased from excerpts quoted in Fenoughty, Susan (1997) *The Garden Classroom*. Unpublished Churchill Fellowship report.

CHAPTER 19

Sustainable schools

Hidden benefits

What does sustainability have to do with schools? Don't they have enough to worry about without anything extra? Can it bring any advantages beyond moral smugness?

Culturally, in one decade, sustainability has grown in the West from unknown concept to fashionable selling point in virtually every sphere of activity. Christianity and Judaism have shifted emphasis from 'subduing the earth' to responsible 'stewardship'. Harmony with nature is central not only to Buddhists: Rastafarians, Sikhs, Hindus and the many shamanistic religions believe the earth is a sentient spiritual being. To Moslems, waste of natural resources has always been a sin. To accountants, any waste is a needless expense. For the planet, it's a disaster – possibly with irreparable ecological consequences.

For children, sustainability is *the* motivating issue of our time. Under pressure of climate change, its inspiration status is sure to grow – for the challenges are acute and time is short. More mundanely, demonstrating care for the environment implies care for those who inhabit it. This affects how children feel themselves thought of. This, in turn, influences their self-esteem, achievement and behaviour. A green image, therefore, means a lot to them.[1]

Sustainability implications for schools

What does sustainability mean for schools? Ethically, economically and inspirationally, buildings should have minimal – preferably zero – adverse impact on climate, minimize other pollution, water-use and other consumption, and maximize ecological benefits. In detail, this means (at least):

- energy-conservative design and construction
- renewable energy – preferably on-site, in view
- materials with low embodied energy/CO_2/pollution/social costs
- natural lighting
- natural ventilation
- minimum transport energy

- water conservation
- rainwater harvesting
- slowed and locally retained rainwater run-off
- grey water recycling
- waste recycling
- healthy building
- organic gardening and local food
- improving wildlife habitat

And – most importantly – raising consciousness.

Is this possible? For all these aspects, there are successful precedents.

Visible solar and greywater systems

Design for sustainability

Heating, cooling and lighting British school buildings produces six million tonnes of CO_2 per year – and costs £400 million. As CO_2 has such a devastating impact on climate, a major responsibility must be to minimize energy consumption. Energy *conservation* is primary. Schools must set examples here – both with low-energy buildings and policies to minimize energy use. Educationally – and inspirationally – they can demonstrate alternative energy generation. This has value well beyond the little energy it saves, as on-site microgeneration has proved to initiate many shifts in attitudes and behaviour.[2] All *visible* sustainability measures encourage this – essential – new consciousness.

Buildings also have 'embodied' environmental costs – mostly energy and pollution resulting from manufacture and transport of their construction materials. Generally, the more local and less processed, the lower they are. Some materials also carry social-exploitation costs. Regionally traditional materials usually have the lowest adverse impacts and best suit local climate and construction skills. Socially, we expect buildings to have benefits greatly exceeding their costs. Environmentally also, they can have 'negative costs'. As wood locks up carbon for the life of the building – and longer, if easily demountable for re-use – timber construction brings a global-climate *benefit*. Non-sustainable forestry, however, can be so destructive that environmental costs can grotesquely outweigh benefits – hence the importance of certified timber. Wood, being a biological material, needs the right environmental conditions for longevity. In cold, dry climates it lasts well, but few species are durable in wet, warm ones. But how long do buildings need to last?

The more buildings are used and the longer their life, the more are costs – both environmental and monetary – spread. British schools are typically designed to last 60 years. As, however, they're only used for about 1400 hours per year,[3] this totals only ten full years of occupation, making environmental costs per hour high. Not all last 60 years. 1960s schools, demolished after 30 years, demonstrate that no building will last if occupants don't value it. If, therefore, schools aren't *delightful* to be in, *climatically comfortable* and *healthy* for occupants, they won't be well looked after, won't last, won't justify their environmental costs.

To be sustainable, something must last. Obviously. But widespread teenage disaffection raises questions about conventional education in a changing world. Education *has* changed over the years, and undoubtedly *will* change – many times in a building's life. This makes *adaptability* and *alterability* vital for building longevity. Climate change is another major factor. Globally, the world is warming, but regionally, the consequences are unknown: will we swelter? Enter a new ice-age? Will we see desertification? Or flooding? Can we assume familiar weather patterns? Or should we anticipate 'extreme events'? To cope, buildings will need to be *climatically robust*; and easily *thermally adaptable*.

Heating, cooling and energy issues

Climate-change is a major issue for the survival of society as we know it. What does this mean for design? Energy conservative design is crucial. Fortunately, this is relatively straightforward. (In theory! It's demanding in detail[4].) But schools are special cases. They're densely but intermittently occupied, so heat-loads fluctuate. Lots of children give off lots of heat. Even north-facing classrooms, chilly when empty, can overheat when full. To buffer temperature swings, fluctuating heat-loads need thermal mass. In cool climates, this can't be left unheated or rooms are chilly, increasing condensation and mould risk. Also it responds too slowly if thermal boost is needed. Schools, therefore, require a balance between thermal storage, background heating and short-term response.

Slow(ish)-response systems include radiant walls and floors. Being low-temperature, these suit heat-pump-boosted geothermal heating. (The input:output efficiency of heat pumps is 1:3 – appealing, but they're normally powered by electricity. If fossil-fuel generated, at an efficiency of 3:1, nothing is gained.) Boilers can deliver fast response. Of these, woodchip (pellet) fuelled ones are carbon-neutral.

Biofuel-powered Combined-Heat-and-Power makes energy, economic and educational sense – but what to do with heat in summer (when solar can heat water)? Or with power during winter holidays? Likewise, building-use limited to the school year eases summer overheating problems, but what to do with solar hot-water in summer holidays? And what if schools are used as community-resources out-of-hours? This – and four-season use – brings up multiuse and security subdivision issues. These have heat-zone and thermal-regime implications.

Between the requirements of background heating, unpredictable weather and occupant heat-inputs, school heating can't be left to chance. Nor, with changing climate, can it be precisely planned. This all adds up to the need for a coordinated energy *strategy*. One robust enough to cope with unpredictables. While technical systems can be precise, they're generally designed on the basis of predictions. This tends to limit flexibility if circumstances change or something wasn't predicted. Robustness, on the other hand, while usually more crude, implies that buildings do the thermal-balancing work *on their own*, with nothing sophisticated to go wrong.

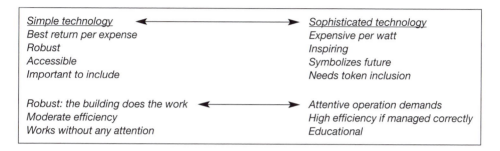

Simple technology ⟵⟶	*Sophisticated technology*
Best return per expense	*Expensive per watt*
Robust	*Inspiring*
Accessible	*Symbolizes future*
Important to include	*Needs token inclusion*
Robust: the building does the work ⟵⟶	*Attentive operation demands*
Moderate efficiency	*High efficiency if managed correctly*
Works without any attention	*Educational*

Energy conservative design

Insulation is central to energy conservation; also it's inexpensive. A whole industry has grown up specializing in insulating old buildings. *External* insulation must resist weather but is less disruptive to install. (Breathable systems avoid trapping moisture in walls.) Crucially, it maximizes thermal mass indoors – unsuitable for rarely heated churches, but advantageous for schools. *Internal* insulation reflects body heat so feels warmer, hence pin-board on an external wall, though providing negligible insulation, increases comfort. Internal insulation, however, maximizes thermal fluctuation – good for churches; disastrous for schools.

For super-insulated buildings, avoiding cold bridging is more significant than adding more insulation. Air-tight construction, likewise, requires painstaking detailing and good workmanship. Insulation isn't limited to building materials. Even at a depth of 3 feet (1 m), earth is closer to annual average temperature than to seasonal extremes; also there's no

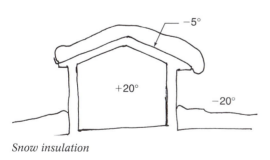

Snow insulation

wind-chill. Snow is a much neglected insulation material. Though free, it needs shallow or rough-textured roofs, climbing plants or wall-hugging bushes to keep it in place. (It's heavy, but deep roof insulation gives room for increased structure.) Vines and vegetated roofs also trap air, giving a small insulation benefit (greater under snow). As they shade and transpire moisture, their cooling contribution, however, is significant.

Air-lock draught-lobbies minimize draughts. It is equally important – as all doors are often open at the same time – to restrict simultaneously used entries to a single building side. Microclimate-sensitive location, reinforced by judiciously placed trees, shrubs and

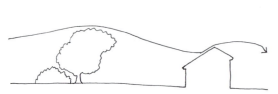

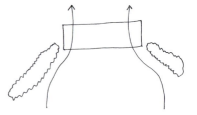

Windbreaks sheltering buildings   *Breeze-channelling for cooling*

fence-screens can further reduce wind at entrances. As wind-chill magnifies cooling, planting, landscaping – and buildings themselves – have a microclimate-modifying role. In cool climates, play, sitting and social spaces need wind-shelter; buildings need wind-break protection and wind-shedding form. In hot climates, shrub and building form can catch, channel or even induce breezes.[5]

Movable insulation – from multilayer curtains to insulated shutters and demountable insulation panels – can ensure windows lose effectively *no* heat. Internal shutters are easier to operate and needn't resist weather. External ones add security, don't require swinging space and clear internal window-sills, don't trap warm air (causing condensation when cooled) and sleeping cats (causing worse problems) but are more expensive, prone to weather-damage and harder to access.

Solar heating

Solar-heating is free. Even without intent, it provides 10–20 per cent of British building heating, more in sunnier climates.[6] Doubling this isn't difficult. Large south-facing windows – in Britain, around 40 per cent of wall- or 30 per cent of floor-area[7] – are suffi-

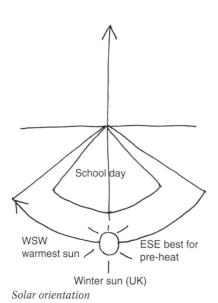

WSW warmest sun

ESE best for pre-heat

School day

Winter sun (UK)

Solar orientation

cient. Halving the heat-loss of buildings, however, is easier, cheaper and more effective – an essential first step. To warm more than it cools, glazing normally needs to face within 30° of south (or, for pre-heating, south-southeast), and north-facing windows should be small. But different building uses require different orientations. Homes ideally face south; schools, needing pre-heating, face south-southeast. Most after-school play-gardens need mid-afternoon (southwest) sun. (Some, of course, need morning sun; some, leaf-shade).

Solar heating is unpredictable – sometimes too hot, sometimes too cold. Conservatories, atria and passages can tolerate fluctuating temperatures, so buffer the climate of adjoining rooms. If walls, floors and ceilings can rapidly absorb and store heat, temperatures remain relatively stable. Heat-storing materials are generally heavy: masonry, earth or water. While 24 hour storage needs some 4 inches (100 mm) (8 inches: 200 mm, if both sides are exposed).[8] Some 1 inch (25 mm) – a double layer of half-inch (12 mm) plasterboard (sheetrock) – suffices for most short-term buffering.[9] Unpredictable weather, such as prolonged cold or grey skies, requires more thermal storage, but efficiency declines with depth. 'Eutectic' chemicals, by melting, store heat in low-temperature 'latent' form – more efficient, but also more complicated. Water convects, storing heat in its entire volume. But are black water drums attractive? Most people prefer to look at brick, stone, slate or earthen materials. The rapid heat-absorption – and release – of clay make cob, adobe or rammed-earth walls effective heat buffers. Though easy to carve names into, these are equally easily invisibly repaired. As it is *surfaces* that transfer heat, niches, folded walls, ledges and steps increase surface-area, hence efficiency. Heat-stores incorporating built-in seats give delicious conductive warmth. Thermal storage is easy to incorporate in new buildings. It's often adequate – but uninsulated – in old ones. In recent ones, however, it's usually scanty. Normally more disruptive than difficult to retrofit, it's easy, however, to demonstrate at a small scale.

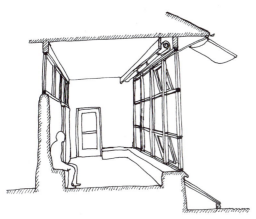

Heat-stores as built-in seats

Buffering needs lots of thermal storage, but to store *heat*, surfaces should be directly sun-warmed; air is only at room temperature. Dark surfaces (attractively coloured, not necessarily black) – or (more expensively) thermally selective ones – absorb more radiant heat. On what does sun fall, when? Is light reflection critical here? Or are these potential solar-heat stores? Are pictures stuck to these walls, or carpets on floors, shading and insulating them? Identifying, exposing – and perhaps colouring – thermal storage is yet another consciousness-raising job for children.

Few old buildings were designed for solar heating. Can we improve them? Exposing, and colouring dark, sunlit masonry increases warmth-absorption. Adding conservatories and glazed passages transform cold external walls into heat stores. Can this make much difference? In often-cloudy Glasgow, conservatories and super-insulation added to substandard council houses cut fuel bills by 90 per cent.[10] But can schools in dull climates really be solar heated? Even in the 1950s, one was built near Liverpool – not the sunniest part of Britain.[11] Even with the primitive knowledge, technology and materials of that time, it was dramatically successful.

Cooling

In moderate climates, cooling never used to be an issue. Climate change, however, is rapidly pushing it to the fore. In fact, by UK Climate Impacts Programme predictions, lightweight buildings will need air-conditioning by 2021, and even heavyweight ones by

2061.[12] New buildings can be designed for passive cooling, but what about old ones? The simplest solution is to add air-conditioners – but these have massive environmental costs. How else can old buildings keep cool?

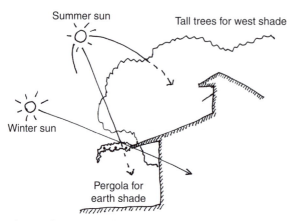

Planting for summer shade, winter sun

The essential first step is shading. Roof overhangs can shade summer noon sun while not hindering low winter sunlight. But sunlight warms things – and powers all life – through *time-delay processes*, so bricks and tarmac radiate the sun's warmth long into chilly evenings and hottest and coldest weather is long *after* the solstices.[13] As most deciduous leaves open in late spring and stay till autumn, foliage shade better matches *thermal* need. But trees, shrubs and vines grow. As *their* preferred size and shape may not match *our* requirements they need constant attention. Fortunately, pupil-powered pruning for shade – and wind-breaking – involves geometry, biology and art. Otherwise, it's called 'child-labour'.

Weather isn't constant. It varies from day-to-day. These variations are best controlled by moveable shades such as shutters, awnings, sun-shades, adjustable-angle slatting or sophisticated adjustable reflector-shutters. Like everything else, shades warm up in sunlight. Indoors, the heat they radiate compromises effectiveness – critical in hot climates, though less significant in cool ones. Outdoors, warm shades hardly matter. Shades are yet more devices for children to operate. The simpler, even cruder, they are, the easier can children see how they work – important for motivating involvement.

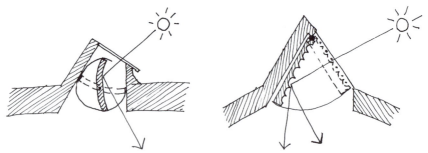

Child-controlled light-reflector/shutters. Left, by Edward Cullinan. Right, by William McDonough: closed, this reflects sun onto water-tubes. Open, it scatters light into the room

Even in cool climates, occupant heat can overheat rooms. Schools often need cooling as well as heating. Solar-heated schools, especially. Large areas of south-facing glass are prone to freeze–fry syndrome. Glass roofs make this many times worse – sweltering under high-angle summer sun, bitter in winter! Even in Britain, unshaded southwest-facing conservatories boil on summer afternoons. Generous ventilation and summer afternoon shade are essential.

Hot air rises – the key to sun-driven cooling. Ceiling levels determine whether it can escape or gets stuck in warm pockets. Cold air sinks – so cold ceilings (cooled perhaps by groundwater pumped through embedded pipes) are more effective than cold floors. Also heat on the head is exhausting; on the feet, just sweaty! In hot, dry climates, high-level intruder-proof openings can flood interiors with cool night air. Being heavier, this 'ponds' in the lowest places, cooling the building fabric. Lightweight buildings can't store coolness for long enough so need thermal mass added. To retain this 'coolth', openings need closing by day, and windows shading. But buildings only perform as well as they're managed. Theoretically, children can do this, but as operation is often outside school hours, microprocessors – or, preferably, a caretaker – can better maintain constant temperature. Automation, however, can't feast on the huge palette of light qualities that blinds and reflectors access. Manipulating light (even for thermal reasons) brings delight – fostering awareness.

Ventilation

Air movement cools us. (Above 32°C, however, cooling declines sharply. Over 37°C, though still evaporating sweat, it *adds* heat.) In most climates, therefore, ventilation – driven by wind (the most effective), height or solar warmth – is the easiest way to cool building occupants. Cross-ventilation – especially by wind, however light – usually works best. Smaller openings to windward, larger to lee, dampen gusts. (But where is 'windward'? This needs observation. Cooling breezes are more often driven by land-heating than by prevailing wind; also topographic deflection and turbulence can alter wind direction from where you might expect it.) Less rain drives in through wind-shielded windows. (Rain-bearing winds are more predictable in direction.) High-level hopper windows keep draughts above table top level, but for still conditions, wind-scooping, side-hinged ones catch more air. *Thermal*-driven ventilation flows from cool to warm – shady to sunny side or cool floor inlet to warm ceiling outlet. Like chimneys, increasing *vertical* difference between openings accelerates air-flow. Height is more effective – and much more

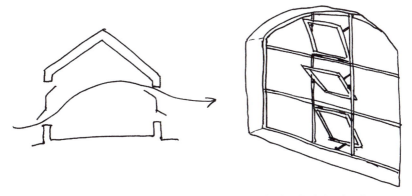

Multiple ventilation options: low and high ventilation, draught-free high-level or hopper openings, cross-ventilation and wind-shielded opening-direction against rain driving in

economical – than heat. Solar-chimneys utilize both heat and height – and, with cowls, wind as well – maximizing efficiency.

But what will the weather be? Too hot? Too cool? Windy? Rainy? Still? Mixed systems with many options best cope with varying conditions and needs. This means *high* and *low* vents on opposite – ideally all – building faces; windows (or vents) sheltered from driving rain by shrubs and trees; others where hedges deflect wind towards them; ridge and tower extract vents; and wind-catching tower inlets. Such multiple 'adaptive opportunities' ease comfort control in all weathers.

Water issues

Despite water being indisputably our most precious resource, ever since Thomas Crapper invented flushing toilets we've used it to transport waste, so accord it no value. Even drought-prone countries use flushing toilets. Yet even in rainy Britain, there often isn't enough water. With climate change, water conservation is becoming increasingly crucial. Conservation measures include rainwater harvesting, grey-water recycling, 'xeriscape' landscaping (using drought-tolerant plants) and gardening with mulches. Water-saving appliances, spray-taps, long- or short-flush cisterns, waterless (but air-flushed) urinals or even dry toilets, reduce demand. Economy of use is fundamental. This, however, is more a matter of consciousness than of gadgets. Gadgets only *improve*, never *remedy*.

In Britain, rainfall closely matches water use. Disposed of as a nuisance, it causes floods. This is another aspect of rainwater – also climate-change related. Much flooding is man-made. Unpredictable weather – itself, partly resulting from human activities – is only part of the reason for floods. Natural landscape provides many cushions to absorb rain: forests, marshes and even, to some extent, lush grassland. Rivers' elongated routes dampen the effect of flood surges. Impermeable roofs and paving, conduited rivers and straight drains accelerate rain run-off, compressing it into short time periods. This makes floods.

The more porous or puddle-trapping are ground – or living-roof – surfaces, the less run-off there is. Water-permeable paving, soakaways and balancing ponds keep rainwater local. This prevents distant problems – floods – and maximizes local benefit – plant fertility and, in winter, aquifer recharge. Yet another potential eco-job for children is to observe where water runs off land and dig interception swales to re-route it for irrigation or groundwater replenishment.

For irrigation, rainwater makes plants grow faster than chlorinated tap-water ever can. (Thunder-rain even more so.) Rainwater butts, therefore make sense near any garden. If *children*, not teachers, control the taps, they quickly learn there's only a limited amount. Carting, bucketing or siphoning this water to garden beds links rain to plant-growth. It's also good balance exercise.

Rain runs off all hard-surfaces – easy to collect. A mere 1/2 inch (1 cm) of rain provides over 2 gallons (10 litres) per 10 square foot (square metre). But how much is clean enough for use indoors? The first rain washes dirty ground and roofs. Devices can divert this to irrigation – subsurface if heavily polluted. The rest can be used indoors – for instance, for toilet-flushing. For laundry, rainwater, being 'soft', is actually better than most tap-water.

But how to store rainwater? For irrigation or 'streams', ponds – with fluctuating water levels – are simplest. In hot countries, however, open water evaporates fast and is algae prone – unattractive and dangerously slippery. Tanks, securely lidded, are more efficient and safer. As these are normally unsightly above ground, they can be integrated in noise-screens or foundations, or used as retaining walls.

Tanks as retaining walls

Micro-organisms flourish in warmth, so, after filtering (using extra particle- and UV-filters if required) – water should be kept below 18°C, and in the dark.[14] (Above 24°C, legionella bacteria – potentially fatal – thrive.) This implies underground tanks. What about heavy metals? Fortunately, these are indeed 'heavy', so – usually bound to particulate – sink. As they only accumulate a half-inch (12 mm) per year, outlets can be just above tank bottoms.[15] Water-quality deteriorates if stored for long, so tanks need to overflow regularly to flush themselves clean. For potable water, this restricts storage to little over 5 per cent of annual rainfall; for lower quality water, around 40 per cent.[16] As Legionnaires' disease is caught by inhalation, poor-quality stored water isn't suitable for spraying. For indoor uses, tanks need (a little) topping up with mains-water whenever they're nearly empty.[17]

How much water can we get from rain?

Annual yield (gallons/litres) = roof area (plan, ft^2/m^2) × rainfall (inches/mm) × filter efficiency (80–95%) × collection coefficient (flat roof: 50%; slate: 80%).[18]

Travel

Road traffic doubles every decade. Despite improved fuel-efficiency, exhaust CO_2 increases annually. A generation ago, nearly all children walked or went by bus to school. Not now. School transport by car significantly congests – and pollutes – cities. Most British children would rather cycle or walk, were it safe to do so – an urban planning issue.[19] Bicycle theft is another deterrent. Secure cycle-sheds – doubling as noise and exhaust screens – locked during school hours, overcome this. Many American high-school students drive to school. Although the independence this brings is appealing for them, it's bought at high environmental cost. Also, for schools, parking land is expensive. Subtractive parking charges – exorbitant for single-occupant cars, but reduced per passenger – can help limit this traffic. (Such charges can have a transparent basis: parking land, construction and maintenance; rain-forest preservation; and contributions to eco-charities.)

Transport CO_2 isn't only an issue of child-car-miles. Everything coming into schools has a transport cost. Sea-, rail-, road- and air-miles have differing CO_2 costs. This is particularly relevant to food: local fruit travels perhaps 30 miles by road; imported, perhaps 3000 miles by air. From how far away does everything – from building materials and furniture through stationery and equipment to school meals – come? Asking this question won't guarantee the lowest CO_2 option, but it will guarantee an attitudinal shift – much more effective in the longer-term.

Eco-schools

What are eco-schools? Definitions range from schools that compost garden-waste and recycle paper to those dedicated to every aspect of sustainability. But eco-schools are nothing new. They date from the 1980s in Sweden; and even in appallingly polluted Moscow, from the early 1990s. In Germanic-Nordic countries, they're relatively common. Close relatives are Steiner schools, organically gardening, composting and using non-toxic, natural materials since the 1920s, and Froebel kindergartens – the original 'children's gardens' – from 1840. (The first kindergarten actually dates back to 1695.[20]) Just as 'the emotional damage caused by alienation from nature' – only visible in the second and third generations of town-dwellers – fuelled the 1920s and 1930s German 'Back-to Nature' movement,[21] contemporary schools' 'lack of relevance to life and overtaxing academic syllabus' has spurred the burgeoning 'Nature School' movement.[22]

Nature Schools need nature. Cities rarely adequately provide this. Whatever their benefits, however, rural schools mean more private transport and social insularity. If eco-schools are to contribute to sustainability, they can't transfer energy savings from buildings into child-miles. Most importantly, they must be available to all – urban, village and rural dwellers, both environmentally committed and wholly unaware.

Sustainability requires consciousness reform – in everybody, every child. Can this happen? Is it an unrealistic hope? More to the point: can humanity survive another century without this? Can the school *environment* help this come into being? Can any school, however urban, afford *not* to be sustainable – an everyday demonstration and inspiration to its pupils?

Notes

1 Titman, Wendy (1994) *Special Places; Special People*. Quoted in Marshall, Alan (1999) *Greener School Grounds*. Learning Through Landscapes.

2 Sustainable Consumption Roundtable (2005) *Seeing the Light: The Impact of Micro-generation on the Way We Use Energy*. Quoted by Elliot, David (2006) All Change: the New Low Carbon Building Programme. In Building for a Future. AECB spring 2006, Llandysul.

3 Royal Institute of British Architects (2001) *A Sustainable School: The Winning and Commended Schemes in an RIBA Competition*. RIBA.

4 See, in particular, Roaf, Susan (2001) *Eco-house*. Architectural Press; and Day, Christopher (2002) *Spirit & Place*. Architectural Press.

5 For more on cooling breeze induction, see Day, Christopher (2002) *op. cit.*

6 RIBA (2001) *ibid.*

7 RIBA (2001) *op. cit.*

8 Roaf, Susan (2001) *ibid.*

9 (2003) *Building for a Future*. AECB. There is concern however, that unless the two sheets are thermally linked, they won't work as intended.

10 BBC Radio 4, 20 September 2005.

11 In Wallesley, Cheshire. While cynics say low ventilation means it's actually sweat-powered, this solar design worked so well its back-up boilers were never needed. Half a century later, there are now draught- and heat-loss-free techniques for more generous ventilation.

12 Research by ARUP, cited in Masonry construction may benefit from global warming! *Building for a Future* 16(2) Autumn.

13 In Britain about 40 days later, as were Celtic equinox and solstice festivals.

14 Budgeon, Roger and Hunt, Derek (2004) Water: don't waste a drop. *Building for a Future* 14 (1), Summer, AECB, Llandysul.

15 Budgeon, Roger and Hunt, Derek (2004) *op. cit.*

16 Budgeon, Roger and Hunt, Derek (2004) *op. cit.*

17 Budgeon, Roger and Hunt, Derek (2004) *op. cit.*

18 Budgeon, Roger and Hunt, Derek (2004) *op. cit.*

19 51 per cent of over seven year olds, according to a SUSTRANS survey cited in *Positive News*, winter 2003.

20 Seth, Ann (translator) (2003) *The History of School Gardens in Germany, Environmental Education*. NAEE (UK), Summer 2003.

21 Heyer (1931) *Gartenkunst*. Quoted in Seth, Ann (2003) *op. cit.*

22 Seth, Ann (2003) *op. cit.*

Environment to serve and inspire

CHAPTER 20

From ends to means

What is education for? This highly contentious issue used to be simple: education was a ladder to better jobs.[1] Nowadays we're less sure. Should education turn out cyber-intellectuals for the new knowledge-based economy? Media-specialists, because most students want to do this? Or plumbers, whom we all need? To add complication: will any of these skills match the needs of a fast-changing world? Would discernment, grasp of essential principles, resourcefulness and adaptability be more useful?

Even if we're only concerned with vocational aims, some skills are necessary for getting a job:

- the ability to focus. This only happens when inspired; never when bored, disinterested;
- the ability to relate different kinds of information. This requires insight into the *essence* of any situation;
- the ability to see consequences. This is inseparable from ethics;
- the ability to think outside the box. This requires flexible thinking;
- the ability to be practical. This gives purposeful direction to thinking.

Children only want to learn if their *interest* is aroused. *Inspiring* places support this.[2] Uninspiring ones de-motivate. There's also the issue of low attention. Background sensory stimulus mitigates this. Changeless uniformity and sensory – especially visual – monotony further weakens it. These are design issues for any kind of education.

But should we perhaps worry less about what facts and skills we want children to learn, but more about how we want them to *be* when they're old enough for experience to shape inspiring ideas into achievability? Should education focus, perhaps, not on facts but on *relationships*? These give meaning to otherwise separated accumulations of knowledge. (Another factor influencing attention.) Should children learn that *listening* ensures validity better than competitive assertion. On the principle that 'Education is what is left when you've forgotten everything you learnt', this would mean the full fruit of education isn't reached at 18 years of age, but in the second half of life.

This is about education. But what does any of this have to do with children's environment? Educational theories and practice constantly change. They flow through fixed buildings and places like water between river banks. Just as river banks shape water flow, how can these buildings support life-development aims? For children to mature into creative-thinking, practically resourceful, responsible and compassionate good listeners, able to relate different modes of knowledge, what physical environment should we surround them with? A related question is: what are children ready for, need, crave, when? What moods of place suit different ages of children? What sort of spaces, colour and light support their developing consciousness?

Clarity of thought may depend on logic (traditionally taught through mathematics) but creative thought needs insight and recognition of relationships. Symbiotic relationships – a fundamental characteristic of nature – are as essential to buildings as they are to landscapes. Without these, neither are ecologically sustainable, nor pay their way. If achieving multiple aims is an everyday principle, constantly in view, relationship-thinking becomes the norm. Mutually reinforcing sensory experiences both feed this and help us meet the world – and consequently think – in many, diverse ways. Insight requires mobile, parallel thinking, constantly relating different strands. Educationally, crafts enliven technical understanding through artistic exploration. In the classroom, however, one-sidedness is easy, but in the arts the inter-relationship of feeling, thinking and doing is unavoidable. Whether children practice arts is a curriculum decision, but whether arts *enthuse* them is, in part, influenced by environment.

Flexible thinking depends on open listening. This is fed by exposure to multiple viewpoints and, particularly, *ways* of thinking – this is one reason why learning foreign languages is so important. Teamwork, from performance arts and sports to building and landscaping work, teach cooperation. Multicultural and multi-age playgrounds add social dimensions. While monoband community restricts social challenges, diversity develops viewpoint mobility. This highlights the need to bring polar groups such as young and old, privileged and under privileged, able-bodied and disabled, into constructive – not frictional – relationship. Ensocializing design fosters this. Indoors and out, design and furnishing affect how children meet, learn socialization skills and establish social identity.

The broader, more multilayer our thinking, the more flexible, creative, multistrand and inter-related are our several kinds of intelligence. Creativity and imagination are intertwined, feeding each other. Both are fed by exploratory learning. While second-hand images – particularly TV at an early age – inhibit imagination, sense-rich places with plenty of things and places to discover, enjoy, investigate and play with, encourage it.

For children, the ever-changing outdoor world – nature – offers richer exploration opportunities than buildings – which are fixed in purpose. Whether for play, adventure, building dens or growing vegetables, natural surroundings – from gardens and parks to farms, forests and wilderness – have educational, therapeutic and irreplaceable developmental benefits. Many teachers consider that children learn more from outdoor activities than indoors. Many school-opposed children – disruptive vandals indoors – become cooperative, enthusiastic and quick-learning in activity-based, nature-nurtured, surroundings. Fresh air and physical activity help; so does engaging with *living* things, systems and processes. But, more significantly, in an age when buying whatever we need is so easy, unshielded contact with nature's forces demands resourcefulness.

Resourcefulness requires both practical skills and imagination. Traditionally, it used to be learnt in workplaces characterized by changing situations, such as farms and ships, not in classrooms. Exploratory play and challenge – natural to children – encourage resourcefulness. The more opportunities for adventure – particularly 'found' amongst natural elements, not pre-planned in play-equipment – the better. Unlike abstract thought, resourcefulness depends upon being well-grounded. Virtual reality and dependency culture don't encourage this. Making, mending and 'fixing' things do. Discarding things says we owe them no responsibility Mending them says they're worth something. Mendable construction and furnishings support this attitude.

The values imprinted in our daily environment shape *our* values. Steiner expressed this more strongly than many of us dare publicly admit: 'Many people believe that the materialism of modern times comes from so materialistic literature being read ... What the eye sees is much more significant, for it influences the dynamics of the soul on a more or less unconscious level ... How different it was from our days to walk down the streets of the middle ages ... People saw façades of houses that had been constructed from something that was felt and thought in the soul. A piece of soul was in each thing, and when the human being passed among such structures, soul forces flowed towards him too. Just compare that with a city of our day'.[3] Surroundings that hurt our soul say art doesn't matter. Soul-nourishing beauty encourages it. This means soul-refreshing beauty is no mere luxury. Steiner continues: 'People will never develop full human substance, able to face the demands of life, if they have not learned to take the path of beauty, and through beauty to attain the truth'.[4] Until the emotional self-awareness of the teenage years, however, few children are *consciously* aware of beauty. Nonetheless, *unconsciously*, it affects them deeply. It is an essential foundation for reverence.

Responsibility isn't sustainable if merely *thought*. It must be *felt*. Reverence and compassion, natural to small children, are the foundation of moral inspiration. While heartless environment breeds cynicism as they age, gentle surroundings offer a model for human behaviour. Learning to care for the environment, for people and for life, is about the journey from instinctive wonder-filled reverence to self-directed consciousness. Environmental responsibility starts with love. Through understanding, it develops the innate reverence of infanthood into conscious care. Animals touch children's souls. Even in street-hardened louts, these bring out compassion – an important step towards responsibility. This makes care for living things *developmentally* important – especially for urban children. As care means attention to protection, food, habitat and behavioural needs, it lays the basis for ecological thinking.

Recognizing the great life-renewing cycles of nature, where food comes from and the foundations of life in substance, water, air and energy, substantiates ecological understanding. Subliminally, but more potently, how places encourage us to use them teach lessons – and values – by example. In such ways, children learn about sustainability through daily experience. Thinking green can become so routine, it permeates every action.

Every generation of children grows up under the shadow of crisis: economic collapse, pandemic, war, nuclear Armageddon, terrorism. But this generation's crisis is different. Climate change seems imperceptibly slow, but relative to full-spectrum ecological adaptation, it's devastatingly fast. Bio-communities, human society and built environment can only *partially* adapt in time. The inevitable result will be multiple interwoven crises – mostly beyond timely prediction. Depending on outlook, this is either a petrifying fear or a stimulating challenge.

Because fear freezes development, we owe it to children to prepare them for challenge. The inevitable social, demographic, economical and ecological traumas will bring entirely *new* challenges. These will need *new* skills, *new* thinking, insightful, balanced and flexible. For children, this can – indeed must – be an inspiring century opening up! Essential to meet these challenges, however, are both anchoring confidence in personal identity and thought mobility, both stability and life. Metaphorically, they need the qualities of both the straight and the curved. These in turn are hugely boosted if children grow up in an environment developmentally and soul-nutritionally appropriate. An environment *for* children.

Notes

1 Hence the Welsh word for school is the same as for ladder: *ysgol.*

2 I am indebted to Sandra Farnström (2001); dissertation in Umeå University.

3 Steiner, Rudolf (1914) *Der Baugedanke des Goetheanum.*

4 Steiner, Rudolf (1994) *Ways to a New Style of Architecture.* (1914 lectures) Rudolf Steiner Press.

Bibliography

Aepli, Willi (1955) *The Care and Development of the Human Senses*. Steiner Schools Fellowship of Great Britain.

Alexander, Christopher et al (1977) *A Pattern Language*. Oxford University Press.

Alschuler, Rose H. and Hattwick, La Berta Weiss (1947) *Painting and Personality*.

Amons, Christie (2005) Lecture at *The Integrity of the Child* conference. *Anthroposophy Worldwide* 3.

Andersson, Olaf *Living Water*. Architectural Press.

Aries, Philippe (1962) *Centuries of Childhood*. Jonathan Cape.

Aronsson, Karin (1981) *En spännande situation där någon är i fara och där någon kommmer till hjälp*. Lunds Konsthall (exhibition catalogue).

Arq, Concepcion Laguna (1995) The children, the green area and the sense of community in Mexico City. *International Play Journal* 3 (2).

Bachelard, Gaston (1976) *The Poetics of Space*. Beacon Press.

Bachler, Käthe (1989) *Earth Radiation*. Wordmasters.

Baldwin, Cecelia (2004) The meaning of gardens. *New View*, spring.

Barrington, Rupert (1971) *The Bird Gardener's Book*. Wolfe Publishing.

Bartlett, S., Hart, R., Satterthwaite, D., de la Barra, X. and Missair, A. (1999) *Cities for Children: Children's Rights, Poverty and Urban Management*. Earthscan and UNICEF.

Bayes, Kenneth (1967) *The Therapeutic Effect of Environment on Emotionally Disturbed and Mentally Subnormal Children*. The Gresham Press.

BBC Radio 4 (2002) *The Learning Curve*, 25 June.

BBC Radio 4 (2002) *Today* Programme, April.

BBC Radio 4 (2002) *Today* Programme, 2 May.

BBC Radio 4 (2002) *Today* Programme, 8 May.

BBC Radio 4 (2002) *Today* Programme, 28 May.

BBC Radio 4 (2002) *Today* Programme, 29 May.

BBC Radio 4 (2002) *Today* Programme, 9 August.

BBC Radio 4 (2003) 23 June.

BBC Radio 4 (2003) *The Learning Curve*, 10 June.

BBC Radio 4 (2004) *Today* Programme, 6 May.

BBC Radio 4 (2005) 20 September.

BBC Radio 4 (2005) *Farming Today*, 4 March.

BBC Radio 4 (2005) *Today* Programme, 15 July.

BBC Radio 4 (2006) *The Sound Hunter*, 11 February.

BBC Radio 4 (2006) *Today* Programme, 15 June.

BBC Radio 4 (2006) *Today* Programme, 12 September.

BBC Radio 4 (2006) *Today* Programme, 19 October.

BBC Radio 4 (2006) *Today* Programme, 30 October.

BBC World Service (2005) *Making a Change*, 23 January.

Bettleheim, Bruno (1950) *Love is Not Enough*. Macmillan.

Bettelheim, Bruno (1976) *The Uses of Enchantment*. Thames & Hudson.

Bidsrube, Vibeke (1993) *Children and Square Metres*. Paedagogisk Bogklub.

Birren, Faber (1978) *Color & Human Response*. Van Nostrand Reinhold.

Bochemühl, Jochen (2003) Lecture at *On the Edge of Landscape* conference. Pishwanton.

Bockemühl, Jochen (2005) Reported in Rohde, D. (2005) Chemists Conference at the Goetheanum: bridges of understanding. *Anthroposophy Worldwide* 10/05.

Budgeon, Roger and Hunt, Derek (2004) Water: don't waste a drop. *Building for a Future* 14 (1), Summer, Association for Environmentally Conscious Building, Llandysul.

Building Green. London Ecology Unit (1993).

Caldicott, Helen (2006) BBC World Service interview, 25 October.

Ceppi, Guilio and Zini, Michele (1998) *Children, Spaces, Relations; Metaproject for an Environment for Young Children*. Reggio Children.

Chillman, B. (2005) Ask the experts. *Learning Through Landscapes*, Building Design, March.

Chillman, B. (2005) Secondary thoughts. *Learning Through Landscapes*, Building Design, March.

Controller and Auditor General *Good Stewardship: National Audit Office Examination of Value for Money at Grant Maintained Schools 1995–96*. Report HMSO (HC 697).

Crowhurst, Lennard S.H. and Lennard, H.L. (2004) *True Urbanism & the Healthy City*. IMCL Conference, February 17-1 2005, Carmel CA.

Curwell, March and Venables, eds (1990) *Buildings & Health: The Rosehaugh Guide*. RIBA Publications.

Dagens Nyheter (2001) 1 September.

Daily Telegraph (2006) Letter by 110 childhood professionals, 12 September.

Daniels, Robin (1999) Depression – a healing approach. *New View* 4th quarter.

Davy and Bittleston, eds (1975) *The Golden Blade*. Rudolf Steiner Press.

Day, Christopher (1998) *A Haven for Childhood*. Starborn Books.

Day, Christopher (2002) *Consensus Design*. Architectural Press.

Day, Christopher (2002) *Spirit & Place*. Architectural Press.

Department for Education and Skills (2003) *Growing Schools*. DfES.

Dubos, Rene (1973) *The Biological Basis of Urban Design*. Ekistics.

Dudek, Mark (1996) *Kindergarten Architecture*. Spon.

Dudek, Mark (2000) *Architecture of Schools*. Architectural Press.

Dulux advertisement (2005) *Architecture Today* September.

Dunér, Sten and Katarina (2001) *Den Gyllene Trädgården*. Prisma.

Dyck, James A. (1994) The case for an L-shaped classroom. *Principal* November.

Elliot, David (2006) All change: the new low carbon building programme. *Building for a Future*, spring, AECB.

Elton report to the UK government (1989).

Enns, Cherie C. (2005) *Places for Children*. University College of the Fraser Valley.

Environmental Campaigns (ENCAMS) (2002) Kids confess to causing a mess! *Review*.

Fairweather, L. and Sliwa, J.A. (1970) *'Architects Journal' Metric Handbook*. Architectural Press.

Families, Festivals and Food. Hawthorn Press.

Farnestam, Sandra (2001) *Arkitektur i skolan*. Unpublished dissertation, Umeå University.

Fenoughty, Susan (1997) *The garden classroom*. Unpublished Churchill Fellowship report.

Fenoughty, Susan (2001) *The Landscape of the School Grounds*. Comenius.

Fenoughty, Susan (2002) *Outdoor Education: Authentic Learning in the Context of the Landscape*. Comenius.

Fenoughty, Susan (2006) *Seven Stages to Develop the School Site as an 'Outdoor Classroom' & Place for Play*. suefen@blueyonder.co.uk

Fiske and Maddi (1961) *Functions of Varied Experience*.

Flinspach, Jürgen (1985) *Waldorfkindergärten Bauen*. Unpublished translation by Luborsky, Peter (1988).

Ford, Brian (1998) *Sustainable Urban Development through Design*. Royal Institute of British Architects CPD lecture at Cambridge University 12 February.

Fredholm, Kerstin, *Sjuk av Skolen*. Brevskolan.

Gapell, Millicent, Sensual interior design. *Building with Nature*.

Gardner, Howard (1983) *Frames of Mind – The Theory of Multiple Intelligences*. Harper Collins.

Gerard, R.M. (1958) *Differential Effects of Colored Lights on Psychosociological Functions*. University of California Press.

Gissen, David, ed. (2002) *Big & Green*. Princeton Architectural Press.

Glaser, Karen (2003) Written in the womb. *Building Design* 23 May.

Goethe, Johan Wolfgang von (1810) *Zur Farbenlehre*. Translated as *Theory of Colours*. John Murray (1840).

Goodnow, Jacqueline (1977) *Children's Drawing*. Fontana/Open Books.

Gordon, Aenghus (2003) Lecture at *On the Edge of Landscape* conference, Pishwanton.

Green, Jeff (2006) Sensing the world and ourselves. *New View*, Autumn.

Guepin, Mathias (1995) Community supported agriculture. *News from the Goetheanum* 16 (3) May/June.

Hagender, Fred (2000) *The Spirit of Trees*. Floris Books.

Hall, Alan (1997) *Water, Electricity and Health*. Hawthorn Press.

Hall, E. (1976) *The Anthropology of Space*.

Hart, R. (1993) Summer in the city. *International Play Journal* 1, 3 September.

Heaf, David (2006) Summary of articles. *Archetype* 11, September.

Health News (2001) *Higher nature*. Summer.

Hertzberger, Herman (1969) *Harvard Educational Review: Architecture and Education*, 39.

Hill, Julia Butterfly (2002) *The Legacy of Luna*. Harper San Francisco.

Hinds, Jonathan (1995) Breathing walls. *Architects Journal* 26 January.

Hobday, Richard (2000) The healing sun. *Building for a Future* 10 (1) summer. AECB, Llandysul.

Holdsworth, B. and Sealey, A. (1992) *Healthy Buildings*. Longman.

Holloway S. and Valentine, G., eds (2000) *Children's Geographies: Playing, Living, Learning*. Routledge.

House of Commons Education and Skills committee report.

Huckle, John *Burning Isues in Primary Education: EDUCATION FOR SUSTAINABILITY*. National Primary Trust.

International Archives of Occupational and Environmental Health.

Jacobs, Jane (2000) *The Nature of Economies*. Random House.

Jarvie, Catherine (2003) Noises off. *Observer Magazine* 27 April.

Jennings, Sue (1995) Playing for real. *International Play Journal* 3 (2), May.

Johnston, Jacklyn and Newton, John (1992) *Buildiing Green*. London Ecology Unit.

Kandinsky, Wassili (1970) *Concerning the Spiritual in Art*. (*Om det andliga i konsten*). Konstakademien.

Kaplan, R. and Kaplan, S. (1989) *The Experience of Nature: A Psychological Perspective*. Cambridge University Press.

Kaplan, S. (1995) The restorative benefits of nature: toward an integrative framework. *Journal of Environmental Psychology* 15.

Kellog, Rhoda (1970) *Analyzing Children's Art*. Mayfield Publishing.

King, Shawn (1996) Managing the blooming algae. *The IPM Practioner* XVIII (7), July.

König, Holger (1989) *Wege zum Gesunden Bauen*. Ökobuch Verlag.

Kuhfuss, Werner (1979) *Evoloution genom Lek*. Järna Trykeri.

Küller, Rikard (1974) Arkitekturpsykologisk forskning. In Acking, Carl-Axel *Bygg mänsligt*. Askild & Kärnekull Förlag.

Lantz, H (1956) Number of childhood friends as reported in a life histories group of 1000. *Marriage and Family Life.*

Lee, Terrence (1976) *Psychology and the Environment*. Methuen & Co.

Lennard, H. and Lennard, S. (2000) *The Forgotten Child*. Gondolier Press.

Liddle, Howard (2005) in *Building for a Future* Spring. AECB, Llandysul.

Lifeways North America, http://www.waldorfhomeschoolers.com/waldorfplay.htm

Lillard, Paula Polk (1972) *Montessori – A Modern Approach*. Schocken Books.

Lindström, Sylvia, Berefelt, Gunnar, Wik-Thorsell, Anna Lena *Livets träd: Världen genom barnets ögen*. Rabén & Sjögren.

Littlefield, D. (2005) Funds and games. *Learning Through Landscapes*. Building Design, March.

Littlewood, Michael (2004) Natural swimming pools. *Building for a Future* 14 (1), Summer.

Lohrmann, Iris (2003) Learning from nature in the urban landscape of Berlin. *Environmental Education* 73, Summer.

Löwenhielm, Gunnar (1999) *Rum för en ny skola*. ARKUS No 33, *Arkitektur och skola: om planera ett skolhus*. Byggförlaget.

Lundahl, Gunilla, ed. (1995) *Hus och Rum för Små Barn*. Arkus.

Marcus, Claire Cooper (1995) *House as a Mirror of Self*. Conari Press.

Marshall, Alan (1999) *Greener School Grounds*. Learning through Landscapes.

Martin, Nick (2005) Can we harvest useful wind energy from the roofs of our buildings? *Building for a Future* 15 (3), Winter.

Mason-Hunter, Linda (1989) *The Healthy Home*. Pocket Books.

Masonry construction may benefit from global warming! (2006) *Building for a Future* 16 (2), Autumn.

Matin, D., Luca, W., Titman, W. and Hayward, G., eds (1990) *The Outdoor Classroom*. Learning Through Landscapes.

May, Neil (2006) Green materials and energy efficiency – is there a conflict? *AECB Yearbook 2006/7: The Sustainable Building Guide*. AECB.

McDonald, E. (1976) *Plants as Therapy*. Praeger Publishers.

Meyerkort, Margaret (Unpublished) *Kindergarten architecture and equipment*. Compiled By Elvira Rychlak.

Meyerkort, Magaret and Lissau, Rudi (2000) *The Challenge of the Will*. Rudolf Steiner College Press.

Ministry of Education (1952) *Moving and Growing*. HMSO.

Ministry of Education (1961) *Village Schools*. Building Bulletin No.3, June.

Modern Barndom 3, (1996) Reggio Emilia Institutet.

Mollison, Bill (1988) *Permaculture: A Designer's Manual*. Tagari Publications.

Montagu, A. (1971) *Touching: The Human Significance of the Skin*. Harper & Row, McGraw Hill.

Morgan, Chris (2006) Healthy heating. *Building for a Future* Autumn, AECB, Llandysul.

Neihardt, John *Black Elk Speaks*.

Newberry, Beatrice (2002) Natural born learners. *The Times Magazine*.

Nordström, Maria (1990) *Barns boendeförställningar i ett utvecklinspsykologiskt perspektiv*. Doctoral thesis, Statens Institut för byggnadsförskning, Lund University.

Nute, Kevin (2006) *The Architecture of Here and Now: Natural Change in Built Spaces*. Proposal for: The Architectural Press.

Olds, Anita Rui (2001) *Child Care Design Guide*. McGraw Hill.

Palmer, Sue (2006) *Toxic Childhood: How the Modern World is Damaging Our Children, And What We Can Do About It*. Orion.

Patten, Angela, *New View*.

Perspective September/October (1993)

Petrash, Carol (2005) Creating a seasonal garden: bringing nature inside. *Messenger*, the Waldorf School of Mendocino County, 16 November.

Piaget, Jean (1982) *Barnets själsliga utveckling*. Liber förlag (original 1964).

Planverkets Rapport 77 (1987) *Sunda och Sjuka Hus*. Statens Planverket.

Pollard, A., ed. (1987) *Children and their Primary Schools*. Falmer Press.

Prohansky, Ittleson and Rivlin, eds *Environmental Psychology: People and their Physical Settings*. Holt Rinehart and Winston.

Roaf, Susan (2001) *Eco-house*. Architectural Press.

Robinson, F. (2005) Grounds for concern. *Learning Through Landscapes*, Building Design, March.

Roszak, Theodore (2002) *Ecopsychology: Eight Principles* http://ecopsychology.athabascau.ca/Final/intro.htm.

Royal Institute of British Architects (2001) *A Sustainable School: The Winning and Commended Schemes in a RIBA Competition*. RIBA.

Royal Society for the Protection of Birds (2002) *Ponds for Wildlife*, RSPB.

Sandven, Jostein (2003) *Kroppslig erfaringsdanning – uteskole arbeid med rom*. Paper to Freskerutdanningskurs, 23–25 May 2003.

School Bullies and Bullying at School, http://www.bullyonline.org/schoolbully/school.htm

Scott, William B. (2002) *Aviation and Space Technology Journal*, 6 May.

Shin, Dongju and Frost, Joe L. (1995) Preschool children's symbolic play indoors and outdoors. *International Play Journal* 3 (2), May.

Skanze, Ann (1989) Vad betyder skolhuset? Skolans fysika miljø ur elevernas perspektiv studerad i relation till barns och ungdomars utvecklingsuppgifter. Doctoral thesis, Stockholm University.

Steiner, Rudolf (1916) *The Sense Organs and Aesthetic Experience*. Rudolf Steiner Press.

Steiner, Rudolf (1916) *The Twelve Senses and the Seven Life-Processes in Man*.

Steiner, Rudolf (1996) *The Foundations of Human Experience*. (1919 lectures) Anthroposophic Press.

Steiner, Rudolf, *Faith, Love and Hope*. Rudolf Steiner Press.

Steiner, Rudolf, *Riddle of Man, his Earthly and his Cosmic Origin*. Rudolf Steiner Press.

Studies in USA by Heschong Mahone Consulting Group (2004) Cited by Monodraught. In *What's New in Building*, September.

Sustainable Consumption Roundtable (2005) *Seeing the Light: the Impact of Micro-generation on the Way we Use Energy*.

SUSTRANS survey (2003) *Positive News*, winter.

Talking Pets: Pets are Good for People (1986) Pedigree Petfoods, Burton-on-Trent.

Tate Modern Catalogue (2002) *Who's Afraid of Red, Yellow and Blue*?

Thomas, Derek (2002) *Architecture and the Urban Environment*. Architectural Press.

Thörn, Kerstin, *Att bygga en skol*. Västerbotton, Västerbottons Museum.

Titman, Wendy, *Special Places; Special People*.

Tulley, Mark (2006) *Something Understood*. BBC Radio 4, 11 June.

Uijlings-Schuurmans, M, *Environmental Education in Primary Schools*. Alkmaar College of Education.

Underwood, Guy, *The Pattern of the Past*.

van Eyck, A. (1962) *The Medicine of Reciprocity Tentatively Illustrated*. Architects' Year Book 10.

Venolia, Carol (1988) *Healing Environments*. Celestial Arts.

Vernon, M.D. (1962) *The Psychology of Perception*. Pelican Books.

Vilma, Luule, *A Teaching for Survival*.

Vision in Action 4 (1) (2001).

Vygotskij, Lev Semënovic (translated by Lindsten, Kajsa Öberg), *Fantasi och kreativitet i barndom*. Daidalos.

Way, Emma (2005) Ask the experts. In *Learning through Landscapes*, Building Design, March.

Weigert, Hannes (translated by John Barnes) (2004) Transforming our relationship to nature. *Anthroposophy Worldwide* 8, October.

West Devon Sustainable Schools Project. http://www.westdev.co.uk/Pages/schools2.htm

Wyon, David (1992) User control of the local environment. *Building Services Journal* June.

Zajonc, Arthur (1993) *Catching the Light*. Bantam Books.

Index